Higher Ground

Martin Moran is one of Britain's most accomplished moun-
taineers and guides. Born on North Tyneside he pursued a
mountain path from boyhood. After studying geography at
Cambridge University he and his wife Joy moved to Sheffield
where Martin trained as a chartered accountant, consoli-
dating his climbing experience with an ascent of the Eiger
North Face and new alpine-style routes in the Himalaya.
In 1985 he qualified as a British and International IFMGA
Mountain Guide and moved to Lochcarron in the North-
West Highlands.

Martin and Joy Moran have expanded their mountaineering school from running local climbing courses in Wester
Ross and Skye to holidays and expeditions in the Swiss
Alps, Norway and the Indian Himalaya. He has made over
a dozen pioneering ascents in the Himalaya and climbed a
hundred new winter routes of high standard in Scotland.
Martin has authored five other books including *The Munros
in Winter* – which recounts his ascent of all 277 Scottish
mountains over 3000 feet in height in a single winter, and
Alps 4000 – the story of his first continuous traverse of all
the Alpine 4000 metre peaks. Martin and Joy have two
grown-up children, Alex and Hazel.

By the same author

The Munros in Winter
Alps 4000
Scotland's Winter Mountains
The Magic of Wester Ross and Skye
The 4000m Peaks of the Alps – Selected Routes

HIGHER GROUND

A Mountain Guide's Life

Martin Moran

SANDSTONEPRESS
HIGHLAND | SCOTLAND

First published in Great Britain and the
United States of America in 2014
Sandstone Press Ltd
Dochcarty Road
Dingwall
IV15 9UG
Scotland

www.sandstonepress.com

Editor: Robert Davidson
Copy editor: Kate Blackadder
Indexer: Sara-Jayne Donaldson
Technical support: David Ritchie

The publisher acknowledges subsidy from Creative Scotland
towards publication of this volume.

ISBN: 978-1-908737-55-7
ISBNe: 978-1-908737-56-4

Cover image by Leon Winchester
Cover design and plates by River Design, Edinburgh
Typeset by Iolaire Typesetting, Newtonmore
Printed and bound by Totem, Poland

To all my clients and colleagues in the mountains,
with thanks for enriching my life

CONTENTS

Part Four
NORWEGIAN LIGHTS

Part Five
INDIAN PIONEER: THE HIMALAYA

Part Six
REFLECTIONS

MAPS AND DIAGRAMS

ILLUSTRATIONS

1. Martin climbing into The Ramp on the Eiger North Face 1938 Route (photo: Dave McDonald)
2. Dave McDonald at the bottom of the Eiger North Face
3. Andy Nisbet on the Hydnefossen (Hemsedal, Norway)
4. Paul Tattersall sets out on pitch two of The Godfather on the first ascent
5. Loch Carron from Stromeferry summit with Fuar Tholl and Sgorr Ruadh in the distance (photo: Clarrie Pashley)
6. Joy – eight months pregnant with Alex – inspects our new home at Achintee in November 1986
7. David Litherland descending from the Täschhorn on the Domgrat traverse – September 1989
8. David on the final climb to the Dom with the Domgrat behind
9. Martin at Montenvers after a solo ascent of the Aiguille Verte in September 1987
10. Ben the cook leads pitch one on the Emosson Dam
11. Joy on the Bossons Glacier during an attempt on Mont Blanc in 1984
12. Joy at the helm on the sea crossing from Knoydart to Rum
13. Martin guiding Eva Groenveld on the East Ridge of the Inaccessible Pinnacle in May 2013
14. Martin on Sgurr Dubh Mor looking to the northern half of the Cuillin Ridge during a November traverse
15. Alan Colley climbing the East Ridge of the Inaccessible Pinnacle during a two-day traverse
16. Our oldest client: Stan Dow at 74 on Aonach Mheadhoin in Glen Shiel

ACKNOWLEDGEMENTS

I would like to express my appreciation to all who have contributed to the final text, in particular: Andy Nisbet for his contribution to Chapter 12; to Keith and Pru Cartwright, David Litherland, Fran McDonald and Des Winterbone and many others for checking and reviewing relevant parts of the script; Ric Singerton for his artwork for the maps and diagrams; Dave Ritchie for his work on scanning photographs; to Robert Davidson of Sandstone Press for his trust and editorial guidance; and finally to Joy, Alex and Hazel for their companionship, tolerance and inspiration through my long absences climbing mountains and writing about them.

Part One

FORMATIVE YEARS

Chapter 1

BEGINNINGS

Only a hill; but all of life to me
Up there between the sunset and the sea.
Geoffrey Winthrop Young

I never especially wanted to be a mountain guide, but it was the hills that opened my soul to the wonders of existence. By the age of eight they had become a major part of my dreams and imaginings. I was born into an aspirational household that was making the post-war transition from working to middle-class status. Neither of my parents had the least inkling towards outdoor adventure. My mother was a dreamer, but was tied by the conventions of a housewife's life. My father was provider and disciplinarian with scant time to spare from his career as financial accountant to a company in Wallsend on North Tyneside. Like so many of their generation both Mum and Dad sacrificed personal indulgence to give my brother and me the best possible starts in life, but their greatest contribution to my cause was unwitting.

Both parents had distaste for the conventional seaside holiday of the 1960s, and instead we were taken on touring trips in the Lake District and Scottish Highlands. My eyes were first opened to the hills through the back windows of a Vauxhall Victor. On Kirkstone Pass I saw grim crags rearing up into the mists on Red Screes. In Glen Lyon I marvelled at pencilled torrents which plunged from hidden heights. I urgently needed to find out what was where, to define and contain the world, and so became obsessed with maps. I accumulated a collection of Ordnance Survey One Inch sheets and became a devotee of Wainwright's guidebooks. The strange Gaelic names of the Highlands – Sgurr nan Clach Geala, An Teallach, Bidean nam Bian – evoked a mix of fear and enticement.

Soon I was scampering up hillocks and hummocks during Sunday picnics in the Cheviot Hills. Langlee Crags and Humbleton Hill briefly meant all the world to me, but by now I had found the mountain bookshelf in North Shields library and my horizon widened. On a family drive to Devon the billowing masses of summer cumulus became my own Himalaya, every cloud cap a new and unfathomable summit, and with excitement came fear. One night in bed my imagination passed from the hills to the whole of the Earth and up to the sky. The stars stretched into a yawning and terrible abyss. Suddenly I sensed the ultimate truth and in a spasm of panic rushed downstairs to the arms of my mother. I now knew that a search for the absolute was futile, but I was not deterred from the quest.

From fell-walks and camps to rock faces and bivouacs, the hills gave me solace and inspiration through my teenage years. All else in life seemed dull by compare and I won revelations of a life beyond the plain.

By December 1978 I was married and living in Sheffield. So far the magic of Scottish winter mountaineering had eluded me. I was steeped in the works of Bill Murray and the legends of Tom Patey[1], Jimmy Marshall and Robin Smith[2]. The sublime experiences described by Murray in *Mountaineering in Scotland* convinced me that it was in this genre that the true force lay. Yet my previous trips north had all ended in storm or retreat through want of courage.

Lacking a ready partner I resolved to make a weekend visit to the Cairngorms alone and absconded from a tedious accountancy audit in the early afternoon. We owned a seventeen-year-old Ford Anglia, inherited from my late grandfather. I dropped Joy, my wife, with her family in Durham and drove north through torrential rain, battling self-doubt and loneliness. The 350-mile journey seemed interminable but the rain petered out to be replaced by snow showers, which fired mesmerising volleys of white daggers across the headlight beams. On the climb from Glen Shee to the Cairnwell thick banks of powder snow defeated the car. I parked and bedded down on the back seat, my mood morose but still determined.

A snow-plough appeared at 7.00 am and, tucking in behind, I surmounted the pass in triumph. My perseverance had paid off. Remembering the joys of a summer crossing as a fifteen-year-old

Scout I was drawn to the Cairn Toul-Braeriach massif. The hike up Glen Dee was a soulless trudge and the hills were shrouded behind the veils of falling snow, but I kept my head down and climbed Cairn Toul from Corrour bothy without a stop. On the summit the visibility was less than twenty-five metres, so I took a direct descent past Lochan Uaine and cramponned delicately down the frozen water-slide of its outflow stream. Just before darkness I found the squat stone-clad Garbh Choire bothy, and settled in for the sixteen-hour night. Tomorrow's likely outcome would be another dull trudge back to the car and yet another disappointment, but at least I was secure and warm.

In such expectancy I overslept my alarm by an hour. The bothy door opened to a morning of absolute clarity. The mountains shone under a white blanket of fresh snow. I couldn't get packed quick enough. The snow was dry and aerated making the 600m climb to Braeriach an exhausting struggle, but what recompense there was in the views of the snow-plastered corrie walls around me. On reaching the summit, my sight ranged westward across the upper Spey valley to the white rump of Ben Nevis, which sailed on the skyline sixty miles away.

Anxious to squeeze every moment of pleasure out of this precious day, I ploughed down to the Pools of Dee in the jaws of the Lairig Ghru, straight up the east side, and on to Ben Macdui. Already the sun was slipping from my grasp. I pounded over the summit and descended towards the Luibeg Burn. Midday's glare faded to a pale pink alpenglow, which flushed the high tops for a magical half-hour until the heavens turned to indigo, leaving only the western horizons with a fringe of light. The immensity of the vision moved me close to tears. A blanket of freezing fog gathered in the glen as I jogged down the icy track. Once more I saw the Universe for what it is, infinite and pitiless; I could feel the sting of death in the barren frost, and yet was utterly happy. The paradox is inexplicable. Back at Linn of Dee the Ford Anglia's engine fired first time and a wind of elation carried me home.

Notes

1. Tom Patey was one of the great characters of post-war Scottish climbing – raconteur, musician, satirist and formidable pioneer. He died in 1970 in a fall while abseiling from the Maiden sea-stack off Scotland's

north coast. The anthology of his writings *One Man's Mountains* was an inspiration to the new generation of the 1970s.

2. Edinburgh climbers Jimmy Marshall and Robin Smith took Scottish ice-climbing to a new level. In a single week in February 1960 they put out five new routes on Ben Nevis including the magnificent Orion Face Direct, establishing grade V as the high-water mark of aspiration for the next generation. Smith's mercurial career and untimely death at the age of twenty-three added to the aura of his climbs.

Chapter 2

TRIAL BY EIGER

Dave McDonald sat wedged between rucksacks in the back seat of our Renault 6 throughout the drive to the Alps. The fields of France baked in late-summer heat. There was no discussion of an acclimatisation route, no agonised dissection of weather forecasts. Our Eiger pact was already sealed. We turned east into Switzerland through Bern and Interlaken and camped in Lauterbrunnen. While Joy resigned herself to a few days of solo walking, Dave and I packed the kit and took the train to Kleine Scheidegg. At 12.30 pm on 30 August 1981, thirty-six hours after leaving Sheffield, I saw the Eiger and its fearsome north face for the first time. An hour later Dave was leading me across the screes and meadows under the huge limestone walls bounding the face.

For Dave, the North Face of the Eiger was something of an obsession. Through the 1960s he had climbed many of the hardest rock faces in the Dolomites and the Western Alps, including the Philip-Flamm route on the Civetta and the Walker Spur on the Grandes Jorasses. Dave grew up in poverty in Felling on the south bank of the Tyne. He trained as a toolmaker, developed uncompromising socialist politics and found in climbing the outlet he needed to express his energy, anger and creative talent. He had tried the Eigerwand in both summer and winter. Now in his mid thirties and settling down with his wife Fran, Dave wanted the Eiger albatross off his back.

I hardly considered myself the sort of chap that Dave would court as a partner. In fact, I was more than a little shy of him. By reputation he was hard-climbing, hard-drinking and ferociously argumentative. Earlier in August we had met for a preparatory weekend of rock climbing in the Lake District. I was taken aback that, far from putting me through a psychological trial, he treated me with warmth and considerable respect, yet his broad balding brow, tapered jaw and cropped moustache betrayed a man on a mission. He was decisive in action and razor-sharp with quips and observational humour.

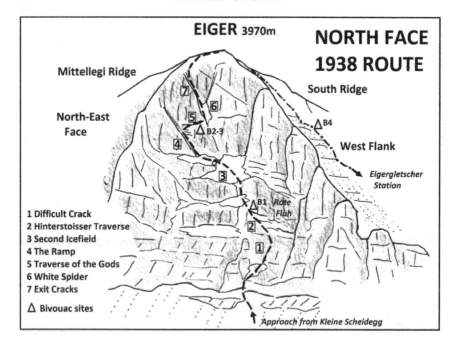

EIGER 3970m

NORTH FACE
1938 ROUTE

Mittellegi Ridge

South Ridge

North-East
Face

B4

West Flank

Eigergletscher
Station

B2-3

Rote
Fluh

1 Difficult Crack
2 Hinterstoisser Traverse
3 Second Icefield
4 The Ramp
5 Traverse of the Gods
6 White Spider
7 Exit Cracks

Δ Bivouac sites

B1

Approach from Kleine Scheidegg

Under the centre of the north wall he stopped, craned his neck back and scanned the maze of shattered pillars and terracing above. I could rely on Dave to master the complexities of the lower face. He set off climbing solo at a formidable pace. There was no suggestion to use the rope. The first significant difficulty of the route is the Difficult Crack which sits under the massive rock shield of the Rote Fluh. Dave found a route to avoid this on the left and forged on, still without a rope. The limestone rock was variously brittle or sloping. Climbing in big boots with a heavy sack I felt terribly insecure.

We moved left along a ledge under the Rote Fluh. Dave stopped and ferreted in a rock cleft, producing a bag of gas cylinders and food.

"We stashed these when we retreated in winter."

We added a gas cylinder and some powdered drinks to stretch our resources to three nights. At the infamous Hinterstoisser Traverse our rope was summoned into service. This was the pitch where, in 1936, Andreas Hinterstoisser's party burned its bridges by failing to leave a rope in place, not realising that the traverse was irreversible. When forced to retreat they were trapped on the face in line of falling stones and in a gathering storm. Their only option was to abseil straight downwards over rock overhangs. Hinterstoisser and Angerer fell. Rainer froze to death, jammed by his rope against a karabiner. The last survivor, Toni Kurz, spent a night hanging free from his rope and perished just a few metres above a rescue party.

Old fixed lines offered a handrail on the traverse and the water-worn rock offered vague flutes and pockets for the toes. We performed a delicate dance poised two thousand feet above the sunny meadows of Alpiglen. A little higher we found the overhung niche of the Swallow's Nest and set up a bivouac. We were now on the edge of the central amphitheatre of the face and I spent much of the evening attuning myself to the scale of tomorrow's challenge.

I snuggled in my new goretex-covered sleeping bag while Dave assembled his self-made tower stove, which he hung from a piton in the roof of the cave. Dawn came chill but clear. Dave led on to the First Icefield at 5.20 am and yesterday's dynamics were repeated. Dave forced the pace with an intent that bordered on aggressive while I struggled to follow. In 1981 the effects of global warming were not yet apparent and it was still quite normal to attempt the Eigerwand in summer in expectancy of a good cover of ice on the crucial links. However, we now faced bare rock slabs covered in verglas on the Ice Hose. Dave hauled on an old piece of rope, then disappeared up the slabs above. Suddenly, there was a scraping and a clatter. I braced on my anchors expecting a fall, but instead one of Dave's axes flew down and disappeared into the abyss. We could continue with three axes between us but our comfort margins had significantly narrowed.

I tried to second this pitch with style to save energy but couldn't find any purchase for my crampon points. There was a runnel of ice to the right but the ropes forced me ever leftwards. When I fell Dave yelled at me to climb the rope. There was no pause, no mercy shown. Was it me being timid or was Dave unduly anxious to get this climb over and done?

My turn to lead came on the Second Icefield. Here there was a cover of snow on top of a sheet of old ice. To save time we dispensed with belaying and moved together, keeping a couple of ice screws between us for running protection. We noticed two parties on the face above us, one at the top of the Ramp and the other in the Exit Cracks. Traversing along the top of the ice field we reached the crest of the Flatiron where Mehringer and Sedlmayer perished on the first attempt on the face in 1935, their ledge ever since known as Death Bivouac.

From here the commitment was total, the feasibility of retreat diminishing with every leftward stride that we made across the central bowl. The tiny Third Icefield was sheet ice and I felt vulnerable traversing across with just one ice axe. The exposure was giddy. The ice slipped into a void that led the eye straight down to the clustered hotels of Kleine Scheidegg. We gained the protection of the Ramp soon after midday, leaving the open expanses of the icefields for the enclosure of a gully. The morning's urgency lifted. When we looked back we were dismayed to see two other climbers setting out across the Second Icefield where there was now a serious risk of stonefall as the upper face loosened its ammunition in the sun.

Halfway up the Ramp we found an anorak and sleeping bag embedded in the ice, and wondered how or why these had been abandoned. Throughout the climb there were grisly reminders of past epics and tragedies. The number of twisted old pitons was bewildering. We led through to the top of the Ramp and at 2.00 pm stopped at a ledge to make a brew of tea. All was going well. An afternoon mist had gathered around the face, rendering a distinctly spooky ambience but this was not a particular cause for concern. The Eiger usually draws its curtain in the afternoon hours.

We continued from the Brittle Ledge up a steep rock wall to the Traverse of the Gods. This tiny balcony leads back right into the centre of the face and makes the crucial linkage with the White Spider. The Traverse was dry and easy. Despite the exposure we romped across in twenty minutes, but were brought to an abrupt halt at the sight of small stones fizzing down the Spider. The temptation to tackle the last thousand feet of the face that evening was considerable, but we played a prudent game. Besides, there was nothing to suggest any change in the weather. We retreated back over the Traverse to a three-foot wide ledge that offered some shelter for a bivouac.

As we prepared for the night the mists parted, but instead of the anticipated sunset, we saw an armada of thunderstacks sailing straight towards us from the north-west. For a minute we stood transfixed. Dave broke our silence.

"Why does it always happen to the good guys?"

The air became charged with humidity. With malign stealth the cumulo-nimbus towers enveloped the foothills, ridge by ridge, and marched into the Grindelwald valley. The storm hit the face just as we clambered into our tent sack. All hell let loose. Vicious cracks of lightning were instantaneously followed by heart-thumping peals of thunder. Within seconds, volleys of hailstones hammered against our nylon bag. For thirty minutes the hailstorm raged and then snowfall commenced. The lightning flashes and thunder growls were now muffled by a thickening blanket of swirling snowflakes. The first sloughs of powder snow trickled over our heads, then intensified into regular avalanches that built up cones of snow behind our necks.

Ensconced in my new sleeping bag and securely tied to belays I let my feet dangle over the edge and eventually drifted off to sleep. Whenever I stirred I heard Dave fidgeting, tossing and turning. His old down sleeping bag and threadbare underwear were no match for the creeping chill. Morning brought a mournful grey light and the gentle patter of dry snowfall. We were pinned by a foot of fresh snow. Powder avalanches swept the face on both sides. Progress seemed unlikely. Starved of sleep, Dave commenced a soliloquy of wry Geordie humour.

"I've just worked out," he piped up, "it'll take us forty-four abseils to get back down the face."

On this point I thought he might be serious. I clung to the hope that we could climb out as soon as the storm abated. The Exit Cracks posed a formidable technical obstacle but seemed preferable to making a traumatic series of abseils from rotten pegs. If we went down the avalanches would increase in volume. We would have to climb back across the ice fields with a significant chance of being swept off the face. In 1981 helicopter rescue was only possible at a few points on the face. The bottom of the White Spider was one such place, but without a clearance we couldn't signal for help.

At midday the snow turned to rain and fleetingly the clouds parted to reveal a tormented sky. The air masses were in perpetual motion and we watched their display with keen eyes, knowing that they held our destiny. We were fortunate that we had picked up the extra gas at the start of the route. We could brew up every three hours. While I still nurtured dreams of success Dave became despondent. The composure that enabled our rapid climb the previous day had gone. Even his wit deserted him. Re-organising his sitting position he dropped a mitten. I let my temper fly before telling him that I had a spare.

At nightfall another set of cloud stacks drifted in from the west while dense grey stratus obscured the northward view. Only the westerly breeze gave any hope of improvement. Food and gas were virtually exhausted. My optimism was beginning to falter but again I slept for long intervals while Dave fretted in a damp gloom. We had to get out the next day or most likely we'd perish.

At 4.00 am I peered out of the frosted vent of our bag. Joy of joys; a mass of stars shone over us and the Eiger was perched above a sea of white cloud. We agreed to go on. At 6.20 am I led off across the Traverse. Every ledge and cranny was choked with powder snow and the protection pegs were obscured. The twenty-minute romp of two days ago now took us two hours. Protection was so scant that a slip would probably have been fatal. The Spider was silent. We abandoned any lingering thoughts of rescue and climbed three ice pitches to the start of the Exit Cracks.

With the vigorous hacking of ice, tingling warmth returned to fingers and toes. A sense of wellbeing and normality returned. We had only to use our climbing skills and master the last quarter of the face. There were no longer any "ifs" or "buts". High in the Exit Cracks a steeper cleft posed a serious test of my new philosophy. This was the famous crack where, after a similar storm in 1952, the legendary alpinist Hermann Buhl had made the climb of his life to lead a *corde européenne* of French, German and Austrian climbers to safety. His clothes and ropes were frozen and he had already spent two nights bivouacked without liquid. For four hours Buhl teetered on the edge of exhaustion in leading the twenty-five-metre pitch. An iced fixed rope of uncertain vintage now hung down to the left of the corner.

Many times I had read the account of Buhl's feat in Heinrich Harrer's history of the Eiger *nordwand*, *The White Spider*. Now I felt awed to be faced with the challenge. I ignored the rope and started up the crack, climbing cautiously from one bridged resting place to another. Dave glared up from the belay. My purist approach was irking him.

"Climb the f**king rope, will you," he snapped.

"You can't trust old ropes; I think the crack is safer," I replied.

While Dave fulminated I made a couple of aid moves on jammed nuts and rested just a couple of metres from the top.

"For Christ's sake will you climb that f**king rope?!" he screamed.

"You keep your opinions until you've followed it," I yelled back, but I was sufficiently ruffled to grab the rope for the last moves. Dave seconded in humble silence and immediately admitted that it was hard. He followed another fixed line diagonally downwards to the bottom of the exit chute. Again, it was my lead. Fog had rolled in and light snowfall sent an endless stream of spindrift down this glassy half-pipe. Rarely able to look up, I braced my cramponned feet on either side and with alternate pressing on my outstretched palms I bridged up the gully. Once embarked there was no possibility of reversing the moves. For a hundred and twenty feet I monkeyed up the cleft without any sign of respite. My only protection consisted of two dubious nuts. Teetering on the edge of self-control and now some forty-five metres out from the belay I peered through the sifting powder and spotted a ledge and piton out to the right. The day was saved.

Dave led through up tiled slabs towards the summit icefield. As I followed, the pick on my axe snapped. We were now reduced to one working axe apiece. Our nerves were taut, the climbing delicate and protection imaginary. With a final effort of concentration we climbed the ice slope and emerged in thick mist on the final section of the Mittellegi Ridge. The moment we raised our axes above the crest their metal heads emitted a buzz of static electricity. Another thunderstorm was imminent. Propelled by fear we staggered along the ridge and reached the summit in thick mist at 5.10 pm. We paused only to take a compass bearing for the West Flank descent.

The relief to get off the ridge and into the shelter and gentle angles of the West Flank was short-lived. Dry slabs which offer easy scrambling in summer were now banked with powder snow. The angle was just sufficient to guarantee a slide if we slipped. Hopes of getting off the mountain dwindled in the evening gloom. We stopped by a large boulder and made our fourth bivouac. With no liquid and just a couple of sweeties each this would be a long night.

My own sleeping bag was now sodden and I began to worry for Joy. What would she be thinking sitting alone in our tent in the deluge? We'd said we would take two days and now we had been out for four. With sleep improbable Dave recovered his old swagger and began a long tirade against the evils of Thatcherism. I made sufficient response to ensure that Dave maintained the heat of dialectical argument, until he too fell to silent shivering.

Wet snowfall was succeeded by rain at dawn. We packed and

left at 6.00 am. My ventile jacket and lambswool sweater were now saturated. Dave was rejuvenated and I slipped behind as he threaded a line over dicey slabs and down snowy couloirs. Finally, we reached an overlap where we could not climb down. By abseiling the impasse we were committed to the outcome. The ropes ended in a big snow gully. Surely this was the end of the difficulty. We ploughed down and then, to our immeasurable joy, the cloud lifted and we saw the roof of Eigergletscher Station a couple of hundred metres below.

At the station we shook hands with sincerity and mutual gratitude. Wherever one of us had faltered the other had been strong. Without that interdependence we might not have come through. On the train the uniformed ticket collector gravely stamped our tickets and looked unkindly on the seeping mass of ropes and sacks on the carriage floor. Dapper businessmen with newspapers under their arms got on at Wengen, shrugged imperiously and sat as far away from us as they could. We had landed from a different planet.

Meanwhile, Joy could no longer stave off her fears for our safety. That morning she drove to Grindelwald police station and reported us missing on the Eiger.

"Yes," said the officer. "I think there are two men who have fallen there."

He took a note of our names and went through to the back-office. There was an excruciating delay of several minutes before he wandered back out.

"No, these men were from New Zealand. We recovered their bodies yesterday."

They could only have been the pair that was following us across the Icefields on the first day. While Dave squatted in his tent porch and cooked a fry-up I waited pensively for Joy's return. We didn't betray our feelings but dropped straight into the minutiae of domestic life as though nothing had happened in the last four days.

Next morning Dave marched into Grindelwald rail station. He knew that we'd had a close escape and was sensible to all that Joy had been through. Emotionally shaken and pining for Fran, he headed straight for the ticket counter.

"A single ticket to Besançon, please," he demanded.

"But Dave, why do you want to go to Besançon?" I queried.

"Once I'm at Besançon, I'm in France, and once I'm in France I know my way home." The logic was incontestable. In an hour he had gone. I little guessed that the Eiger would be his last big alpine climb.[1]

In contrast I was buoyed by our success. I had proved myself equal to the Eiger. Had I done enough to be worthy of a career in the mountains? On returning home I battled inner doubts then steeled myself to phone the secretary of an organisation of which I had recently become aware, the Association of British Mountain Guides.

"How do you become a mountain guide?" I asked, and with those words my fate was sealed.

Notes

1. Dave McDonald was killed in December 1985 in a collision on the A69 near Brampton while returning from a weekend working on his house in Keswick. His wife Fran, eight months pregnant with Jeff, and three-year-old daughter Jenny, escaped unhurt. His obituary in the *Newcastle Journal* described him as "Super-Geordie".

Chapter 3

TESTS AND TRAUMAS

In 1982 the Association of British Mountain Guides (BMG) was establishing its reputation as the premier body of mountaineering professionals in Britain. The BMG was accepted as a member of the International Federation of Mountain Guides' Associations (IFMGA) in 1979, so that British Mountain Guides carried the same badge, status and working rights as their French or Swiss counterparts. The BMG would only accept applicants who had extensive experience of technical climbing, mountaineering and ski-touring. The training scheme was rigorous, involving several courses and two major assessments over a three-year period. At that time the BMG President was Pete Boardman, the leading Himalayan activist[1,] and the sixty-strong membership of qualified Guides included many of the country's best-performing climbers as well as leading instructors from the national outdoor centres.

Faced with such a reputation my trepidation was understandable. Not only did I question my worthiness as a climber, but I was also acutely aware that I was entirely self-taught. While many applicants to the BMG were already qualified mountain instructors I had never coached or led anyone in the mountains in my life. I felt as though I was jumping from the ranks of mediocrity into the realm of the elite, but Secretary Colin Firth was both approachable and helpful. I submitted a four-page list of my mountaineering experience together with references from my best-known climbing partners and my application was accepted. I was as much surprised as thrilled.

The commitment to doing the Guides' training scheme was clearly incompatible with a full-time accountancy job, but I managed to secure three months' unpaid leave a year from my employers. Colin suggested that I get some experience working as a voluntary or apprentice guide before presenting myself for the summer test in

North Wales. The British Mountaineering Council (BMC) ran a series of subsidised courses in both Scotland and the Alps, aimed at giving young people a structured introduction to the mountains. The BMC Training Officer, Chris Dodd, was a fell-running friend and he arranged two weeks of work for me in the French Ecrins massif in August. Along with fellow-apprentice Kevin Flint I travelled to the village of Ailefroide at the head of the Vallouise where a woodland campground housed several hundred trekkers and alpinists. The 4102m Barre des Ecrins sits at the head of the valley. The courses were directed by John Brailsford, an outdoor pursuits lecturer at Bangor University and a notoriously ebullient character. He was mad-keen on cycling and biked from Wales to the Alps each summer with his students. John took his guiding skills straight from the French template. When Kevin and I produced our rock-worn crampons for inspection John took one look and snapped:

"Get them sharpened; all twelve points."

After a gruelling late-night filing session we followed John to the Glacier Blanc for what he described as an école de glace. We were amazed by the precision and discipline of John's école. For several hours the course students were grilled on every form of footwork on crampons and then inducted into the techniques for crevasse rescue. By the end of the day we were hoisting each other out of crevasses by a system of prusik knots and pulleys. John supervised proceedings wearing corduroy breeches, checked shirt and white cap. Our dishevelled attire and self-conscious shufflings on the ice looked pathetic by compare. Clearly, there was a great deal to learn in this guiding game.

John was assisted by a second guide, Harold Edwards, who worked in the Lake District. Harold was relaxed, affable and completely free of hauteur. We youngsters felt sufficiently comfortable with him to assume a primacy in our fitness and technical prowess. On the walk up to the Ecrins hut the path takes a serpentine course, tackling a 500m high slope in a series of long zigzags. The tedium of the ascent demanded some action.

"Let's see how fast we can do it," I said to Kevin.

We dashed off, jogging the gentle inclines and thrusting hands down on knees to power round the steeper bends. Harold quickly disappeared from view. Soon my heart was pounding to its maximum and I deeply regretted my indulgence over a lunch which churned half-digested in a tightening gut. We arrived in a state of near-collapse at the top of the path only to find Harold lounging on a boulder.

"Did you go up the long way?" he laughed. He had quietly nipped up a direct route cutting out the zigzags. I never again made the mistake of underestimating an older guide.

Throughout the Ecrins fortnight I enjoyed the company of the students. Instructing and guiding seemed natural and I could not deny a certain pleasure in my status as an expert. Many on the course were tousled university students, but each had some chink of individual charm. Others were plainly eccentric. Two Oxbridge graduates turned up wearing tweed jackets, white shirts and ties. Contrary to our advice they insisted on maintaining this attire on all ascents. We nicknamed them Whymper and Winthrop[2]. Whymper described himself as a "mathematical modeller". Winthrop possessed a naïve geniality and was full of bright ideas. As we plodded up the glacier towards the Barre in the moonlight his quivering voice perked up from behind:

"I'm sure we're going wrong; I can see the path across the glacier over there."

We turned to see that Winthrop's "path" was actually the deep black slit of a crevasse. There was reassurance to realise that many folk, while personally competent, actually need guides to find the way. Perhaps guiding really would be a worthwhile career.

In preparation for the summer assessment I spent long evenings puzzling over Bill March's textbook *Modern Rope Techniques in Mountaineering*. The most intimidating part of the test consisted of a demonstration of improvised rescue techniques using only rope, slings, karabiners and 5mm prusik cord. I was not intuitively adept at knots and pulleys. There seemed to be dozens of different systems. Without real practice I remained utterly confused so I badgered Joy to overcome her aversion to heights and subjected her to a couple of evenings hanging in a harness off Burbage Edge while I performed rescue manoeuvres.

On 22 May 1983 six of us assembled for the assessment at Plas y Brenin outdoor centre to be informed that the rescue test would take place on day one at Tremadog crags. We worked in pairs, each with an assessor. I lashed myself to belays on the cliff-top. My companion,

Dave, was then lowered off an overhang. Assessor Nigel Shepherd allowed me twenty minutes to secure Dave, abseil down to him, administer first aid, put him in a chest harness and then hoist him to the cliff-top, with the assumption that he was unconscious all the while! Knots such as the autobloc, klemheist and sheetbend were to be employed. No university or accountancy exam was ever like this!

I successfully secured the loaded rope with a releasable autobloc and prusiked down to Dave. I glanced across to the other teams. Another candidate, John, had turned out in a stylish Swiss ski sweater complete with white chest bands in an attempt to seduce his assessor, but was now running back and forwards from his belays to the edge of the crag completely unable to work out a plan of rescue. While John went into meltdown, I crudely harnessed my man, prusiked back to the top and yanked him five metres up the cliff on a 3:1 pulley hoist. At this point Nigel commanded me to stop. I had cleared the first hurdle.

After a day climbing HVS and E-grade rock routes at Gogarth we were sent straight to the Glyders for a night navigation and bivouac exercise. The night was clear and we worked our way by moonlight to a sheltered bivouac spot near the Bwlch Tryfan. My new assessor, Dave Walsh, maintained a dour countenance despite our ministration of hot stew. The pressure level rose further with the gathering of a thick damp mist at dawn. We were asked to find and climb the Very Severe Direct Route on Glyder Fach in boots and with rucksacks. Dave was meticulously critical throughout the approach and I began to resent his pernickety attitude. Direct Route was a good climb. "We should be enjoying this!" I thought. I led the crux chimney with angry determination and was delighted when Dave slipped off while seconding the crux. This brought a temporary relaxation of tension, and Dave allowed me a brief smile as we finished the route.

The fourth day tested our general mountain sense and environmental knowledge. Ski-sweater John and I were assessed by Rob Collister, who said he would pretend to be an eccentric botanist in search of rare plants on the crags of Cwm Glas. John got us lost on the approach and then we displayed our embarrassing lack of knowledge of mountain flora. Asked to identify lady's mantle, roseroot and *saxifraga oppositfolia* we offered only blank stares and suggested that anything purple might be saxifrage, but we kept Rob safely roped while he taught us some elementary botany.

I took an icy pre-breakfast dip in the Brenin lake to freshen me for the final trial, the rock-coaching day. We went back to Tremadog. My "mock" students were a teacher and pupil from St David's College. They were hardly the novices I had expected. Both seconded Hard Very Severe routes with ease. My assessor Bill Wayman directed me to a climb which was appropriately called Grim Wall. Having acquitted myself on this I choose an E1-grade route called First Slip as a finale, thinking this would delight my team and secure me a pass. This was not a wise selection. I had never done the route, the crux was 5c in technical difficulty and I hadn't bargained that Bill would climb up the route behind me. With Bill scrutinising every move I tackled the crux groove facing the wrong way and ended up stretching my hamstrings in an unlikely bridged position. My calf muscles commenced the involuntary shake, known as "disco-legs", that often plagues the novice climber. An urgent repositioning and desperate finger-fight got me back into balance, but both Bill and students had seen me struggle.

We abseiled off and I felt a dizzying wave of relief. The test was over. The teacher shook my hand and with crushing condescension he said:

"Well, it's obvious you haven't done much instructing but perhaps you'd like to get some experience helping the school from time to time."

The real verdict came back at Plas y Brenin. I was given a clear pass and my joy was unbounded.

In June I drove out to Chamonix to further my guiding apprenticeship with Terry Taylor, a well-known guide from North Wales. Terry was hampered by fused ankle joints, the result of injuries sustained in a terrible fall on Clogwyn Du'r Arddu in the 1960s, but his zeal and enthusiasm still burned bright. In those days there were no rules about non-qualified staff taking groups on the alpine peaks[3]. Although I had passed the summer rock test I had taken no assessment in the Alps. The judgement of competence lay with the supervising guide, and Terry was willing to trust me with a bunch of school students from a college in Leicestershire. For a trainee this was a wonderful opportunity to gain genuine experience.

The course was run from a wild camp in the woods behind the Grands Montets lift station in Argentière. Terry pitched a large frame tent as his base for the summer and the students camped nearby. The ski-station toilet solved our sanitary needs and we lived in harmony with the mountains. In that spirit Terry took us all on an open bivouac on the Glacier des Rognons on the second day. A storm arrived as we were bedding down behind a snow-wall and we were treated to a night-long display of pyrotechnics. The kids slept undisturbed and awoke covered in ten centimetres of fresh snow. Terry's operation was often described as "cheap and cheerful", but he promoted the ethos of simple mountain living that was to be slowly submerged by the subsequent boom in commercial climbing.

After a week of training and acclimatisation the weather became very hot[4] and I was tasked with the oldest and most able trio of students to make a traverse of the 3824m Aiguille du Chardonnet via the Forbes Arête. This classic *assez difficile* (AD) route starts from the Albert Premier Hut and gains the beautiful turreted arête by a snow bulge known as La Bosse. At that time the hut guardian was a surly disciplinarian by the name of Nicholas.

Knowing we had a long day ahead and fearing a rapid deterioration of snow conditions after sunrise, I asked for a 1.00 am reveille. He insisted that nobody was to get up before 2.00 am, but I decided to break the rules anyway. We got up at 1.15 am and ate a cold breakfast. Just as we crept on to the porch Nicholas appeared in the doorway. We were caught!

With his rebuke still ringing in our ears we climbed up the Glacier du Tour. The outlines of the peaks gleamed in silvery moonlight, but the air was warm and the snow-crust thin and fragile. We approached the shadow of the large ice-cliff that guards the left side of La Bosse and I began to feel uneasy. Suddenly the tracks of yesterday's climbers disappeared under the debris of a recent ice avalanche. We were a hundred metres from the safety of La Bosse. My heart started to pound.

"We can't hang around here; run," I said, and we dashed madly across the swathe of ice blocks. On gaining the ridge we paused to regain our breath and saw several splinters of ice break off from the sérac. Clearly, the whole cliff was unstable. In the twilight we noticed a dozen other climbers approaching the danger zone. I began to feel vaguely sick as we continued. Just before we reached the summit ridge a mighty roar sounded from below. I looked down to see the talus of a massive fresh avalanche covering the approach slope. The

sérac, the size of a three-storey apartment block, had completely collapsed. Other climbers were frantically scouring the debris.

I said nothing, hoping that my three seventeen-year-old students
might not realise the import of what had happened, but when
helicopters arrived on the scene half an hour later there could be no
doubt. The boys looked dumbfounded. For a second I felt horribly
trapped but quickly decided that the wise course was to press on and
divert our thoughts in the concentration of climbing. Another loud
report and prolonged rumble sounded a few minutes later. A second
sérac to the right of La Bosse had disintegrated[5]. There was mayhem
among the rescuers as a new wave of ice swept past a few hundred
metres away from them.

Our summit moments were solemn. I estimated we had less than
two hours to descend the North-West Ridge before the sun would hit
and trigger new avalanches. We had to be quick but to dispense with
belays and short-rope three students on 40° slopes was potentially
treacherous. Eventually, I decided to abseil the steepest section. A
helicopter made a close scrutiny of our team as we descended. Perhaps
a head-count was being made. Feeling proud that we were accomplish-
ing our descent unaided, I signalled that we didn't need to be rescued,
failing to realise that Terry, the other students and their teachers could
be waiting at the hut under the supposition that we were dead.

We moved into intense sunlight as a final bergschrund barred
access to the safe slopes of the glacier. Old tracks ended at its edge.
A bridge of snow had collapsed. Almost frantic with fear I pulled
the lads along a shelf into a pocket of shade and from an ice screw
lowered them one by one across the cleft. I abseiled behind and we
fled the mountain.

Terry was waiting above the hut among a throng of journalists
and television cameras. His face was wrought by stress. Five had
died. Had we left the hut twenty minutes later the total would have
been nine. Terry had seen the collapse while approaching the neighbouring Aiguille du Tour with his group and had been one of the first
on the scene.

"I saw four figures above but couldn't be sure it was you; but I
always thought you'd make it."

After a day of subdued spirits the course went on. Young folk are
not readily susceptible to trauma. Even faced with such an event the
average teenager believes in his immortality. I was older, but still

able to cast off the shock. Since that day I have always trusted my intuition. Never would I forgo an early start on an alpine climb.

The British guides' winter assessment is generally regarded as the toughest of the courses. In stormy weather the Cairngorms provide a wild arena in which to be examined. I was not to be spared. The test was based at the Glenmore Lodge national outdoor centre. I was paired with Choe Brookes, a lanky and laconic Mancunian who was a brilliant climber but hadn't much clue about mountain guiding. Bob Barton, one of the senior instructors at the Lodge, was to be our assessor. "No-nonsense" would be the kindest term to describe his examining style.

The first morning produced winds gusting to 70mph. Before we even reached our training ground in Coire an-t Sneachda we had to assist in the recovery of the body of a walker who had been blown off the neighbouring Fiacaill Ridge. Undeterred, Bob asked us to demonstrate our personal skills by soloing across a clutch of grade II gullies on the corrie headwall. Then we staggered over the plateau and into the shelter of Coire Domhain where large snowdrifts accumulate each season. We were instructed to dig a snow-hole for our lunch-break.

Backsides in the air, Choe and I began a frantic burrowing session, and in twenty minutes had fashioned two shallow rabbit-holes. Bob sniffed dismissively and ushered us over to view his own creation. By dint of cutting out several blocks of windslab, scooping out the interior and then replacing the bricks, he had fabricated a wind-tight snow coffin in which we could all sit in communal gloom and chew our sandwiches.

I felt well prepared for the afternoon's navigation session, having weather-proofed my map with plastic laminate. On being ordered to navigate to a meaningless knoll near the top of Hell's Lum I opened my map with a flourish only for a sudden wind gust to snatch its slippery panels from my mittened hand. Choe produced his map. As he tried to pin it to the ground, another rogue gust came along and tore it from his grasp. Bob gave us a long frost-caked stare and compounded our misery by refusing to lend us his own map. Only then did we remember that we had packed an old one-inch scale map as a spare. Clinging grimly to this we completed our exercises and got Bob off the plateau.

We were descending the Twin Burns route under Coire an Lochain when Bob announced that we would finish the day with some short-roping practice. The snow was brick-hard. I took the first turn and tied Bob on to the rope two metres below me. As we descended he repeatedly attempted to throw himself down the 40° slope while I clung desperately to the rope and plunged my axe pick into the slope to prevent a slide. I could only admire his trust in my ability to hold him. The consequences of a fall would have been grisly.

On day two the winds were accompanied by a full-bore blizzard. Other assessors took their candidates to low-level venues or cancelled their day altogether, but not Bob. We were given our brief.

"Just assume I'm a rich American client and I want to climb a grade IV route."

We tumbled out of the minibus into the storm. The ski car park was covered in sheet ice and I immediately fell flat on my face.

"That never happens to my American guide," came the taunt.

We directed Bob towards the only route we thought might be safe to climb, Patey's Route on Aladdin's Buttress. Windslab was fast-building on every slope. Even the short approach to Patey's Route looked unstable. Choe and I conferred. A sound mountaineering judgement at this point might not only gain us some "brownie-points" but would also save us the trouble of climbing the route.

"Look, Bob, conditions are just too dangerous; there's no way we can guide you up here."

"OK folks, so we'll drop this game. I'm just Bob again and I want to do this route!"

As a full-time Lodge instructor Bob could judge the conditions to the finest margins. We took the precautions of hand-railing rocks along the base of the cliff and went one at a time across any open slopes. Climbing the route was the easiest bit of the day and we abseiled back down. Night was falling and we were far behind our estimated finishing time. Bob tore ahead through the drifts while we wallowed in his wake.

The car park was snow-bound and empty, and we had to descend to Glenmore forest before a bus came out to fetch us. On entering the Lodge drying room every stray hair and every stitch of clothing, ropes and rucksacks was thickly caked with rime and snow. We nearly fainted in the heat. I had never willingly climbed in worse conditions.

I emerged from the week with a pass in all sections, except rope management, for which I was asked to do a one-day reassessment. Somehow the snow-hole and navigation fiascos had been forgiven. Having survived the heat of battle, I emerged from the assessment a more resourceful leader. The true worth of the qualified guide is only proven when the going gets tough. That's when the training really counts.

After completing two ski-touring courses and a first-aid certificate in the same winter I was left exhausted and somewhat depressed. For the past six years I had pursued my personal climbing with total obsession. The guiding courses and work apprenticeships were sapping my energies. On one hand I resented the diversion, but on the other I began to see life in a more selfless way. Service as a guide could provide its own fulfilment without the continual need for individual achievement.

I completed my summer alpine apprenticeship in Arolla in the Swiss Valais Alps under the supervision of ex-Marine Mick Tighe. Mick was well known for giving nervous trainees a hard time, but for some reason he seemed to like me and took a hands-off approach. For a week he just let me go off and do what routes I wanted, then decided to follow me up the classic rock ridge of the Dent de Tsalion. The morning was chill, and, keen to impress Mick, I forged ahead at an immodest pace. I was wearing Damart gloves, popular with Yorkshire grannies for their thermolactyl warmth but not renowned for grip. Halfway up a rock groove my hand slipped and I slid headfirst to rejoin my students at the belay.

In mid-fall my kneecap had sliced against a rock flake and my team now beheld a deep gash that was oozing blood. I bound the knee and declared an immediate retreat. I had to keep my injured leg straight to avoid tearing the wound further, but could climb down with belays. We passed Mick, who considered that I was coping so well that he didn't need to assist. While he completed the climb I spent five hours hobbling down to Arolla. The doctor in Evolène applied eight stitches but omitted to prescribe antibiotics. Within three days the wound became badly infected and red streaks of septicaemia were racing up towards my groin.

Every day for the next week I underwent agonising sessions of cleaning and sterilising the wound. Effectively crippled, I cancelled my work for the rest of the summer. My impetuosity had cost me dear. Falling off when guiding is not a smart idea and it didn't happen again for twenty-five years.

Thankfully, I was given credit for my earlier alpine work with Terry and the BMC and was passed through to a final day of reassessment with Alan Kimber in March 1985. I was asked to guide Tower Ridge on Ben Nevis as far as Tower Gap and then evacuate my team by abseils into Observatory Gully. The weather and conditions were benign and Alan was supportive. Without hesitation he passed my day. I was a British Mountain Guide. I drove homewards into the night and slept in the open in a layby in Strath Fillan. The freedom of the hills was mine! I intended immediately to abandon my career in accountancy and within six months Joy and I began a new life in the North-West Highlands.

Notes

1. Peter Boardman died on Everest in 1982 attempting the first ascent of the NNE Ridge in alpine-style and without oxygen.
2. Edward Whymper of Matterhorn fame, and Geoffrey Winthrop Young, a doyen of British mountaineering through the early twentieth century.
3. Only Aspirant Guides who have completed winter assessment and alpine training are now allowed to take groups in the Alps and they must always be supervised by a qualified Guide. What is lost in freedom is gained in prudence, but with such regulation it has become more difficult to give trainee guides experience of independent work before they qualify.
4. 1983 was the first of a string of heat-wave summers in the Alps and heralded the beginning of the glacial retreat which has continued to the present.
5. The Forbes Arête tragedy was the first of several in the Mont Blanc range. The monitoring of such hazards and implementation of a warning system could have saved many lives. Many similar tragedies have occurred before dawn, just when climbers must pass such dangers. A possible explanation of such timing could be that ice adopts a plastic form when warm and is able to withstand massive gravitational forces; so that the sérac merely extrudes a little rather than collapsing during daytime heating. The cooling at night then causes the ice to contract and to fracture catastrophically in the twilight hour.

Chapter 4

NORTH-WEST FRONTIER

Motorists who drive the Road to the Isles from Fort William towards Kyle of Lochalsh often choose to turn north at Auchtertyre on to the Wester Ross scenic route. After passing through undistinguished moorland and planted forestry for six miles the road sweeps eastwards up to a marked crest – the Stromeferry summit – where a car-stopping vista unfolds. Vertiginous forested slopes drop to a broad fjord, a mile in width, which stretches inland to a fertile strath. In turn the strath is swallowed by the darker trench of a glen. North of this fault-line the skyline is decorated by a ring of bright quartz-capped hills. These are the first bold thrusts of the Torridonian mountain range. The north shore of the loch is fringed by a long straggling village, backed by linear crofts which blend gently into the landscape. On a crisp spring day the expansive scene is resonant of renewal and freedom. This is Lochcarron and in 1985 we decided to make it our home.

Lochcarron is not known as a centre of mountaineering, but has a pivotal position between the mountains of Torridon and the Isle of Skye. Through recent months Joy and I had toured the Scottish Highlands during our expedition to make the first ascent of all the Munros[1] in a single winter. Of all the areas we visited, Wester Ross had evoked the strongest passions. The north-western seaboard stands in full exposure to the power of the Atlantic storms but also harbours many pockets of intricate beauty. Beaches, bays and native woods contrast with barren headlands and a wilderness interior. The peaks are singularly impressive with their alternating tiers of sandstone and quartzite, and at that time their climbing potential was barely explored. Very few winter climbs had been recorded and dozens of cliffs still remained untouched. The maritime climate might be turbulent but could produce a bewitching array of light and atmospheres that no continental mountain ranges could match. For sure life would be hard, but had I wanted a safe ride I could have stayed an accountant.

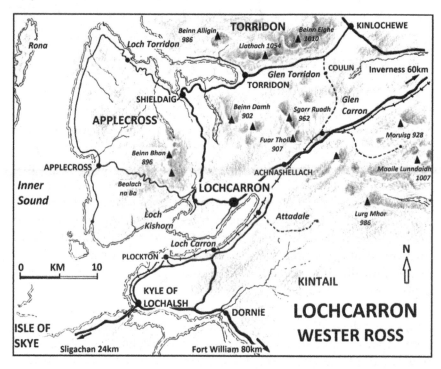

Romantic fancy did not blind us to the practicalities of running a mountain-guiding business. The geography had to be right. Lochcarron had fast access to the Cuillin of Skye, the hills of Kintail and Lochaber as well as all the peaks of Wester Ross. The Applecross plateau could become an instant playground thanks to the 600m Bealach na Ba road pass. The area also had good links from the south. Although thirty miles of the route were still single-track road Inverness airport was less than two hours' drive away, and the Kyle of Lochalsh railway offered a reliable public transport link. We reckoned that we could tempt climbers to forsake the honeypots of Aviemore and Fort William. Most importantly, there were no other mountain guides or instructors operating in the region. We would be pioneers.

I embarked on the venture with missionary zeal. Combining new-won guiding skills with my love of climbing, I wanted to take my clients out of their comfort zone to a new level of experience where the mountains would become as special for them as they were for me. Already I had seen guides in the Alps who merely went through the motions of mountaineering without a spark of passion. I was determined never to give in to the dread curse of tedium, and truly believed that I could inspire a genuine improvement in the ability, confidence and courage of each of my clients.

In September we rented a cottage on Slumbay shore near Lochcarron village and plotted our first season. There were no half measures. Winter courses were to be six days in duration. Camping, bothying or snow-holing would be obligatory on at least one night. We could accommodate three guests each week in our tiny cottage and Joy would provide home-cooking and packed lunches. We printed a sepia-tinted four-page brochure illustrated by black and white photos of An Teallach and Skye's Inaccessible Pinnacle. The prices were ridiculously low. The Winter Mountain Exploration course weighed in at an inclusive price of £150. For technical climbing at a 2:1 ratio the price top-up was all of £35. We weren't going to get rich quick on these deals, but nonetheless we were thrilled when the first bookings came in.

Heavy snows swept in over Christmas and the mountains were plastered white when our first groups assembled. Our nearest major hill was 907m Fuar Tholl, *the cold hole*. The "cold hole" in fact refers to a high corrie on the mountain's south-east flank which is clearly visible to travellers in Glen Carron and gathers any snow blown in on a west or north wind. The corrie has an impressive 200m-high sidewall and a short steep snow gully at its apex. I earmarked the place as the ideal training venue.

The first day of a winter course should offer an assessment of avalanche risk followed by an intensive coaching session in the use of ice axe and crampons. This would lead to the construction of snow belays and practice in basic rope-work as preparation to the ascent of a short grade I or II gully to the summit. With the addition of three hours for walking in and back out, this was quite a lot to squeeze into the eight hours of solstice daylight, especially in a foot of fresh snow. We ploughed upwards in single file and after three hours of trail-breaking reached the lower lip of the corrie. It was immediately clear that the powder snow was too deep for any meaningful training. We made the avalanche assessment which was positive in the sense that it indicated high risk on all steep slopes.

Instead, I suggested that we climb the ridge bounding the east side of the corrie to gain the summit. Toil became torment as the snow deepened into thigh-high drifts, and two of the students were lagging. A lunch break brought only a brief respite. The day was turning into an unmitigated slog. I felt guilty that I had offered virtually no coaching. Only a summit could give us any consolation. On gaining the corrie rim at 3.00 pm we broke into the golden glare of December's setting sun. Below us Loch Carron was bathed in a hot fusion of light and liquid while the surrounding hills, already stripped of the sun's brief glow, lay peacefully in greying slumber. I could tell that my students were mesmerised. What matter the training manual? What matter the long cold descent to come? This was what the people came to see.

The winter of 1986 developed into one of the finest in living memory. After a succession of storms and blizzards a Scandinavian anti-cyclone set in for five weeks. We saw a golden eagle soaring on the wind shear over Beinn Bhan's plateau, watched airborne powder avalanches cascading off the cliff of Coire na Feola and were blown off the Horns of Alligin by a Force 10 southerly. After successfully surviving an overnight expedition in the Fannaich hills I planned another snow-hole in the northern corrie of a remote Munro south of Glen Carron called Maoile Lunndaidh. One of my students was suffering from a stomach bug and the six-mile walk-in amounted to a "kill or cure" prescription. Instead of exploring the slopes to find the deepest drifts in which to dig, as is wise, we stopped at the first available snow-bank. The snow was mousse-like in consistency. After scooping out three metres our shovels hit the ground. By now it was dark. I decided to commit to what we had and we fashioned a fragile snow-house. Hardly had we got our invalid sheltered in his sleeping bag than half the roof collapsed. We tried to shore up the gap with a stack of overlapping snow briquettes but they simply disintegrated. At 7.30 pm our snow-hole had been downgraded to a starlit bivouac. We crouched under a constant barrage of spindrift and couldn't coax our stoves to light. My survival instincts then kicked in. I remembered passing an unlocked outhouse at Glenuaig Lodge two miles away and ordered an immediate withdrawal. By midnight we were laid out in a dry barn, fed, watered and mightily relieved. Maoile Lunndaidh was saved for the morrow.

By mid-February the ice climbing conditions in Torridon were magnificent. On the technical climbing course it was time to test my brochure enticement of *visits to remote corries with the potential for new routes*. One such venue was the east face of Tom na Gruagaich on Beinn Alligin, a tiered sandstone wall nearly 300m high, broken by three shallow couloirs where icy cascades had formed. My clients, Mick and Nigel, had proven themselves solid climbers over two days of training, and I judged that I could chance their skills on virgin ground.

We went for the left-hand couloir which led direct to the summit. Initial icy steps led to a steep ice groove and then a vertical fifty-metre barrier pitch. I could arrange good rock belays on the terraces between each tier. The boys rose to the occasion, seconding the grade V crux wall without any falls. They shared my excitement of pushing out a big new line. A narrow gully led over several shorter steps to the top. We emerged in a night of perfect calm at 6.15 pm. The embers of daylight coupled with a rising moon to cast a silvery light over the Hebridean seas. We called our climb Crown Jewel in celebration of Beinn Alligin's translation as *peak of the jewel*. I had inspired my clients to surpass their inhibitions and push their technical standards on a new route. Crown Jewel fulfilled all my hopes for my new guiding enterprise.

Two days later we climbed on the Applecross cliffs, and I assumed that if my clients could second grade V with aplomb they could lead a short grade IV under my supervision. I arranged all the protection runners except for a knife-blade piton which Nigel placed. I then soloed up the crux ice bulge and secured myself on a ledge with a spare rope ready to lend assistance and advice as necessary. The psychology of working with students in this way is delicate. The presence of a friendly instructor may seem reassuring but in practice can put unwanted pressure on the leading client. Nigel set off nervously. I soon realised that he didn't want to be in this predicament but gently coached him on to the bulge. Here, he forgot the need for good footwork, lost control and pulled up on arm strength alone. One axe popped out and I was powerless to help as his second hand lost its grip, then slipped through his wrist-loop. Leaving his glove in his loop he lurched backwards. The piton came out, and he tumbled a further five metres, giving his helmet a glancing blow on the way. He was unhurt but his confidence was shot. I had badly misjudged. After every day of sublimity there comes a hangover. I was simply expecting too much of my clients.

I tried to rescue the situation on the last day with another ambitious plan to hike a thousand metres up and over the top of Torridon's highest mountain, Liathach, to climb in the Trinity Gullies. We were all mentally exhausted. The inspiration of the Crown Jewel day had evaporated. The biting wind, the sheet ice on the ridge and the lack of protection on the climb sorely taxed my residual patience. We finished by wading through thick cakes of rime on the Northern Pinnacles and I was heartily glad to see the summit cairn. Again we were caught by darkness. Subconsciously blaming Nigel's fall for my stress, I let petty irritation boil over when he made a trivial mistake in map-reading on the descent and roundly berated him. If only we had admitted our fatigue and worked as a team. The mountains offer many moments of glory but they sorely punish the impetuous. I was still too young to know.

The cold weather came to an abrupt end at the beginning of March. Among our guests was an ingenuous and totally inexperienced couple from Suffolk, Sheila and Tom, who were not deterred from asking to climb an ice gully. I chose the most accessible and sheltered route, a grade III called Deep Gully in Coir' an Each on Beinn Bhan. A big south-westerly blow was due to come in during the day and strong gusts on the approach walk portended the storm. As I led the 25m ice pitch, waves of spindrift and stinging hail strafed the gully. Sheila responded with a tortoise-like crawl up the ice, Tom with a manic windmilling of both axes. By the time they had reached me the storm was upon us. We were trapped. At the top I looped all spare rope around my shoulders and tied us together three metres apart. We staggered up 30° slopes of frozen snow.

Every few seconds a miniature whirlwind birled down the slopes. One of us would be blown sideways and the others would be dragged down by the linking rope. We became dangerously tangled. My spectacles were completely fogged so I stuffed them in my jacket and stared blankly into the maelstrom. I feared that we might slide off and fall back down the gully but had lost all sense of direction. Sheila and Tom were plainly terrified; I was seriously perturbed, and yet the only way we could progress was to untie.

"Get down on your knees and crawl. Keep right behind me and

cling to my harness," I yelled. We inched across to meet a thick shroud of fog on the open ridge. Here the wind roared at a steady 80mph. By leaning hard into the gale and forming a tight shield we maintained ungainly progress until a line of old footprints showed us the way to the sheltered descent slopes. Though we were no longer in the teeth of the storm Tom still gripped my arm.

"Thank you for saving our lives," he said. "We'll never forget what you've done for us."

I was tempted to bask in the glow of their gratitude, but conscience stopped me. In truth I had taken them beyond the thin white line.

The long winter season brought a progressive strain in domestic life. We bid one group goodbye on Saturday morning only to welcome their successors five hours later. Joy and I began to get frustrated that we could never have a good argument. The intensity of having our guests with us for seven nights a week even extended to the breakfast table. Though doubtless well intentioned, some guests perched me on a pedestal, from which there was no escape. The questions were unceasing.

"Martin, what's the most difficult climb you've ever done?"

"What's your favourite Munro, Martin?"

"Martin, what was it like climbing with Chris Bonington?"

Faced with such a barrage on a dark winter's morning I nearly choked on my muesli.

As business grew we started employing other instructors. Lochcarron was in the twilight of its Klondyke period when a huge oil rig was constructed in the nearby Kishorn yard[2]. There were hundreds of construction workers lodging in the area and the social scene included regular pub discos. One morning after a big "do" at Strathcarron Hotel Joy opened our spare bedroom door with a cup of tea to find an uninvited female visitor sharing our guide's bed. Joy kept her cool.

"Would your friend like a cup as well?" she asked politely, but she was boiling inside.

"That's it," she vowed. "There'll be no more clients or guides staying here next year."

I readily agreed. The guide-client relationship is enhanced by a polite degree of separation. In any event Joy was pregnant by the time our second season started. In autumn 1986 we made two big commitments. I resigned my membership of the Institute of

Chartered Accountants, thus making an irrevocable commitment to full-time guiding. Then we bought a cottage in the crofting township of Achintee, which lies on a raised beach at the head of Loch Carron.

The self-discipline of training, whether it was running, pull-ups, or weight-lifting, became a vital part of my new life. Without it, pressures and insecurities soon built up and left me swimming in self-doubt. On Christmas Day and with our baby imminently due, I ran up the Apple-cross pass from Tornapress bridge. The Bealach na Ba is regarded as the finest mountain drive in Britain, and is so well engineered that its 600m ascent is evenly graded throughout its six-mile length. For both runners and cyclists it is a gruelling test of stamina. The fifty-minute Bealach dash sent me into a prolonged endorphinous glow, which was just as well. Joy went into labour that evening and it was not until just after midnight on the 28th when Alex arrived.

Any suggestion that I should take some paternity leave was frivolous with a fledgling business to run and no savings. The New Year courses were vital to our cash flow. A day after Alex's arrival I was up on Fuar Tholl with the first of our groups. Our car broke down the day Joy came out of hospital. Luckily, our village ambulance was doing a run to Inverness the next day. I spent the morning leading a navigation exercise and Joy and Alex arrived home at 2.30 pm. Hardly had the driver put Alex in his carry-cot down on our kitchen table than I was pestering him for a lift to pick our car up from the garage.

"But don't you want to see your beautiful baby?" he asked with withering West Highland charm.

The dynamics of our family life were etched at the outset, but, happily, we now had some peace. A significant increase in bookings affirmed my initial vision for the school. We were getting the benefit of increasing consumer wealth as the boom of the later Thatcher years took off. Adventure holidays were a new and attractive concept for the young middle class. We had entered the outdoor market at an ideal time. An additional boost came from the publication of *The Munros in Winter*[3], which was the perfect advertising vehicle. To handle groups of up to ten a week we rented a nearby shooting lodge, Carron Lodge. Courses were trimmed to five days, and we employed a couthy local lady, Mrs Thomas, who could cook hearty meals that satisfied a bunch of hungry climbers. Mrs T's thick broths, steak and kidney pies, Sunday roasts and jam roly-polys quickly acquired their own reputation. Joy supervised the domestic arrangements and handled our bookings while I worked on the hill.

Nineteen-eighty-seven was another vintage winter season but the climate changed abruptly thereafter.

Global warming, Scottish-style, began in 1989. The shift in the balance of weather patterns from cold dry easterlies to mild wet south-westerly airflows was dramatic. For whole weeks there was continuous rain. My diary extracts lost their former verve and hinted at despair.

Sun Jan 15th 1989: Non-stop deluge; probably four inches in 24 hours, and very warm. Struggled to find motivation but got the courses out and walking. Took my team out over Beinn Liath Mhor; force 9 on top; enjoyed it once the commitment was made . . .

Mon Jan 16th 1989: Still rough but colder; walked in to Fannaich bothy; no chance of fording rivers so could not follow the path; wild torrents pouring off the hills; reached bothy at 5pm; chimney blocked; couldn't sleep due to smoke on the lungs.

For lack of snow we were often forced to rock climb in atrocious weather.

Wed Feb 3rd 1989: Over to Skye but washed off Cioch West after one pitch

Thurs Feb 4th 1989: Out to Ardheslaig crag; downpour commenced on arrival; gave up after one route; surely it can't get any worse than this?

When the air-stream swung to the north-west, damp blizzards set in. The passage of every cold front was followed by wild squalls, which hurled volleys of white hail, known as *graupel*, over the ridges, making it impossible to face into the wind. During such storms, we had to cower on the ground and wait for a clearance. Climbing conditions were correspondingly grim. The cliffs became caked in soft rotten ice, which collapsed at the swing of an axe.

Wed 24th Jan 1990: Croydon Chimney on Sgorr Ruadh; turf stringy, ice rotten, desperate chimney half-way up complicated by avalanches of graupel; hoisted my students over this impasse; vicious

downdraughts on top pitch – further hoists needed; on top in a light-
ning storm at 5.15pm; thigh-deep drifts and knee-deep heather all the
way back; a real winter battle.

Wed 28th Feb 1990: Checkmate Chimney, An Teallach: main ice
pitch soft mush; weighty spindrift avalanches in top gully; furious
squall on reaching top; took an age to undo frozen knots, zips and
buckles; non-stop blizzard all the way back; Braemore road just
passable; a mind-sapping day, times when I felt blind anger at the
constant trials and torments.

In 1990 the weather reached its nadir. In the previous 125 years
the maximum January to March rainfall total in Fort William was
1149mm. This was smashed in 1989 with a three-month total of
1518mm and a staggering new record of 1754mm was attained in
1990. The psychological effect was insidious. Mountaineers revel
in the contrasts of experience, but with the mountains continually
clasped in the grey pall of storms, aesthetic pleasure was denied. As
guides we bore the pressure of providing for paying guests, and every
day we faced increased risks going up on the hilltops. I now had
a regular team of guides working for me – Simon Jenkins, Kevin
O'Neale, Paul Potter and Martin Welch. Their efforts were heroic.
Simon was the most stoical of guides but towards the end of his
twelve-week stint his phlegmatic humour waned and even he became
visibly traumatised. I developed a stress-induced gastroenteritis to
add to habitual insomnia.

Clients must have wondered at my jaundiced pallor, lack of energy
and frequent diversions off the path. I had once believed that I could
become habituated to continual drenching; 1990 proved that the
weather would always win.

Meanwhile our clients, revelling in the elemental experience of the
winter mountains, but assured of escape at the end of their five-day
holiday, would comment:

"It must be wonderful having your job; out on the mountains
every day."

Our final release from Atlantic storms coincided with the arrival
of our second child, Hazel, on 12 April. A glorious spring took root
and I felt as though I had entered a Garden of Eden. Many had
warned that I wouldn't handle Scotland's west coast climate, and, in
truth, I had only just passed the test.

Notes

1. The 3000-foot (914m) mountains of Scotland as listed in Munros Tables by Sir Hugh Munro in 1891. The original number of Munros was 282, but the Tables have been revised several times in light of re-surveys and topographic reassessment. In 1985 the number stood at 277; in 2013 the total was back to 282.
2. The Ninian Central rig was built at Loch Kishorn between 1975 and 1979 and at that time was the largest mobile structure ever built. At its peak the yard employed 4000 workers but by 1986 this had dwindled to 500. The site closed in 1987.
3. David & Charles (1986) re-published by Sandstone Press (2010)

Chapter 5

THE LEARNING CURVE

A little learning is a dangerous thing
Alexander Pope

The summit crown of the Aiguille Verte hovers dream-like above the forests of Argentière. On a fine evening a pink alpenglow will, for a brief half-hour, lend the peak divine aspiration. Clusters of granite spurs make a fierce stockade surrounding her citadel of ice.

The other-worldly beauty of this mountain is an entrapment to the unwary. Unlike the nearby Mont Blanc there are no easy routes here, no ways that can be tamed by bolts or fixed ropes. To linger in her couloirs in the heat of a summer's day is to court the hand of fate. The mountaineer must employ combined faculties of style and speed to realise the ascent by night and quit her slopes in the brief hours of morning shade. Nowhere are the moments of summit glory more precious than on the Verte.

Graduation as a mountain guide offers a gateway to travel the length and breadth of the Alps in pursuit of the most beautiful mountains and the most elegant routes. In 1985 the Aiguille Verte was my most-wanted mountain. I now advertised my own series of courses and for a third summer Joy and I camped wild in Argentière woods, where the Verte maintains her vigil, luring the susceptible while deriding any want of courage. The *voie normale* on the Verte takes a broad couloir on the south-east flank and was first climbed by Edward Whymper and his guides Christian Almer and Franz Biner in June 1865, three weeks before Whymper's Matterhorn ascent. The Whymper Couloir is 500m high and receives the full blast of the morning sun. A safer but more technical route, the Moine Ridge, was established on the second ascent, which was made just a week later.

No guides of my acquaintance had dallied on the Verte. The peak was far outside the scope of the usual training courses, and required a 1:1 guiding ratio to achieve the required speed. A young Czech student, Martin Vesely, was the only applicant on my first advanced Alpine course. With a new business to promote I was unwilling to cancel any course on grounds of financial viability. Martin turned out to be a fit and able climber and, unbeknown to him, I saw his potential and trained him for an attempt on the Verte during our second week together. The summer of 1985 was another hot season and in mid-July a considerable volume of spring snow still lay piled on the ridges. I reasoned that we could use this snow to speed an ascent of the Moine Ridge.

The climb commences from the Couvercle Hut, perhaps the most delectable spot on the French flanks of the Mont Blanc massif, possessing a stunning panorama of the Grandes Jorasses, Mont Blanc and the Chamonix Aiguilles from its flowered meadows. We found ourselves the sole candidates for the Aiguille Verte and obeyed the recommended *reveille* of half past midnight. Outside the air was warm and muggy, the temperature well above zero. In such conditions the snow surface may crust temporarily through radiational heat loss but there is no proper freezing of the snow-pack. The guardian got up to bid us farewell and as he too sniffed the air he remarked:

"I think you will take a long time."

Throughout the ascent of the Talèfre Glacier our boots broke through the fragile crust into calf-deep granular snow. By dawn we had lost half an hour on my projected schedule, but I reasoned that we could recover such a minor loss by climbing well on the ridge. On gaining the crest we found many obstacles completely covered in granular snow which collapsed under body-weight. Digging, wading and swimming I fought onwards with increasing desperation. Our self-imposed seven-hour time limit slid far beyond our grasp but the summit drew tantalisingly close. I could see its unblemished corniced flute just two or three hundred metres away, but we were deflected by a succession of gendarmes. The towers could not be climbed direct and flanking manoeuvres took us on to collapsible banks of slush. Ten hours after setting out and just seventy metres below the top, I realised that we had climbed far beyond the point of safe return. The mountain cast off its last remnants of allure and was unmasked as a baking cauldron of peril. A fraught retreat ensued. I lowered Martin wherever I could find a belay and stuck out my neck to climb down many sections of vertical slush which offered neither grip nor protection. Soaked down to the puddles in our boots we staggered into the Couvercle Hut at 9.00 pm. The guardian gave us a late supper, served with a knowing smile.

In eventual victory the Aiguille Verte still exacted a heavy price. I returned alone two years later to solo the Nant Blanc Face, a *très difficile* (TD) route pioneered by the local guide Armand Charlet in 1935. A route-finding error forced me to climb under the overhanging sérac which fringes the summit ice-cap. Finding there was no escape, I was forced to aid-climb the ice, leapfrogging my two ice screws above a giddy drop, poised 2000m above the green meadows of Argentière. I reached the summit in baking heat at 2.00 pm, and was forced to bivouac for fifteen hours before I could descend the Whymper Couloir and get off the mountain. Some lessons are hard-learned.

Later in the summer of 1985 I returned to the Couvercle with a student group to attempt the traverse of 3856m Les Courtes. This offers an elegant expedition in miniature mould of the Aiguille Verte but without the scale and commitment. We had already been slowed by crampon failures when a cold wind caught us on the narrow final arête. Here, the weakest of the group, Roland, had an anxiety attack. For ten minutes he sat in a snow-step, shaking and weeping, while I tried to coax him back to his feet. I reasoned that the onward traverse was the best option. A retreat would take us across snow-slopes exposed to the sun and would either stigmatise Roland as cause of the failure or else allow him to wallow in self-pity. I did not wish to encourage either trait. As I had hoped, we recovered an air of normality once we moved on. Thankfully, I had one strong student in Steve and he led us down to the Col des Cristaux, one of the loneliest spots in the Mont Blanc range.

Our way back to the hut first descended a slope of granite boulders. I was moving ahead to check the correct route when I heard a yell from behind and the rope pulled tight. Steve slumped on the rocks squirming with pain. A sling that was hanging on the back of his harness had snagged on a spike and exerted a sudden twisting jerk in his nether regions as he moved forward. Initially we treated the mishap with schoolboy humour, fully expecting a rapid recovery. Steve was wearing a Troll Whillans harness[1]. The Whillans was the first manufactured sit harness offering leg support, and was a revolutionary advance in climbing technology when first introduced in 1970. Before then, climbers used only a waist-tie so that the load of a fall was directed entirely through the abdomen and the climber could slowly suffocate when hanging free. However, the Whillans itself had a significant flaw. The flat crotch strap left the male user distinctly vulnerable, and rumours were already circulating in the climbing community.

After five minutes Steve blanched and succumbed to a spasm of involuntary shivering. Almost as quickly he broke into a hot purple flush. The cycle of shock continued unabated. I was perplexed and increasingly distressed as to why Steve showed no improvement, but he refused to allow any examination. Faced with the emergency Roland discovered hidden reserves of strength. While he tended and reassured Steve I pondered the predicament. We were alone. Mobile phones did not exist, we had no radio and the hut was three hours' away. If I went for help I would have to leave my three students alone at 3500m, and to cap the brew a big storm was forecast for that evening.

I had a few prescription painkillers in my medical kit in case of an incident of major trauma. As these were opiate-based their unqualified use broke the law and would leave me without defence should they have malign consequence, but as I saw things our only chance was to drug Steve sufficiently to get him up on his feet and off the mountain.

"Take three of these," I ordered

After ten minutes the spasms subsided and he regained something of his natural colour. We had bought ourselves a breathing space. With Steve tied tight and close to me the other two gently led the way down rocky ribs to the Talèfre Glacier and over three kilometres of flat ice. Steve became so nauseous and fevered that we virtually had to drag him up the final slope to the hut. At 5.00 pm we helped him inside. I was still naively incredulous that so small a tug could produce so violent a reaction. We put him to bed and called the guardian, who peeled back Steve's underwear. A shockingly distended and swollen organ the size of a snooker ball was revealed. The diagnosis was instant.

"Testicule étranglé; hélicoptère."

The situation was now obvious. Urgent surgery was required to restore blood flow. Within forty-five minutes a helicopter arrived and Steve and I flew down over the Mer de Glace to be met by a waiting ambulance at the Chamonix helipad. A little later the thunderstorm broke with a vengeance. By getting off the hill we had probably saved more than one testicle. As a guide I have never abandoned the conviction that to move is to survive, whatever the pain and complexity involved.

Steve was quickly restored to normal function. When I visited him the next day he was sitting pink-faced in his hospital bed tackling a steamed artichoke, but we didn't bargain for the deviousness of the media. The Chamonix news agencies devised a suitably dramatic press release and the next day's edition of the *Birmingham Evening Post* ran the headline:

"Worcester climber castrated in 6,000 foot fall in the Alps."

I hoped that he'd told his girlfriend about his recovery before she read the story.

The Brenva Spur of Mont Blanc is a compelling objective. This snow ridge bounds the majestic east face of the mountain and was first climbed a day after Whymper's Matterhorn ascent in the momentous year of 1865. The route represented a major step forward in the standard of alpine snow and ice climbing, and was not surpassed in difficulty for twenty years. Even today the climb is graded *difficile* (D). Having suffered rejection by the Aiguille Verte the Brenva became my prime objective when my next technical course assembled. My clients, John Blore and Martin Lister, proved their worth on two training climbs and soon succumbed to my persuasive charms.

A complex approach adds significantly to the seriousness of the Brenva climb. We left the Aiguille du Midi cable station on a hot mid-August afternoon, crossed the Vallée Blanche and climbed into the Combe Maudit. To get to the Brenva we had to climb over the Frontier Ridge and descend to the head of the remote Brenva Glacier. On the Ridge crest a decrepit Italian bivouac, the Trident Hut[2], offered shelter until the midnight hour. The hut became improbably crowded with other parties, all aiming for a variety of routes across the Brenva Face, and sleep was impossible. With relief we retrieved our kit from the chaotic pile in the hut and headed out into the moonlight at 11.30 pm. A short descent brought us to the glacier and we traversed into the shade on the Col Moore at the base of the

Spur. A triangular rock buttress guards access to the snow ridge. The climbing here was awkward and serious. Unable to see the easiest route we blundered up steps of grade IV standard. The arête was obvious once gained, but we could sense the growing voids on either side, and the angle imperceptibly rose from 40 to 55°.

We had been climbing blind for nigh on six hours when the first dawn light appeared over the hills of Piedmont. At last we would see where we were and could perhaps enjoy the situation, but the appearance of the sun was accompanied by a bitterly cold breeze. The hour after dawn is often the coldest in the alpine day. The sunlight triggers immediate air motion on the eastern faces of the peaks, and a rising anabatic breeze streams over the ridges and down the west flanks where the cold night air is still sinking. I had climbed through the night lightly clad and now we were stranded on slopes of glassy ice, cut to the bone yet unable to stop and put on extra layers. Though bathed in resplendent sunlight I could feel my body heat rapidly draining. Involuntarily, the circulation to my hands and feet was cut. Frostbite and hypothermia were minutes away. We teetered across the icy slopes to a final outcrop of rocks where we could take off sacks and get to our warm clothing.

The dressing operation took fifteen minutes in which time three other parties passed us. Now, they were splayed in varying states of anxiety in the exit cleft, their predicament notable for the absence of any belays. I probed ways of getting past but séracs barred alternative routes. We moved to the side, tied in to ice screws and waited until the way was clear. The cleft posed a glassy ice pitch close to Scottish grade IV in difficulty. My arms were so cold that I could barely grip my axes. Not until we had surmounted the barrier and gained the gentle summit slopes did circulation return. The resultant "hot aches", as the blood pushed back through the capillaries, were protracted and exquisitely painful. Only then could I cheer up and ponder our success.

I was completely overwhelmed that a route first climbed with nailed boots and metre-long alpenstocks in 1865 had taken so much out of me. Today we had been unlucky with both the wind and the icy conditions, but if a grand classic established in the Golden Age of Alpinism of the nineteenth century could prove so demanding, a rich potential for similar adventures all over the Alps was affirmed.[3]

I arrived back at our tent in the woods late in the afternoon in a state of complete exhaustion, stretched out on my sleeping bag and dropped into a stupor. That moment of abandonment to sleep is perhaps the greatest joy in the cycle of an alpine climb. As I was sinking into the capacious depths of slumber I was jerked back to consciousness by a sharp and insistent voice. I opened my eyes to see a pair of creased blue-serge trousers standing at the tent door. Above them towered a poker-faced gendarme.

"You are breaking the law; no camping is allowed. You must move now."

The authorities in Chamonix had finally decided clear the wild campers from their valley.

Our idyll in Argentière woods was over. The alpine life would never again be so beautifully simple.

With inspiration from the pioneering feats of early alpinism and reserves of enthusiasm to expend I wished only for more clients to share my passion. In April 1986 we received an enquiry for guiding in the Alps from a gentleman by the name of David Litherland. I intimated interest and by reply a three-page typewritten letter of engagement arrived in the post. This prospectus listed a mouth-watering selection of classic courses on the high alpine peaks. A final paragraph detailed a financial arrangement that he trusted would be satisfactory. Although his tone was strictly formal David's willingness to commit his alpine career into my care was quite affecting. He became my first private client. A private arrangement usually compels the guide to attempt specific climbs. The guide's control over route choice can be compromised, but presented with David's wish list I was not inclined to complain.

Although the worth of mountain training courses was widely accepted, back in the 1980s there was much prejudice against the private use of guides. The self-taught post-war generation of working-class climbers regarded payment for such services as blatant cheating. Yet many of this hard-core were now training to become guides themselves. As for the traditional mountaineering elite, the Alpine Club held an ambivalent position. Their early members had all used local guides to achieve the pioneering ascents of the 1850s and 60s. Many regarded Albert Mummery as a dangerous radical when he promoted the idea of climbing guideless in the 1880s, but by the mid twentieth century most Alpine Club members climbed independently irrespective of their financial means, and those who did use guides generally kept quiet about their tactics.

Employment of a guide removes some of the commitment and logistical difficulty of a climb, but to do the sort of routes that David proposed requires ability and tenacity at both ends of the rope. For the climber pressed for vacation time yet ambitious to achieve great climbs there is practical sense in booking a guide. Any compromise in ethics may be repaid by a higher success rate. David was in his mid forties; his partners from younger days had given up alpine climbing and, as a senior business development manager with Shell, he could afford to indulge his desire to re-engage in mountaineering.

We met in Täsch in the Zermatt valley at the end of August. David had driven direct from London. He hadn't climbed in the Alps for many years, yet wanted to go straight up to the Rothorn Hut at 3198m and then climb the 4063m Ober Gabelhorn. His vaulting ambition was quickly grounded by the effects of altitude. We struggled as far as the forepeak of Wellenkuppe, itself a decent achievement for a first climb, but turned back with a sense of failure. An attempt on the Nadelhorn on a bitterly cold wintry morning brought similar anti-climax. Our consolation was an easy subsidiary top, the Ulrichshorn, which even had a wooden bench on the summit to mock our pride.

David finally found his fitness on the South Ridge of the Dent Blanche. For poise, beauty and classical challenge the Dent Blanche rivals any of the peaks of the Zermatt ranges. We approached from the Val d'Hérens and enjoyed a magnificent four-hour climb from hut to summit. Although the climb went well, David showed some nervousness traversing under the crux pinnacles of the ridge and frequently questioned me as to the correct line of the route and the coming difficulties. As I had never climbed the mountain before I judged it best to tell David what he wanted to hear rather than attempt objective replies. I also became acquainted with David's passion for photography. He climbed with a metal-cased Nikon SLR camera round his neck and a daily allowance six rolls of slide film in his pockets. Whenever I was leading over a tricky but scenic passage the rope pulled tight and he called:

"Can you hang on a minute?"

This became the mantra of every day. I would turn to see David setting up exposures and apertures and I would fume with impatience.

He probably thought me young, pushy and unduly obsessed with getting the climb over in minimum time. He might reasonably have accused me of demanding too much from him. I based our standards of performance on the grades and quoted times of the current Alpine Club guidebooks[4], not realising that both were seriously underestimated.

These initial tensions set the dynamics of our future climbing partnership, but to our credit we quickly established an easy social relationship. We shared a grammar school-Cambridge education, and I teasingly stoked David's political and environmental polemics. David later made his objective the completion of all the 4000m peaks of the Alps, sixty-one by the Blodig-Dumler list[5] then in current use, within a timescale of ten to fifteen years. With this stimulus each of our climbs became part of a mission and I quickly became as committed to his 4000m peaks project as he.

In subsequent years David devoted a month to his alpine ventures to allow for proper training and acclimatisation. By 1989 we had built a foundation of solid climbs, and at the very end of that season, a window of fine weather opened. The lure of the *grande course*[6] was irresistible. I offered David several options and he chose the Domgrat, a traverse of both the 4545m Dom and 4491m Täschhorn, respectively the fifth and eighth highest mountains in the Alps. These two peaks crown the Mischabel range between Zermatt and Saas Fee and possess an uncanny angular symmetry. The linking crest is razor-sharp, chillingly remote and graded *difficile*. In late September solitude was guaranteed.

On the afternoon of the twenty-first we took the cable car from Saas Fee to Längflue and engaged with the complex ascent to the Mischabeljoch Bivouac Hut. Autumnal snows lay heavy on the Fee Glacier. We wallowed for an hour and on the steeper final climb the whole slope settled several inches under our weight with a deep audible crack. I crawled fifty metres ahead on all fours trying to spread my weight until I reached safer icy ground. Already we felt committed.

We left the haven of the bivouac hut at 5.15 am on a cold calm morning. The ridge to the Täschhorn was in perfect condition. All recent snow had melted off thanks to the southerly aspect. Remarkably, we didn't need crampons, for the rock was dry and any snow crisp but yielding. We were on top by 9.30 and without a second thought embarked on the Domgrat. Instantly, conditions changed.

The overlapping slabs of the Täschhorn's North Ridge were coated in powder snow. No longer could we move together. I took belays and asked David to place protection runners and belays as he climbed down. Because of the fresh snow he moved with hesitancy, unsure of the correct line. With rising irritation I barked instructions from above. Sometimes he couldn't find any anchors and I was forced to back-climb long sections, crimping tiny edges with gloved hands where a fall could not be entertained. We took nearly four hours to descend 250m to the Domjoch, which is as inaccessible a place as one can find in the Alps. Near-vertical ribs and runnels plunged hundreds of metres to the flanking glaciers. Escape was not an option. I rued our earlier haste. If only we had paused and pondered back at the Täschhorn.

The onward ridge broke into a series of decomposing towers linked by arêtes of rotten snow where protection was illusory. When one tower was vanquished another would pop up in its place. I weaved David through this sensational terrain with growing stress. At times I boiled with frustration at the constant demands of route-finding, leading, digging, chivvying and reassuring; at others I felt starkly alone. David sometimes seemed inordinately slow, but he was merely taking the care that was demanded in such an exacting place. At 5.30 pm I reached the red summit battlements of the Dom and led three superb pitches on solid friendly rock to the summit snows. Perched on the final belay I looked back down the ridge. David stood astride the sunlit crest and behind him the Domgrat scythed through a sea of boiling grey cloud. I should have felt undiluted joy, yet the dominant sensation was that of relief.

After five years as a mountain guide I was thirty-five years old and beginning to know my trade. A little experience combined with a surfeit of enthusiasm is a dangerous mix. I had pulled off several good routes, but too often I had climbed for my own ambition as much as that of my clients. My diary was littered with epics and a few near-misses. Great climbs are not measured merely by success but by the style and harmony of their achievement.

Notes

1. Designed by Don Whillans for the British Annapurna South Face expedition of 1970.

2. During the 1990s Trident Hut began slipping off its tenuous perch and was closed, then removed. A second bivouac hut lies a few hundred metres further north-west on the Frontier Ridge on the Col de la Fourche and is still open.
3. The Brenva Spur was subsequently altered by a massive avalanche, rendering the lower rock buttress unstable, and is rarely climbed nowadays.
4. Many *peu difficile* routes have since been upgraded to *assez difficile*. The timings quoted in the 1970s series of Alpine Club guidebooks edited by Robin Collomb were pitched for guided teams who knew the route, climbing in perfect conditions. More recent editions have made realistic extensions.
5. Karl Blodig was the first man to list and climb all the 4000m peaks of the Alps. His list of seventy-six was refined to a total of sixty-one by Helmut Dumler. Of these fifty-one are recognised as major mountains and this is the target for most mountaineers. In 1993 the Union Internationale des Associations d'Alpinisme (UIAA) published a new list of eighty-two 4000m summits, including most significant subsidiary tops. Every list so far published has inconsistencies and omissions, but the UIAA list is followed by those few climbers who want to say they have done everything!
6. The French term for a major alpine route, most-often applied to the difficult face routes, but equally apposite to long ridge traverses such as the Domgrat.

Chapter 6

BASE CAMP

Joy was working in the LD Mountain Centre[1] in Newcastle upon Tyne when I first saw her in February 1974. I took a temporary job in the shop in my gap year before going up to Cambridge University and started a day before my nineteenth birthday. The staff introductions ended in the ski-wear section where a blonde girl with a fulsome figure was standing next to a fan heater, dressed in blue trousers and a polka-dot pinafore.

"Hello; I'm Joy," she said, and broke into a radiant smile as she shook my hand. Her blue-grey eyes were stunningly large and she was surrounded by an aura of Worth perfume.

I was usually tongue-tied when faced with a pretty girl, but, despite her glamour, she had a warmth and openness that put me at my ease. After a fortnight I dared to ask her out and within a month we were completely in love. Our relationship moved fast. I managed one year at university before it became unbearable for us to live apart. We were married at twenty and set up home at Cambridge before moving to Sheffield in 1977.

As I commenced my training as an accountant Joy might have expected a conventional trajectory of married life, but she quickly had to adapt to the greater force of my climbing obsession. She enjoyed hillwalking, skiing and camping with me and we found a shared love of Scotland, but increasingly she had to endure the brooding intensity of life with a driven climber. Secure in her love I pursued my climbing single-mindedly, and very few evenings or weekends were spared. In response she forged her own identity, taking a secretarial course and finding a job as personal assistant to the managing director of a frozen food distributor. She decided that she wasn't going to hang around crags every weekend so took up road-biking. While I climbed she toured the Peak District, Snowdonia and Lake District, and was regularly clocking rides of a hundred miles or more.

She was inured to a peripatetic lifestyle by the time I became a mountain guide. The guiding profession is not conducive to marital longevity. Surveying my guiding colleagues, the marriages that seemed to work usually featured a stable home base and, frequently, the wives in these relationships had their own career. Often the wife was the main breadwinner, and offered a bed-rock of practical and emotional support to their colourful but wayward partners.

Early decisions were crucial. Our move to Lochcarron was inspired. Joy loved the Highlands as much as I. Instead of planting ourselves in a mountaineering enclave we entered an ordinary community, which did not revolve around the adventure sports scene. Joy could breathe the freedom of social normality. Lochcarron is not physically hemmed in by mountains in the manner of the deep alpine valleys. There is more water than mountain, the landscape is expansive and the climate favours gardening as much as climbing. Joy immediately settled and if I ever felt a yen to move abroad to some more fashionable mountain locale, I quickly counted my blessings.

A guide can be away from home for nine months of a year in pursuit of a decent living. Ski-touring offers lucrative earnings but involves spending an extra six or eight weeks in the Alps each spring. I decided at the outset to avoid that trap. We had the mountains of Skye on our doorstep. Whatever the cost to my knee-joints, I committed my energies to the Cuillin hills each spring.

However, the summer alpine season was not dispensable. We packed belongings and closed our home every June for the twelve-hundred mile journey to Chamonix. Our early alpine courses were based in Argentière and in 1990 Joy suggested that, in the interests of our young children, we should buy a caravan and lodge on Les Chosalets campsite for the summer. Unwisely, I agreed and we invested £3000 in a second-hand van and nearly as much again on all the fitments.

The outward journey took four days instead of the usual two. With the van packed to the gunnels we could barely exceed 50mph. We broke a window attempting a reversing manoeuvre, erection of the awning defeated my best attempts and to complete our misery the electrics wouldn't work. A nadir was reached parked on the A14 near Cambridge. I fiddled with the lighting connections inches from the carriageway while the van was buffeted by every passing juggernaut. We arrived in Argentière at 5.00 am and grabbed three hours sleep. I had just fixed both awning and electrics when my first client arrived. So began a sweltering summer. For several weeks temperatures hovered at 30°C in the valley. Hazel was just four months old, and was continually disturbed by children from neighbouring tents who wanted to play mother. With the heat and cramped surrounds her sleep patterns became erratic and Joy never got a full night's sleep. On return from climbs I brooded in the shade, while Joy managed our home and supervised our course clients who were lodged in a nearby chalet.

Tempers were somewhat frayed as the end of the season approached and we longed for the moment we could commence the homeward journey. On 14 September Joy waved me off on a final day-route up the Aiguille du Midi cable car and began packing for a quick getaway. My client, Mike Kent, was a strong ice climber but had a stocky build that made for slow walking. I took him to the Direct Route up the Triangle Face of Mont Blanc du Tacul. After completing ten pitches of ice his crampon broke as we traversed towards the descent route. Instead of an easy walk I had to organise diagonal abseils to get Mike off the ice and on to easy-angled snow. Panic set in when I checked my watch.

Due to the delay we had only an hour to get back for the last cable car to Chamonix. I towed Mike over the Vallée Blanche so fast that, to use Whymper's words, "he larded the glacier".

As we made a final lung-bursting effort to climb the final arête into the lift station we saw the last cabin slide off down the cable with all the staff aboard. We were trapped for the night with nothing to eat or drink[2] and made a penitent's bed on the concrete stairs inside the station. I tried to wish away the next twelve hours. At least we were warm but the intense dry heat, constant throbbing and diesel fumes from the nearby generator left me with an almighty hangover that was not alleviated by the reception when I finally got back to Argentière fifteen hours late. I found Joy in the midst of a collapsed awning, flanked by two fractious children. The chill was colder than the top of Mont Blanc. Once Mike was safely off home I judged the best course was to blame our predicament entirely on my client.

When we moved our course base from Argentière to Evolène in 1994 I had convinced Joy that I would never set foot in a caravan again. Our move to Switzerland was an exciting new venture. I held a special affection for Evolène as the place of my convalescence from septicaemia ten years previously. Spared the depredations of large-scale skiing development the village has stayed compact and rustic and preserves a peacefulness that is missing from the frenetic environs of Chamonix. The climbs around nearby Arolla were ideal for beginners and Evolène has most of the 4000m mountains of the Alps within the compass of a two-hour drive.

We stuck to our proven formula of lodging our clients in chalets and employing a cook for each season. As the volume of business consolidated we might have gone for growth and tried to become a corporate brand. Such a course was contrary to our instincts. With ten or twelve guests a week we could maintain a personal ambience in the operation and keep direct control on the quality of our service, but with Alex now at school the family could only come out for four weeks each season.

In Joy's absence we needed a good domestic supervisor. Usually we recruited locally in Lochcarron and took the cook out with us, but in 1996 we were forced to advertise. Through the classifieds of *Climber* magazine we recruited a charming but wilful young lad called Ben. He performed well on a trial and we set up shop in Evolène with high expectations. We kitted Ben out with chef's hat and apron, but, alas, his greater passions for running, climbing and then lazing on the veranda took priority over cooking. Even the humble flapjack was incinerated under his care. Apple pies were served with a crust and no filling. Moussaka comprised boiled sliced potatoes and an unadulterated tin of lentils. We knew things were bad when we saw some of our clients eating out in Evolène's restaurants. Joy tried tact and persuasion to no avail. Ben bristled at the hint of criticism, so I tried to humour a response by inviting him to join me on the most unusual climb in the Alps.

The Emosson Dam sits high above the forests of Trient on the Swiss-French border, and is perhaps the most spectacular feat of hydroelectric engineering in Europe. In the 1990s the 140m retaining face of the dam was made into a gigantic climbing wall[3] by local guides with the placement of a line of bolts and hundreds of coloured bolt-on holds. The climb started as a steep slab, moved through the vertical on the third pitch and ended on a 105° overhanging face. Ben helped to lead the lower pitches but became exhausted on the headwall. Watched by a horde of tourists I led the finish, pulled over the overhang of the parapet and belayed to the bounding fence.

Quickly, Ben ran out of steam and with the onset of cramp his fingers uncurled from the holds. His spindly frame was left dangling in space over the void. I tied off his rope, sat back and gloated. At last I had him where I wanted.

"Put your prusiks on the rope," I said impassively.

With two prusiks it is possible to ascend a hanging rope, but after some frantic fiddling Ben dropped his first prusik cord, making further progress impossible. Only a hoist from above could save him. I dropped him a spare loop of rope to make a pulley with 3:1 mechanical advantage and called for assistance. With half-a-dozen bystanders hauling on the hoisting line and a sizeable crowd offering vocal support he was unceremoniously fished out of his predicament and plopped on to the parapet. This shock treatment failed to work. Ben's cooking remained as bad as ever. We vowed never again to make the same mistake. The next time we needed to advertise in 2004 we used the rather more genteel *Lady* magazine, and recruited a professional couple Ian and Jan Whiting. When they retired, Judith Hawtree took on the job with verve and passion, and she eventually moved permanently to Evolène with her husband Mike. Our clients were assured of proper hospitality, and many booked as much for Judith's cakes as the climbing.

Whatever the provocation, Joy has never worried about my own safety on the mountains. Whether I was alone and missing for twenty-four hours on the Aiguille Verte or caught in a terrible storm on Les Droites, and even after I had staggered off Fuar Tholl with a dislocated shoulder, she maintained complete faith that I would always return. She fretted far more about my competence in domestic maintenance.

Christmas normally allowed our family respite from business and clients. In 1997 severe December storms had removed some slates from the roof of our course lodge in Lochcarron. On Boxing Day I was becoming bored with inactivity and decided to go over and fix them. I hoisted my ladder over the roof ridge and hauled myself into position six metres above the pavement, but I had neglected to fix proper roof hooks on the ladders. When I shifted position the three-inch struts slipped off the ridge. The ladder shot off the eaves at phenomenal speed. Once airborne I applied climber's instinct and curled myself sideways so as to take the impact on arms and shoulder.

I bounced on to the road in full view of Alex and Hazel who were playing on their new roller-blades. Joy rushed into the fray, called the ambulance and comforted the traumatised children while I was taken to Inverness. My injuries could have been much worse, but in any event I had a badly cracked pelvis, several broken ribs and a fractured elbow. For the next fortnight she juggled hospital visits with the tasks of entertaining ten guests on our New Year courses and finding staff to replace me for the following two months, not to forget full-time duties as a mother.

Two days into this routine an additional intrusion appeared in the form of the media. The story was manna to news-starved journalists in their New Year doldrums. Within hours Joy was receiving calls, not just from the local papers but from the national tabloids. We were offered four figure fees to tell my story and pose for a picture. Joy's mistrust of the media intensified when she caught cameramen snooping around our house. They were summarily dismissed and we agreed that a policy of non-co-operation would give us a chance to bury the story and avoid any damage to our business.

Our naivety was repaid with a swathe of concocted stories in every paper from the *Daily Record* to *The Times*. The *Sun* carried a full-page feature with parallel pictures of Mont Blanc, the Eiger North Face and my house roof with arrows to indicate relative height differences. My reported injuries ranged from a fractured spine to shattered legs. We missed out on a fat fee but at least preserved our moral sanctity.

In 1991, after a shortened alpine working season, I went to the Indian Himalaya to attempt the first ascent of Bhrigu Pathar in the Gangotri range. This was my first personal expedition since becoming a guide, and I left Joy to mind Alex and Hazel for the six weeks of my absence. We flew to Delhi over the Black Sea and the mountains of eastern Turkey, then passed directly over Tehran city and the snowy summit of Demavend before the envelopment of darkness above the deserts of Pakistan. For hours my nose was pressed to the window. I was captivated, excited and motivated. After seven years away from the Himalaya this adventure was special and surely deserved.

Four hours later I lay awake in a Delhi restroom, my pulse pounding against a hard pillow. What had I done leaving Joy for so long? How could I get through the coming weeks? The pain of separation was twisted by paroxysms of guilt at my abandonment of family. The black-dog night was as bleak as I have endured. Then, come dawn and the renewal of the enterprise, the dark clouds lifted. On this emotional rollercoaster I approached the Himalaya, but once I was in the thick of the endeavour the mountains gained the upper hand.

With our climb successfully accomplished I had several days to kill and went exploring in the Rudugaira side-valley south of Gangotri. A dangerous idea was forming. Three beautiful snow peaks ringed the valley head, Gangotri I, II and III, the highest 6672m in altitude. They were wonderful objectives for experienced clients and, so far as I knew, nobody was then running commercial expeditions in the Indian Himalaya.

The homeward journey was flushed with anticipation. My longing for home was soon to be alleviated and I had a plan for the following year. In Delhi I made preliminary arrangements, booking Gangotri peak with the Indian Mountaineering Foundation and checking travel agencies who might support the trip. Simultaneously, I bought an especially generous range of gifts for Joy, my abnormal largesse hinting at subconscious design.

On a wet October afternoon I arrived back in Inverness. One-year-old Hazel uttered her first words to me from the back seat of the car. As always, Joy had made a lovely meal for my return and with great pride I produced my presents. The children were put to bed and the air was warm, even romantic. At that point I felt my quibble of conscience needed to be aired.

"I've had the idea to run a guided trip there next year. I think it will work."

"So it's decided."

"Well yes; I've booked the peak."

"How can you do that without telling me?"

"But it will make us money, I'm sure."

Joy's fury was volcanic; soon my presents were flying round the kitchen and I was consigned to the spare room. During my sleepless night I noticed a growing churning in my stomach, and by dawn was locked in the toilet with acute food poisoning, contracted from indulgence in a Delhi salad bar. After enduring six weeks without me Joy now had to put up with a further four days of helplessness.

In the fullness of time Joy accommodated my idea of running

Himalayan trips. My brochure for Gangotri peak brought an avalanche of replies. Within a month we had ten bookings plus a waiting list. The early autumn was always a depressed period for business. Work in Scotland was sporadic, the weather often awful and we battled against an overdraft until the fees for forthcoming winter courses began to flow in. A Himalayan trip would plug the gap. So began for me a rewarding and engrossing period in my mountaineering career. The Indian Himalaya had huge potential for exploration, little-known ranges with hundreds of unclimbed peaks. With a vow not to exceed a month in time away I could pursue fabulous objectives while earning a valuable slice of the annual bread.

While Joy might protest against my clumsy and often disingenuous way of divulging plans, never did she stand square in my path. Without that understanding our relationship could not have succeeded, and without the homecomings to Joy and family my guiding life would have lost its compass.

Notes

1. Joy's brother-in-law was Gordon Davison, who founded the LD shop with his partner Peter Lockey, and then created Berghaus which quickly became one of the Britain's leading manufacturers of outdoor kit.
2. The nearby Cosmiques Hut did not open until 1992.
3. Fearful of safety issues and the potential for legal claims the Emosson Dam owners rescinded permission for climbing after five years and both holds and bolts were removed.

Part Two

HOME GROUND: SCOTLAND

Chapter 7

THE MUNRO-BAGGERS

He who first met the Highlands' swelling blue
Will love each peak that shows a kindred hue
Byron (*The Island*)

On 27 February 1986 we languished over lunch on the summit of Bidein a'Ghlas Thuill, the highest peak of An Teallach. To our south-west, across the gulf of the Toll an Lochain, the serrated pinnacles of Corrag Buidhe studded the sky in a raiment of rime ice. The youngster of our threesome, seventeen-year-old Gordon, perched on the concrete trig point and opened yesterday's copy of *The Times*, brought to kindle the fire at Shenavall bothy. The pages barely fluttered. We were pinned under an ocean of dense Scandinavian air. Without a wind to stir the snow the ground had become covered in piles of loose hoar-frost crystals, deposited in the bitter cold of successive nights and now shimmering joyfully in the midday sun. We had waded laboriously through these fragile drifts to reach the summit but, without an onward trail, questioned our capacity to complete the traverse and get to the bothy by nightfall. An Teallach is perhaps the finest mainland peak in Britain, its winter traverse an alpine endeavour, but on this occasion it was not the main event.

Our other member, fifty-five-year-old Glynne, looked beyond An Teallach into a blinding glare of sunlight and snow. Over there, in the inner dominions of the Fisherfield Forest, lay an unassuming peak called Ruadh-stac Mor, and this, for him, was of far greater import, for it was his last Munro. Our loads were dead-weighted by the obligatory sack of coal for the bothy fire so we were heartened to pick up a set of tracks on the climb to An Teallach's second summit, Sgurr Fiona. The fuel of lunch now kicked in. Instead of ploughing we marched forward. The tracks led us over the pinnacles and all the way to the last col. From here we turned south and plunged 900m down to Shenavall. No place in the Highlands has more romantic connotation for the wanderer. The house sits at the threshold of Fisherfield and Letterewe deer forests, collectively known as The Great Wilderness, and looks out over the sandy flats of Strath na Sealga to the turreted peak of Beinn Dearg Mor. Many souls have been saved by the sight.

The bothy was deserted. A bitter night set in as the cold air drained to the floor of the glen. Within an hour we made a home. Candles were lit, the fire had sparked into life and a tuna stew was bubbling. We retired early, and I stirred from my cocoon of warmth at 4.45 am.

Glynne was already up and pacing about in nervous anticipation. We stowed our climbing kit for later collection, and set off at dawn. The distance to Ruadh-stac Mor is seven kilometres, every step drawing us further from sanctuary. We forded the ice-glazed remnants of the Allt na Muice, and picked up the stalkers' path for Carnmore. The temperature was close to −10°C and I was clenched by cold, yet wheatears were singing gaily among the rowans that straggled along the river bank, a harkening sign of the coming spring.

The path soon disappeared under the snows. We toiled up the broad upper slopes to meet the sunlight. On the final cone of the hill Gordon and I let Glynne go ahead to allow him a minute or two of summit contemplation before we arrived. I sensed that the last Munro would bring Glynne as much sadness as joy, the end of a journey that could never be renewed. Champagne would have been an extravagance in such a mood, but we did have a celebration cake, which Joy had iced, and this we shared in a huddle along with a thermos of hot chocolate. Then I gazed back over the wastelands to An Teallach and beyond to the Dundonnell moors. I gritted my teeth. We had twelve kilometres to hike before our next succour.

With Glynne I presided over my first Munro-completion as a guide. A year earlier I had completed my own round, a single-winter completion in eighty-three days that had garnered widespread media coverage. The moment my personal mission was complete, a Munros millstone was hung round my neck. When you become fêted for something the public want you for nothing else. The creative side of me wished to move on, but henceforth I could never escape my destiny as the man who climbed the Munros and now guided them.

Fortunately, I still loved the Scottish hills well, but as years passed and my own peak-bagging zeal waned, guiding the Munros became more about the people than the mountains.

In 1985 I became the 383rd Munroist on the list maintained by the Scottish Mountaineering Club[1]. Twenty years later the entries surpassed 3500, and in 2013 the total exceeded 5200. There are doubtless thousands more anonymous Munroists, who preferred private gratification to public record, plus an army tens of thousands strong who are up and counting towards completion. What had commenced as an esoteric pursuit for the Salvationist[2] members of the SMC a century ago had become a mass movement. Something was afoot in society.

The Munros affliction infected every social stratum. A guide might expect clients to be broadly middle-class, middle-aged, professional people, but the reality was nothing so tedious. In 1990 our advertised age limit on courses was sixty-five, but we ran a Spring Munros course where the planned schedule was relatively gentle. With assurance of a doctor's certificate, and in truth rather desperate to fill an empty booking file, we accepted an application from seventy-year-old Stan Dow, who declared his aim to complete one hundred Munros, while health allowed.

My heart sank on meeting Stan. He disembarked from the Inverness train, a hunched fragile figure with a pinched face, drippy nose and beady eyes, dressed in cloth cap and tweed jacket. He was by no means a young seventy. Though he had lived his life in Perth he had never travelled beyond the Great Glen. He didn't drive and all eighty of his previous conquests were on the Grampian and Perthshire hills with the Post Office hillwalking club. The only other person booked on the course was a thirty-five-year-old chap called Dave. I could only hope he was of modest ability.

Dave pitched up at our lodgings just as Stan was stirring the next day's breakfast over the cooker.

"How d'ye tak' your porridge, sonny?" asked Stan.

If Dave was shocked at the sight of his partner he didn't show it. As pinches of salt were added to the oats the small talk stuttered along.

"So do you do much walking?" I asked.

"No," said Dave. "I'm more into running . . . marathons mainly."

The stock question that confronts every marathon runner rose to my lips. "So what's your best time?"

"Two hours and twenty minutes," he replied. Clearly, we had a problem.

Two days later with stick in hand Stan was inching his way up the tourist track towards Blaven on Skye. Dave had proven tolerant, so long as I coached him in navigation skills. Three and a half hours into the walk we had still only reached 700m and I began to lose the will to live, but I'd packed my rock climbing shoes in anticipation for such a strait.

The Great Prow, one of Skye's historic Very Severe rock climbs was within reach. I asked Dave if he minded staying with Stan and rushed off down a scree gully to the base. The Great Prow follows a bulging crack through the right edge of a massive plate of gabbro. I carefully soloed the 130m climb, then jogged back to the tourist track. In the forty-five minutes of my absence Stan had gained less than 100m in height.

We made the top of Blaven, but something had to be done. I inveigled an elderly friend in Lochcarron, Clarrie Pashley, to take Stan on as a walking partner. While I chased Dave over half a dozen Munros next day, Clarrie and Stan disappeared up Coire Lair above Achnashellach. The weather was cruelly hot and thirteen hours later Clarrie's wife reported them missing. With some anxiety I drove up to the car park to find they had just returned, successful but both in querulous mood, having spent much of the day bickering over the route to their Munro, Beinn Liath Mhor.

I didn't have the heart to tell Stan that he wasn't up to our courses. Such kindness to a client is invariably repaid by undying loyalty. For three more years he came back. By dint of selecting the easiest hills in Wester Ross, we helped Stan to his ninety-seventh Munro. Then he came back a fourth year and adamantly declared he had only done ninety-five; so we built him up to ninety-eight. On his fifth year he was unequivocal that he'd only done ninety-six. I realised that he was playing mischief with us. He didn't really ever want to reach his goal. That year the weather was rough and Stan was getting so decrepit that it was easier to carry him piggyback over any rough sections. We drew a blank on Munros, and, with all options exhausted, even he realised that his climbing days were done.

Statisticians form a particular breed of Munro-bagger. In their fanatical quest for completeness they usually record all 226 subsidiary

Tops[3] as well as the 282 main Munros. The extensions and diversions necessary to take in the Tops add spice to many hill days, but can be a bane when no one else in the party is interested in minor collectibles. Our first Tops man was a mathematician with a phobia for tents and bothies. He insisted that each mountain day must end on clean linen and arrived with a swatch of postbus timetables with which to plot one-day campaigns through the most remote areas such as Knoydart. His agenda was promptly abandoned on his third day when he took fright on the pinnacles of An Teallach.

An attack of vertigo usually strikes on arrival at a narrow crest where there is exposure on both sides, its onset so sudden that an experienced guide can be caught unprepared. The eleven Cuillin Munros on Skye are formidable obstacles for any Munro-collector so afflicted.

The West Ridge of Sgurr nan Gillean is a notorious trap. On the famous gendarme pitch the scrambler emerges from a secure enclosed chimney on to a toothed arête with a sheer sixty-metre drop on the south side. For most, the protection of a rope is required. When tackling this passage with a group, I place the client whom I judge the most confident at the end of the line; but he who talks loudest is not necessarily the most assured. Ian was Lancashire-born but had adopted the garrulous demeanour of his White Rose neighbours on taking residency in Yorkshire. His "been there, done that" voice resounded like a foghorn through three days of Munro-scrambles. Ian exhibited not a single twitch of nerves so I put him at the back on the Gillean climb. With his three rope companions splayed on the pinnacles in varied discomfiture, Ian sank to his knees on reaching the arête and commenced the jabber of panic. He pulled back on the rope, trying to regain the safe confines of the chimney, but the others couldn't reverse. Ian needed urgent reassurance but we were stuck. After several minutes of inertia I ordered Ian to untie from the rope. By all norms of objective logic this was the most dangerous course of action that I could have devised but it was our only escape. While Ian remained in prayerful paralysis I brought the other three up to safe ground, then soloed back with the rope and lowered him down the chimney. With Ian safely anchored on a good ledge at the base, I went back up to complete the climb. Ian had sufficient courage to return the next year to complete his Skye Munros, when he conquered Gillean by its easier South-East Ridge, derogatively known as the Tourist Route.

Paul Ormerod was another client who was occasionally prone to vertigo, and like Ian he too stuttered at the bridge to Skye. Paul was a leading statistician and economist. The ledgers of Munro were as a bible to him and he was an obligatory Tops man, but Paul's *bête noire* became the Inaccessible Pinnacle, hardest of the main Munros, and one of only three that Sir Hugh Munro himself did not climb. A bright day in spring or summer brings dozens of Munro-baggers to the base of this bizarre wedge of gabbro, which overtops the natural summit of Sgurr Dearg by eight metres. In hundreds of ascents of the Pinnacle I have never had a client fail once tied to the rope and embarked on the airy scramble of its East Ridge.

Unfortunately, Paul had twice arrived at Sgurr Dearg in unsavoury conditions and had baulked and bolted before the rope could be tied. Paul was soon to publish a book entitled *Why Most Things Fail*, and it looked likely that he would add personal proof to his theory.

On the third attempt he brought a friend for support, but overnight snowfall left the Ridge in a dangerous, slippery condition. We delayed our approach to the Pinnacle by first climbing the south summit of Sgurr na Banachdich, Paul's last Top on the Ridge. By early afternoon the emergent sun was burning the snow off the rocks and I decided we must strike. With a tight rope and his friend tied close behind to give precise commands as to every foot placement, Paul had no chance to demur. All who reach the top must be subjected to an abseil down the shorter West Ridge, but there is no choice. Having regained safe ground Paul recovered his composure, ruminated a while and said:

"You know, I really fancy doing some of this winter climbing in gullies. It might suit me better."

In 2008 Paul made an academic contribution to Munro miscellanea, co-writing a paper that applied the principles of diffusion theory to the spread of Munro-bagging fever[4]. Far from peaking and then entering a prolonged decline as theory might predict, imitative behaviour fuelled by continuing media attention has sustained the number of people completing the Munros at a rate of 200 to 250 per year since the 1990s. A noticeable trend is a rising age profile of those engaged in the quest. While the young have been diverted to more competitive mountain pursuits such as adventure-racing, sport-climbing and trail-biking, older people increasingly take on the Munros as a retirement challenge. For mountain guides the slow walk to freedom of the aging generation has provided work aplenty, but at a decidedly sedate pace.

My son, Alex, gained his summer mountain instructor (MIA) qualification at the age of twenty-four. Possessed of the energy of youth and a natural instructional flair, he marched out with a smiling innocence when presented with his first guiding clients, one of whom was sixty-seven-year-old retired banker, Arthur Curtis. Typical of the older generation Arthur was pitching his remaining powers against eighty outstanding Munros, several of which were on Skye. One Sunday I despatched Alex to take Arthur up Sgurr nan Eag, one of the easier but most distant of the Cuillin Munros, while I climbed the In Pinn with another group.

The weather was inclined to south-westerly and the forecast drizzle turned into a day-long deluge. Alex possessed a leaking shell jacket and was drenched within an hour, while Arthur plodded onwards, well wrapped and seemingly unaffected by either wet or cold. Alex fulfilled his duty and they completed an eight-hour round trip. I got down a little later and found Alex shivering uncontrollably in the front seat of our minibus, while Arthur sat snug and pink-cheeked in the back, recounting his adventures. As we drove home Alex's chill turned into a fever, and we put him straight to bed with a hot water bottle. There he stayed for the next two days. Meanwhile, Arthur ambled into our dining room, his only apparent concern whether it was to be roast beef or pork for dinner.

When a Munro-bagger is exiled to distant shores, completion becomes a herculean task. Howard Castle-Smith was one of our regulars and he particularly enjoyed the adventure of hill-bagging in the winter season. Howard's avuncular appearance and quiet charm belied steadfast determination. When his company posted him off for five years in Shanghai, Howard pinned his Munros wall-chart to his office wall and, when not organising banquets for Chinese dignitaries, he dreamed. From every available leave period he stole a few days to fly to Scotland. Though often met by dreich or drab conditions he sustained his interest and in March 2005 brought friends and colleagues with him to tackle the three Knoydart Munros.

Winter had ended early and we encountered a remarkable heatwave with daytime temperatures of 20°C. My job as organiser was to provide the easiest and most entertaining path to the tops. We approached on a hire boat at Arnisdale from the north side of Loch Hourn, generously provisioned for a well-oiled night at Barrisdale bothy. Barrisdale has a similar reputation to Shenavall among Scottish mountain-initiates. The beautiful northern flank of Ladhar Bheinn, which is owned and managed by the John Muir Trust conservation charity, lies directly above. Without the luxury of a boat, the approach march is seven miles. Discouraged by Spartan bothy facilities, Howard chatted to Barrisdale's resident stalker and secured a serviced self-catering cabin, more worthy of a corporate group. We dumped our overnight loads and got straight to work on the long and graceful ascent of Coire Dhorrcaill to Ladhar Bheinn.

Dutch lawyer Felix was the gazelle of the team and dashed off ahead. I stuck in the middle with steady Frank, who worked at company headquarters in Pennsylvania. Howard and his best friend Nigel lagged behind. Both carried heart monitors to gauge their progress and I was alarmed to note that they registered 170 after just one hairpin of the path. I spent the climb trying to harness these widely differing paces, while ensuring that heart rates didn't top the 200 danger mark. Felix was commanded to stop at a stream and get his stove going. By the time the rear-guard arrived the tea was brewed. We topped Ladhar Bheinn in late afternoon, and continued on the skyline round to the subsidiary top of Stob a'Chearcaill. Knowing that I could quickly catch up, I sent the team off on the descent and lay down to doze for twenty minutes in the evening sun. When I followed I was shocked to find the foursome strung out on 50° slopes of grass interspersed by outcrops of slabby mica-schist, picking their way down in silent concentration. I had completely underestimated the hazardous angle of the descent but was too late to get out my safety rope. With heart in mouth I shepherded them to safer inclines. Grassy West Highland Munros can be every bit as serious as the rocky arêtes of Skye.

Relief at our safe acquittal from Ladhar Bheinn led me to imbibe far too much of the party's liquid refreshment back at Barrisdale. I staggered off to bed, nearly a bottle of wine to the good, while the others got stuck into a bottle of malt whisky.

On Sunday I awoke at dawn, dry-mouthed and rocked by my companions' trumpeting snores. The greater task remained – to climb Knoydart's other two Munros. In this group hangovers were no excuse for inaction, but our pace up Luinne Bheinn was laboured.

Nigel decided to end his day there, but Howard gazed south over the ragged ridges to the second Munro, Meall Buidhe, and pushed on. From Meall Buidhe we faced an awkward five-mile traverse back to Barrisdale. I employed every trick of map-reading to take us across a succession of hollows and spurs without unnecessary loss of height, and after a nine-hour day we made our returning boat with just minutes to spare.

In 2009 Howard completed his Munros with a family ascent of Cairn Gorm. I have been invited to several Munro completion parties, but these inevitably require the ascent of the chosen hill. With between two and three thousand Munro ascents under my belt I am averse to further punishment and politely decline, but Howard had a much better idea. He invited his most faithful guides, Martin Welch and I, to join the after-climb party at a five-star country hotel near Inverness. The penance of swallowing oysters proved rather less onerous than climbing a hill.

With completion of the Munros many walkers feel a void in their lives. Some channel this want of direction to the Corbetts[5]. Ascending the 2500-foot hills of Scotland greatly extends the scope of knowledge of the country and takes the walker further from the beaten trails. Others go back and start again. Jim Halkett first stood on our doorstep in 1992, a great bear of a man, bald, bespectacled and dressed in tartan shorts and tam o'shanter. He launched straight into a non-stop banter in vernacular Scots, that jumped from Munros to football and the latest movies within a single breath. He might have walked straight out of the pages of the *Sunday Post*. So began a twenty-year friendship. On his first guided day with us he climbed Sgurr nan Gillean to complete his first round of the Munros. We quickly realised that Jim experienced what are condescendingly described as learning difficulties. He struggled to handle three-dimensional movement on rock and was achingly slow on exposed ridges, but he had a rumbustious sense of humour and a pin-sharp memory for every hill in Scotland.

Jim immediately commenced a second Munros round, much of it under our guidance. He managed to save enough from his labouring jobs, first in a distillery and later in an abattoir, to afford our courses. His parents were proud hard-working folk and helped him whenever they could. He was generous to a fault and would always arrive with cash in hand and gifts of whisky and chocolates for Joy. I felt humbly guilty to take what had cost Jim so much. In 2005 he completed his second round on Slioch by Kinlochewe, and a third circuit began. The Scottish hills have defined his life and whenever I am tempted to criticise Munro-bagging as a tedious obsession I think of Jim.

One dewy morning in October 2012 I got up before dawn, oiled Alex's mountain bike and set off from Attadale over the estate track to Ben Dronaig Lodge. The wilderness hills that lie beyond my back garden are an unsung sanctuary. No one would call them special, but the approaching walker is possessed of a sense of freedom and solace the moment the fields of Strathcarron are out of sight. The interior includes two of the most remote Munros, Bidein a'Choire Sheasgaich and Lurg Mhor plus a further Top, Meall Mor, which sits in isolation on Scotland's watershed above the head of Loch Monar.

A tough three-mile ascent of the stony Land-Rover track took me to the watershed at 350m where the craggy pate of Sheasgaich and the sweeping profile of Lurg Mhor are revealed above the Black Water strath. Down in the glen a tiny stand of trees and the cream-painted shed of Ben Dronaig Lodge lent scale to the scene. I pushed my gears into top cog and sped downhill to begin my day's work.

My client, Susan Hawkins, was staying with her husband Brian in the Ben Dronaig bothy. They had done some of their early Munros with me twenty years earlier but Brian had developed motor-neurone disease and was unable to join Susan on her final Munros and Tops. The estate stalker, Tom Watson, had driven them over to the bothy the previous afternoon, so that they could share the experience. I felt something of an imposter to leave Brian at the bothy and take charge of Susan's last Munros day. The weather maintained a lazy flux between trailing showers and shafts of sunlight with the occasional rainbow smudge, the clarity sufficient that we could absorb a sense of place. We went over Lurg Mhor and out on the slippery scramble to Meall Mor, then doubled back to claim her last Munro of Sheasgaich. Back at the bothy Brian met us with a brew of tea and opened a bottle of sparkling rosé wine. After a toast and a glass I left them to their bothy fire and cycled off to chase the sunset.

Whatever else there is to do in the mountain world, Munro-bagging is one pursuit that has no bounds of age, means or ability; and that which is open to all should take due precedence in the greater scale of worth.

Notes

1. The Scottish Mountaineering Club publishes a list of all persons who have reported completion of the Munros in its annual journal.
2. There was an early division among SMC members, satirically depicted as pitching the Ultramontanes, the roped mountaineers who pioneered new climbs, against the Salvationists, who preferred tramping over the hills and were inevitably lured by the challenge offered by Munros Tables.
3. The subsidiary Tops are insufficiently pronounced or else too close to higher neighbours to be classed as full Munros. As with full Munros, there is no scientific definition of what constitutes a Top, and the SMC has made many revisions of the list according to opinion.
4. 'Tradition and Fashion in Consumer Choice: Bagging the Scottish Munros', co-authored with Alex Bentley, *Scottish Journal of Political Economy*, Vol 56, issue 3 (2009)
5. The Corbetts are the 221 hills over 2500 feet in altitude in Scotland, each defined by having a minimum drop on all sides of 500 feet (152m). They were first compiled by J. Rooke Corbett and are published by the Scottish Mountaineering Club along with Munro's Tables.

Chapter 8

FROM SEA TO SUMMIT

At every downward plunge of the yacht's bow a salt-water spume spattered against the spray deck. Ahead, the mountains of Rum rose and fell with the swell but seemed no nearer than they were an hour ago.

"Lee-ho," commanded the skipper as he turned the wheel to port. With cold confused hands the crew obeyed, loosening the hitches holding the genoa to starboard. The bow moved through the eye of the wind, the boom swung across the cockpit and more fumbling hands made fast the sheets on the port side. With the boat back on starboard tack, Eigg hove into view. The crew gratefully sank to their seats. Pallid cheeks and pinched noses poked out from wool hats and mufflers, empty eyes fixed on the horizon.

"Flapjack anyone?" asked Joy, opening the biscuit tin. The suggestion was ill-timed. With a groan and sudden lurch over the side, the first apprentice succumbed. Others looked as though they would soon follow.

In the middle of June we were tacking across the Hebridean Sea against a Force 5 Westerly. For several crew members this was their first experience on the open sea. The mouth of Loch Nevis and Mallaig's busy port lay two hours behind us and the rocky Point of Sleat was slowly slipping away to starboard. Our objective, the inlet of Loch Scresort, was barely discernible on the coast of Rum and we could count on another three hours before we reached its shelter. What had become of our romantic visions of cruising effortlessly from island to island, and how was this party ever going to traverse the Rum Cuillin tomorrow? Only the captain seemed happy.

"Great sail!" he enthused. "Now which peaks are you planning to bag tomorrow?" Rob Teago was not averse to rubbing a little salt in the pride of wounded mountaineers.

Half-an-hour later the sun soothed the bite of the west wind. Some fifteen kilometres to the north, the whole chain of the Black Cuillin, from the soaring screes of Gars Bheinn to the craggy crest of Blaven was bathed in its light. Viewed from the sea the Cuillin looked mysterious, inaccessible and suddenly magnificent.

For me this was a revelation. Too many years of Munro-bashing – driving mindlessly to Glen Brittle, plodding the same paths, queuing for the In Pinn – had devalued the cream of Britain's mountains to the status of "bread and butter" peaks. Thanks to sitting freezing on a yacht with a squirming stomach my respect for the Cuillin was regained. Everyone's spirits rallied with the sight of sunlit peaks and with perfect timing a school of porpoise joined our path. For ten minutes they swam with us, diving under the keel and surfing the crests of adjoining waves. We were enchanted. Purgatory had become pleasure.

Our first Sail and Climb week in 1994 was proving to be a roller-coaster. The idea was sparked by my friendship with a neighbour in Strathcarron, Rob Teago. Now a contented potter, he was also an ex-Royal Navy officer and qualified yachtmaster. He wasn't slow to take up the chance of a week's paid holiday skippering my clients around the Hebrides. Sailors regard the west coast of Scotland as offering the finest yacht cruising in Europe. A boat charter yard at Armadale on the southern tip of Skye offered us a 38-foot eight-berth sloop for the week and Joy agreed to come along as cook. We soon had five clients signed up, some as keen on sailing as hill-climbing, others seeing the week as a means of collecting awkwardly placed Munros and Corbetts.

The voyage started promisingly. From Armadale we motored across the Sound of Sleat and round to Inverie in Knoydart from where we ascended Meall Buidhe. Rob minded the boat and put the dinner on for our return. He possessed a refreshing aversion to climbing hills, adhering to John Ruskin's philosophy that distant homage is more meritorious than physical engagement. After this *hors d'oeuvre* we awoke early to cloudless skies and motored lazily up the still waters of Loch Nevis. On entering the upper reach the cone of 1040m Sgurr na Ciche appeared in hazy silhouette, with the slabby bluffs of Ben Aden to its left and shaggy profile of Garbh Chioch Mhor to its right. Few Scottish mountain scenes are more inspirational than this tableau.

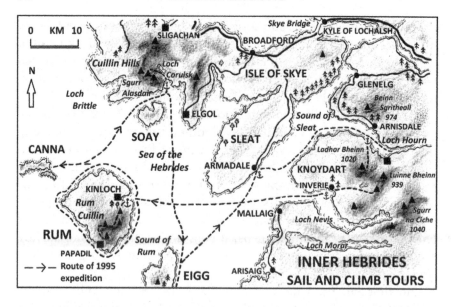

Rob anchored and put us ashore a kilometre from the head of the loch. After crossing the boggy flats of the Carnach glen we romped up bone-dry slabs of mica-schist to Ben Aden, a particularly distinguished Corbett and one of the hardest to reach. Every twist and contortion in the linking ridge to Sgurr na Ciche was a delight. From the summit we looked down at Loch Nevis through binoculars and spotted the yacht, but to our alarm the boat was pirouetting on its anchor. A south-east wind was channelling down from the mountains in a katabatic flow. We wasted no time in getting off the hill. At the loch shore the wind was blowing at Force 6. Despite laying two anchors Rob had been sufficiently worried by the wind to run the boat's engine for several hours lest she broke her moorings. We were unceremoniously bundled aboard and before we knew it were halfway back to Inverie.

Then came the hard sail to Rum. We were so tired on arrival that our sole ambition was a hot shower in the bunkhouse at Kinloch Castle. Next morning low cloud and drizzle deterred any attempt on the Rum Cuillin. By afternoon the weather brightened and a following Force 4 breeze gave us an exhilarating sail through the Sound of Soay, around the back of Gars Bheinn and into Loch Scavaig, an anchorage described in our boat's pilot as one of the finest in Western Europe. A tortuous passage led through a series of gabbro islets, where grey seals lounged, and into the sanctuary of the inner-most pool. The anchorage is safe from the Atlantic swell but prey to katabatic downdraughts from the encircling Cuillin Ridge.

By any aesthetic or geometric yardstick a traverse of the Cuillin should commence here, close to the core of the magma chamber from which the Ridge was formed and around which the peaks are arrayed in a giant horseshoe. Gars Bheinn, the southernmost top, is a rough but simple climb of two hours from the harbour. However, the finest approach to the Main Ridge from Loch Scavaig is the Dubhs Ridge, a whaleback of boiler-plate slabs rising straight from Loch Coruisk, less than a kilometre from the Scavaig jetty.

My last ascent of the Dubhs had involved an eleven-kilometre approach march from Sligachan so it was a delight to be padding up the slabs just half-an-hour after leaving the yacht. Despite a long delay while our team of five made the abseil off the summit of Sgurr Dubh Beag, we completed the route in less than five hours, then scrambled down the chaotic boulder-fields of the Garbh Choire to the shore. On the final morning we sailed out of Loch Scavaig and round the Point of Sleat back to the charter yard in Armadale. I stepped ashore with an overwhelming fatigue. Sailing was not the sedentary occupation that I had imagined. The constant sea breeze and roll of the boat coupled with rapid bursts of energy at each change of tack had sapped the calories. As soon as the boat anchored the mountaineers were disembarked to commence our labours. Six days of the same left me with a prodigious appetite and an insistent desire to sleep.

Nevertheless I was persuaded to repeat the experience. May 1995 brought in a cool north-easterly airflow and the higher peaks were sprinkled with snow. The Rum Cuillin Traverse was our top objective, but the peaks of Knoydart beckoned first. Knoydart is a logistical challenge for land-based Munro-baggers, but not so for the yachting set. A short sail from Armadale took us to a good anchorage in the lee of Eilean a'Phiobaire, 'the piper's island', at the entrance of Loch Hourn. That same afternoon we climbed 1020m Ladhar Bheinn by its north-west flanks, kicking up névé slopes to a summit that was still thick with rime and powder snow, and where a shimmering seaward vista opened to Eigg and Rum. Next morning Rob took us a little further up the loch to Barrisdale bay. While he enjoyed a leisurely sail round to Inverie we traversed Knoydart from north to south over the other Munro summits, Luinne Bheinn and Meall Buidhe.

That night we fortified ourselves for the sea crossing to Rum with an indulgent seafood dinner at the Pier House Restaurant, but happily the traumas of 1994's choppy passage were not repeated. Thanks to a following breeze we fairly flew across the Hebridean Sea with sails offset in a style described by our captain as "goose-winging". We were anchored in Loch Scresort by early afternoon with energies intact for the Rum ridge.

The Rum Cuillins are geologically twinned with their grander neighbours on Skye, but the traverse is shorter and technically easier though still a fine grade 2 scramble. There are two Corbetts enroute – Askival and Ainshval– and three lower tops. The traverse ends at the southern tip of the island and normally the walker must hike seven kilometres back to Loch Scresort along a coastal path via Dibidil. With a nor'easter still blowing Rob felt confident he could find a sheltered anchorage on the south of the island, saving us the return slog.

At this point we discovered that sailors are not immune from statistical fetishism. They might adopt a lofty disdain of Munrobagging but they will jump at the chance of circumnavigating an island. The Scottish sailor's bible is *The Scottish Islands* by Hamish Haswell-Smith, which lists and surveys every Hebridean rock that can support a sheep.

Under further interrogation Rob admitted that there was indeed a "circumnavigation" cult, and that Rum was a treasured objective. He persuaded one of our number to desert the cause of Corbetting, and with a first mate in place set off to sail the western shoreline.

Twenty-two years had passed since my last traverse of the Rum Cuillin when I was a seventeen-year-old Venture Scout. On this bright May day with a following breeze the ridge was a delight. The middle top of Trallval provided the best and airiest scrambling. We managed without needing to rope up and after a blistering ascent of Ainshval we looked down on Harris Bay to see the yacht at temporary anchor. I called Rob on my radio to fix a collection point and to our delight he said he was going on to Papadil, directly under our final summit, Sgurr nan Gillean.

The sight of the mausoleum down at Harris reminded us of the opulence of past owners of the island. The successful Lancastrian industrialist, John Bullough, purchased Rum in 1888, and his spend-thrift son George built the impressive but obscene folly of Kinloch Castle with imported sandstone, then added this miniature Parthenon at Harris as a monument to his family's wealth and power. Meanwhile the last vestiges of indigenous life and tradition were drained from the island, and for many years casual visitors were strongly discouraged. Rum has been a nature reserve since 1957, and is managed by Scottish Natural Heritage, but the magnificent natural environment cannot hide a pervading sense of abandonment. Papadil was once a shooting lodge, but is now a decaying oasis of rambling gorse, untended woodland and sad ruins. Joy and I took a swim in the adjoining freshwater loch and I climbed a little sea stack while we waited for Rob to anchor and bring the yacht's dinghy to shore.

We sailed back to Loch Scresort under the cliffs of the eastern seaboard. The wind blew fresh from the north-east, the sun warmed our faces and the boat surged through the waves at a satisfying five knots. The tradition of yachting and mountaineering in the Hebrides dates from the early days of the Scottish Mountaineering Club, when it was easier to reach much of the western seaboard by boat than overland travel. At Easter 1897 the Club held a Yachting Meet in the Inner Hebrides, and the participants included then-President, Hugh Munro. Walter Barrow recounted the joyous completion of the meet:

The black peaks of Rum stood out against the rich golden light reflected in the glassy surface of a rolling swell. And on the deck of the yacht, members of the Club, headed by the President in Highland kilt and sporran, danced a reel and Strathspey to the drone of the Scottish pipes.

We did not possess bagpipes but caught something of the same spirit. It only needed one of our members to voice his choral pretensions, than we all dropped our inhibitions and enjoined a singsong, the true mark of a happy day.

Chapter 9

CUILLIN HIGHS

*To one whose hands these rocks have grasped, the joys of climbing
unsurpassed*
> Memorial tablet to Lewis MacDonald on the summit
> of Sgurr Mhic Choinnich (now destroyed by lightning)

A few iconic climbs provide the bulk of the income of most mountain
guides. Once I settled in North-West Scotland the traverse of the
Cuillin Ridge of Skye became a regular paymaster. Indisputably, the
traverse is the finest mountaineering expedition in Britain, but one
which exacts an increasing physical toll with every repetition. The
Ridge spans eleven Munros and 2200m of ascent over a distance
of twelve kilometres without ever dropping below 750 in altitude.
A traverse entails half-a-dozen passages of rock climbing to Severe
standard, several abseils and a wealth of exposed scrambling. Complex volcanic geology renders a terrain that is discordant and incred-
ibly rough, alternating between slabs of crystalline gabbro, boulder-
fields of pocked peridotite and slippery ramps of brittle basalt. A full
traverse demands endurance fitness, scrambling ability and mental
fortitude. These are qualities possessed by many mountaineers, but
route-finding ability, logistical skills and local knowledge are also
essential, and this is where the mountain guide comes into play. Any
local guide with the stomach for the fight is assured a steady stream
of traverse business each spring and summer.

The Cuillin Traverse may be popular but is not a prescriptive
assignment where everyone starts in a pack and queues at every
difficulty. Timing, tactics and route-choice are at the discretion of
each group. Most parties traverse south to north from Gars-bheinn
to Sgurr nan Gillean but there is much to recommend taking the
reverse direction. The official route takes the steepest obstacles direct

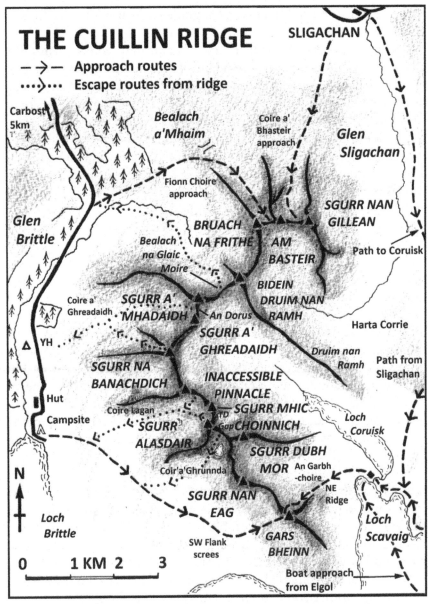

THE CUILLIN RIDGE

— →— Approach routes
····)··· Escape routes from ridge

SLIGACHAN

Carbost
5km

Bealach
a'Mhaim

Coire a'
Bhasteir
approach

Glen
Sligachan

Fionn Choire
approach

Glen
Brittle

BRUACH
NA FRITHE

SGURR NAN
GILLEAN

Bealach
na Glaic
Moire

AM
BASTEIR

Path to Coruisk

Coire a'
Ghreadaidh

SGURR A'
MHADAIDH

An Dorus

BIDEIN
DRUIM NAN
RAMH

Harta Corrie

YH

SGURR A'
GHREADAIDH

Druim nan
Ramh

Path from
Sligachan

SGURR NA
BANACHDICH

INACCESSIBLE
PINNACLE

Hut

Coire Lagan

SGURR MHIC
CHOINNICH

Loch
Coruisk

Campsite

SGURR
ALASDAIR

TD
Gap

N

Coir'a'Ghrunnda

SGURR DUBH
MOR

An Garbh
-choire

NE
Ridge

Loch
Brittle

SGURR NAN
EAG

Loch
Scavaig

SW Flank
screes

GARS
BHEINN

0   1 KM 2   3

Boat approach
from Elgol

but scramblers can devise a traverse that avoids most of the rock-climbing sections. There are several routes of approach, including the option of starting up the elegant Dubhs Ridge from Loch Coruisk to join the traverse at the second Munro. The traverse can be taken in a one-day gamble or a two-day expedition with a planned bivouac en-route. On the Cuillin Traverse a guide can enjoy the freedom of individual expression.

Those who succeed on their first attempt may count themselves lucky. The Cuillin are the first line of defence for every Atlantic weather front. A gentle south-westerly airflow can shroud the Ridge under a blanket of damp cloud, while the rest of Scotland basks in sunshine. The spring months give the best chance of clear weather, but nothing is guaranteed. My first attempt, in 1985, ended in a torrential downpour at a halfway camp in Coire na Banachdich. The weather of May 1986 was so unremittingly bad that all planned traverses were cancelled. Further failure in my third season would be embarrassing.

My first clients in 1987 were an old school-pal, Ian Parkinson, and his friend, Bill. A strong northerly airflow set in on the day of their arrival. The north wind may be cold but it is invariably dry. Bill talked a good climb. Boasts of cranking out sets of one hundred press-ups boded for a blistering pace, but the moment he reached the crest of Gars-bheinn and looked over the Coruisk downfall his bluster ceased. Balancing on knife-edge ridges hadn't featured in his training. By Sgurr Mhic Choinnich his nerves were exhausted and he dropped down the An Stac screes back to Glen Brittle, leaving Ian and me to continue. We established a flowing rhythm over the In Pinn and past the halfway point at Sgurr na Banachdich. The north wind strengthened, tearing the summit clouds into white streamers. At 7.00 pm we gained Bealach a'Glaic Mhor, the lowest point on the traverse, and filled our water bottles from a snow-patch. In the searing wind we couldn't contemplate bivouacking on the crest of the ridge, so we dropped 120m down screes on the south flank of Bidein Druim nan Ramh and banked up a sloping grass ledge with rocks and turfs to produce a comfortable bed. After brews and snacks we bedded down and watched the Ridge fall into black silhouette while the wind boomed through its gaps and eddied down its gullies.

We regained the crest above a sea of cloud at 5.15 am and, without seeing another soul, reached Sgurr nan Gillean by 10.00 am. A second traverse followed a week later and I began to feel some sense of dignity in describing myself as a Cuillin guide.

A one-day traverse is undeniably a worthy challenge but the seventeen-hour schedule imposes a pre-dawn start and a high probability of missing closing time on completion. There is a total commitment, with no margin of time, food or water to withstand any hitch in progress. A well-known hill-runner from Edinburgh, John Blair-Fish, was my first candidate. Though bespectacled and scholarly in facial expression, John possessed the thighs of Michelangelo's David, and was only too willing to show these off, courtesy of a pair of skimpy running shorts. I suspected I was in for a hard time. We decided to bivouac at the start, and, leaving our car at Sligachan, jogged nine miles over to Coruisk and up the North-East Ridge of Gars-bheinn. The Cuillins were to be John's final eleven Munros and my suspicions as to why he had left them until last were confirmed by a twilit screaming fit on Gars-bheinn's summit wall.

We cowered from an easterly gale in a stone shelter on the summit, brewed drinks and dozed until our 5.00 am reveille. The cutting wind persisted throughout the traverse. Rarely could we relax. John needed stern goading and some manual winching on the rope to surmount the difficult pitches, but his grace and speed on the easier sections ensured our arrival at Gillean by 6.00 pm. With relief we left the wind-torn ridge and dropped into the shelter of Coire a'Bhasteir. Checking that John was behind, I shoved my hands in my pockets and ambled down the screes past the Bhasteir gorge, dreaming of a pint of lemonade at Sligachan Hotel. Somewhere on the moors I turned to check John's progress and, to my shock, he had vanished. I waited for five minutes, scanning the surrounding slopes. Had he fallen into the gorge or stumbled on the screes? The standard practice when split from one's companion is to stop awhile, then go back to the last clear landmark. Applying this logic I pushed my weary legs back up the hill, blowing on my whistle and calling his name. After 150m of reluctant re-ascent I reached our last definite point of conference. With rising puzzlement and concern I dashed down to Sligachan. He wasn't at the car. I rushed into the hotel ready to call out the mountain rescue, but there in the corner I spied John, sitting smug, halfway through a plate of fish and chips.

"Where did you get to, John? I waited ages on the path."

"Oh really; well I spotted a good running line off the track on the other side of the shoulder, and I had a great run down."

To complete my frustration he didn't even buy me a drink.

In June 1989 three fell-runners from Leeds booked a one-day traverse "valley-to-valley". We used the conventional approach from

Glen Brittle to Gars-bheinn. This gruelling slog culminates in a 500m ascent of 45° screes. In spring a cuckoo nesting down by the Sound of Soay provides a maddening soundtrack to the climb. The normal time from car park to summit is three-and-a-half hours, but this crew cut a full hour off that target. I was interested to share the nutritional secrets of a bunch of serious athletes.

"I see you're eating a Yorkie bar," I asked one. "What are your rations for the day?"

"Sixteen Yorkies," he replied. "You told us it would take sixteen hours and I eat one every hour."

My guts churned to imagine the metabolic agonies resultant from ingesting this quantity of chocolate. Reaching Sligachan after seventeen hours on the go, I asked whether he had finished them all. He looked embarrassed when admitting that he had only got through eleven, then strolled into the bar for a pint and a bag of crisps.

The majority of Cuillin clients are happy to take the two-day option. In June 1988, Skye temperatures rose to 28°C under an intense anticyclone, allowing us to dispense with sleeping bags for the bivouac. We needed extra supplies of sunscreen but all the shops in Broadford had sold out. On this occasion we also walked in to Coruisk from Sligachan. By the time we had made our bivouac on the broad bealach before the Thearlaich-Dubh Gap, one of the group, James Cox, was seriously afflicted with sunstroke. Instead of stocking up on liquid and calories he spent the evening retching and shivering. I discounted all hope that he could continue. During the night a blanket of fog formed over the cool sea surface and lapped against the hills of Skye at 600m altitude. All the significant peaks on the island and along the mainland seaboard were left protruding like nunataks on an arctic ice cap.

At dawn James asked if he could go on. He had already failed once on the ridge and wanted to grasp the slimmest chance of success. He drank a cup of herbal tea and forced down a few raisins. Aware of the risk of collapse in the event of sunstroke, I agreed only with reluctance and allowed him to wear a sunhat instead of a helmet. The sun rose in an intense golden glare that promised a day-long grilling. For several minutes the silhouetted peaks of the Cuillin were projected twenty miles over the western cloud-sea. We felt like shipwrecked sailors lost on the ocean and marched to war with spirits restored.

The T-D Gap is the hardest obstacle of the traverse. A vertical dyke of brittle lava has been eroded to leave an uncanny chasm, just six metres across and twelve metres deep. This place has an evil reputation that is thoroughly deserved. Usually, it is damp, cold and windy, but today we were blessed with warm dry rock, even at the ungodly hour of at 5.30 am. We made a short abseil into the shadowed cleft. I then wriggled up the twenty-metre chimney on the north side. The rock has become ever more polished in the century since the first ascent. I made fast our fifty-metre rope at its half-way point, hauled up our party's sacks with one end and brought my threesome up one by one on the other. For some the strenuousness of this struggle destroys composure and rhythm, but this team made quick work of the difficulties.

Although unable to eat, James soldiered on and we pushed him as hard as we dared. Lingering snow patches provided vital liquid replenishment. We packed our bottles with slush, which melted in the heat to give cooling mouthfuls. The air shimmered in the heat and refraction from the cloud sea created a mirage effect such that every mainland peak rose in a horizontal stack to twice its normal height. We reached Gillean after twelve hours and dropped gratefully into the cooling bath of fog in Coire a'Bhasteir.

The greatest beauty of the two-day traverse is the bivouac experience. In 1990 I discovered a grotto close to the Inaccessible Pinnacle, which offered a flat bed sufficient for four people. Being conveniently placed near the halfway point this became my standard bivouac spot and each spring we stocked the cave with water ready for prospective ridge travellers. I then became over-confident. Morag was a diminutive lady from Edinburgh, whose chances on the traverse depended critically on minimising her load. I sent a newly qualified guide out with her, and meanwhile stocked the cave with everything from sleeping bags to food and fuel to ensure the most luxurious night. As the guide hadn't previously stayed in the cave I provided him with a detailed sketch-map of the location. I thought nothing could go wrong until a thick mist descended on the ridge mid-way through their first day. Morag and guide reached the In Pinn at 7.00 pm in dreich conditions. The cave lies just sixty metres from the foot of the pinnacle, but the hapless guide was unable to find it. Finally, after two hours of searching, he and Morag sat down to an open bivouac in the lee of the pinnacle with only a scanty nylon

sheet for protection. Heavy rain fell all night and they retreated, in
a bedraggled state, at dawn. On hearing their tale of woe I couldn't
help smiling at the irony, my humour lasting only until I realised
that I would have to go back to retrieve their kit, still lying, dry and
unused, in the cave.

Persistent rain or even damp fog renders much of a ridge a skating
rink. On greasy basalt strata the strongest party is reduced to a nervous crawl, and completion of a traverse becomes implausible. On
a south-north attempt in 2003 we struggled through a damp and
foggy day to gain the In Pinn hotel. Rain set in overnight and even
under the cave roof we were progressively chilled and dampened by
a steady flow of drips. My usual commitment to finish the task had,
for once, vanished. I couldn't wait to get off the ridge come dawn.
Faced with a dismal drizzle two of my team capitulated as expected,
but the third member was a lithe novice from Edinburgh called Jonny
Hall. He stepped outside, sniffed the air and stretched his legs, then
declared:
    "I feel great, so much stronger than yesterday. I'm all for going
on."
    Luckily, he didn't see my face. By the time we had crossed from
In Pinn over the exposed ridges linking Sgurr na Banachdich and
Sgurr a'Ghreadaidh I realised that Jonny was a scrambler of exceptional ability. The dictates of speed mean that the Cuillin Traverse
cannot be completed without doing a substantial portion of the
route unroped. It is to the guide's judgement as to when the rope is
used. That requires acute observation of the members for the first
signs of clumsiness or nervousness. Over the three tricky subsidiary
tops of Sgurr a'Mhadaidh we roped, but I felt sufficiently confident
in Jonny to raise the pace. The weather stayed determinedly damp
and we could see nothing beyond a twenty-five-metre radius, yet we
covered the huge stretch from Mhadaidh to Bruach na Frithe in three
hours. This is usually the section where ordinary mortals get tired
and despondent. There are no Munros to highlight progress and the
terrain is intricate and technical. My spirit revived.
    This was a guiding pace to relish! The Bhasteir Tooth brought us
to an abrupt halt. Just as we entered the home straight this formidable blade loomed out of the mist. There are avoiding manoeuvres,
but Jonny was not to be dissuaded from completing the true traverse.

That meant climbing the Tooth direct by the infamous Naismith's Route, a pitch of remarkable exposure, first led by Willie Naismith, an early doyen of Scottish climbing, in 1898. I grovelled across slimy gangways to the crux move, a bold pull on finger pockets without any nearby protection. My fingers were numb but held their grip, and by 2.00 pm we had surmounted the Tooth, Am Basteir and the summit plinth of Sgurr nan Gillean. With ironic timing the cloud finally broke during our descent, yet Jonny seemed happy with his blinkered traverse of the Cuillin.

However carefully I advertised the trials of the traverse, some still turned up in a state of blissful delusion. When engaged by a team of five "task-force" policemen from Harrogate I expected great things, but on meeting at Sligachan bunkhouse I was dismayed to find several of them kitted out in camouflage gear and Doc Martens' boots. Their bulging sacks sported hanging billy-pans and enamel mugs. I tried to explain that the Cuillin Traverse is not a yomp and a major off-load was actioned. Before we reached Gars Bheinn one of them, a squat and aggressive-looking chap with squashed nose and cauliflower ear, admitted that he didn't really like heights, so preferred to avoid exposed places. We shepherded him along the Ridge, missing out as many of the difficulties as we could. Just beyond the In Pinn we made an open bivouac on a night so cold that the water in our bottles froze. With pride hurt and in a state of some disillusion the human tank and two others dropped out at this point. I completed the traverse with the other two. Back at Sligachan I came face-to-face with the bulldog for a final parting. Bravely, I shook his hand and expressed a muted desire to rope up on future adventures, to which he responded:

"And if I never see you again, it'll be too soon."

Surprise gifts that involve twenty hours of backbreaking labour are a poisoned chalice. When a doting girlfriend signed me up to take her partner along the Cuillin Ridge as his fiftieth birthday present, I withheld my misgivings. She even came along to provide valley support, and drove us to Elgol so that we could take the "royal" route to the Cuillin with a boat trip across Loch Scavaig. From this seaward vantage the Ridge looks at its most impressive and enticing. The Bella Jane dropped us at the Coruisk jetty and within an hour we were romping up the slabs of the Dubhs Ridge. My client professed a considerable technical expertise, so I began with the intention to take him over every available difficulty.

However, his initial high spirits wavered after we loaded up with water at the cave and pushed on into a drizzle at Banachdich. Was his heart really in it? Our bivouac couch under Sgurr Thormaid offered shelter only for head and shoulders. We awoke with our feet in pools of water and waited until a clearance at 8.00 am before departing. Immediately, my man looked nervous on the wet rock and I roped up. At this he became petulant. He clearly regarded my "doggie-lead" method of guiding as something of a humiliation. I thought of his eager girlfriend and of the money she had invested, but her partner evinced no comparable interest. I expended every means of encouragement to get him over all the twists to Bruach na Frithe. At last the sun had emerged and the rock was dry. I thought my task done. I pointed out the last stretch to Gillean, just two hours away, whereupon he airily declared:

"I've done those peaks before, so there's no point doing them. We may as well go down."

I protested the victory that was within his grasp and gently hinted how much his girlfriend wanted him to succeed, to which suggestion he became distinctly obstreperous. We descended moodily to Sligachan and she was there at the car, her devoted eyes expectant of a triumphant return. Our dismal account of abandonment at Bruach na Frithe went down like a lead balloon. I thought it wise to make a prompt departure at that point and left them to it.

For others the Ridge traverse has a seminal significance, a challenge that must not be denied. In 2002 I engaged a north-south traverse with a team of three, Steve, Paul and Polly. They were not strong climbers and overnight rain left the rocks damp, but we went straight to Naismith's Route, which gave a welcome jolt after the tedium of the approach. From the Tooth we traversed out to Sgurr nan Gillean and returned under Am Basteir to collect our sacks for the southward push towards our night's sanctuary at the In Pinn cave. As we reached the triple peaks of Bidein Druim nan Ramh an angry cumulo-nimbus cloud whirled towards us from the sea and within minutes we were pummelled by a furious hailstorm. So sudden was its onset that we couldn't get into waterproofs before we were soaked. The rogue shower left the rocks coated in an inch of white slush.

Martin climbing into The Ramp on the Eiger North Face 1938 Route
(photo: Dave McDonald)

Dave McDonald at the bottom of the Eiger
North Face

Paul Tattersall sets out on pitch 2 of The Godfather
on the first ascent

Andy Nisbet on the Hydnefossen
(Hemsedal, Norway)

Loch Carron from Stromeferry summit with Fuar Tholl and Sgorr Ruadh in the distance
(photo: Clarrie Pashley)

Joy – eight months pregnant with Alex – inspects our new home at Achintee in November 1986

David Litherland descending from the Täschhorn on the Domgrat traverse – September 1989

David on the final climb to the Dom with the Domgrat behind

Martin at Montenvers after a solo ascent of the
Aiguille Verte in September 1987

Ben the cook leads the pitch one
on the Emosson Dam

Joy on the Bossons Glacier during an attempt on Mont Blanc in 1984

Joy at the helm on the sea crossing from Knoydart to Rum

Martin guiding Eva Groenveld on the East Ridge of the Inaccessible Pinnacle in May 2013

Martin on Sgurr Dubh Mor looking to the northern half of the Cuillin Ridge during a November traverse

Alan Colley climbing the Inaccessible Pinnacle during a two day Cuillin traverse

Our oldest client: Stan Dow at 74 on Aonach Mheadhoin in Glen Shiel

James Cox abseils into the T-D Gap –
5am 13th June 1988

Susan Hawkins at her final top – Meall Mor on the Loch Monar hills

The Old Man of Hoy emerges from the morning mists

Red Szell at the belay slings above the crux of The Old Man of Hoy

With daughter Hazel on the summit of Mont Blanc – July 15th 2013

Martin and son Alex on belay during the 2nd ascent of
Genesis on Beinn Bhan
(photo: Nick Carter)

Mont Blanc at dawn – the Brenva Face is directly under the summit

Descending the Three Monts route from Mont Blanc with Hazel

The Matterhorn from the east – Hörnli Ridge on the right , Italian Ridge on the left

Leading up the Moseley Slab on a quiet morning on the Hörnli Ridge

Reaching the summit of the Matterhorn looking east to Monte Rosa

The morning after the Grandes Jorasses – Martin and David outside the Boccalatte Hut

Jules Cartwright at the Sasc Fura Hut with the Badile and Trubinasca groups behind

Jules leads the Fiamma of the Spazzacaldeira in the Bregaglia Alps

Julie Colverd abseiling from the Punta Albigna

Martin makes an awkward diagonal abseil on the Grépon traverse

Des Winterbone follows the *Fissure en Z* to the summit of the Grépon

David Litherland on the West Ridge of the Grandes Jorasses
with the Pointe Marguerite behind

We battled onwards into the liquid light of a moist evening. Progress was achingly slow. The last vestiges of twilight caught us slithering on our backsides down the rock ramps under the Pinnacle towards the sanctuary of the cave, sixteen hours into our day. Once zipped into my sleeping bag I dropped into exhausted slumber for seven hours, while the team anxiously tossed and turned on our stony couch. Mist and drizzle greeted our emergence at 8.00 am. Resolve wavered. We waited an hour for a clearance and then, wearily, we toiled back up to climb the In Pinn. The slow crawl towards Gars Bheinn recommenced, hour by hour, over each and every crenellation of the ridge that I knew so well. This mission meant little to me yet I clung to my obligation to get my team to the end. Often I have commended the adage that hard work is good for the soul but now I passed into another realm of the senses. The Cuillin, my companions for so many years, reflected my despair, but towards my team I could show only steely resolve.

I looked over the sea, saw the western cliffs of Rum plunging into the Minch and sensed all the pain of human existence. When would this end?

Somehow we crossed the T-D Gap intact. The grim plod restarted, out to Sgurr Dubh Mor, across the jumbled boulders of the Garbh Choire, then on to the endless climb of Sgurr nan Eag. Still they kept going at the same laboured pace, their effort as magnificent as it was maddening. Suddenly I felt the need to break free and for five minutes I pounded ahead, driving my heart and lungs to their maximum. Then I lay panting by the summit and briefly saw hope in the skies. Only Gars Bheinn remained, a shattered sabre-tooth rising high above the ocean. I led my team to the top at 6.30 pm, thinking glumly of the long descent and homeward drive. We had been on our feet for twenty-four hours out of the last thirty-two. No traverse had taken so much from me. Then Steve arrived and he promptly burst into tears of joy. I felt both shame and absolution. I had briefly forgotten what this means in the lives of those I guide – the Cuillin Ridge, a monumental achievement, however it is done.

Chapter 10

TWENTY-FOUR HOURS WITH THE GODFATHER

Beinn Bhan has given me more adventures than any of my other local mountains, and yet doesn't even possess Munro status. The 896m summit is the culminating point of the Applecross plateau and, viewed from the south or west, it is merely a broad swell of high moorland, more akin to the Pennines than the sensational topography of Torridon. However, on the north-east side, the plateau breaks into a series of deep glacial corries that together form one of the most dramatic landscapes in the country. The headwalls of these corries are composed of bands of sandstone rising to over 300m in vertical height. They are repulsively vegetated and offer little appeal to the summer rock climber, but in winter they can be transformed into amphitheatres of ice, ringed by lofty balconies and framed by jutting prows of rimed rock.

This magnificent arena was discovered for winter climbing in the late 1960s by Ullapool GP and obsessive pioneer, Tom Patey. He brought Chris Bonington up to climb the most obvious line, the thousand-foot slot of March Hare's Gully (IV). In the 1970s Hamish MacInnes and Kenny Spence led parties up many of the icefalls which can cascade over the precipices during a prolonged cold spell. Some of these serious grade IV and V routes were ascended with students under the auspices of the MacInnes's infamous Glencoe School of Mountaineering. The best icefall in the central corrie, Coire na Poite, is the biggest expanse of vertical ice in country when formed. First ascenders, Norrie Muir and Arthur Paul, gave it the evocative name of Silver Tear.

Coire an Fhamair, 'the giant's corrie', is the right-hand of Beinn Bhan's three central corries and is well-named. The mountain's highest and steepest vertical walls are harboured here. After Patey's death in 1970, another Aberdonian, Andy Nisbet, became the prophet of Scottish mixed climbing, in which rock cracks and turf are used as climbing material as much as snow or ice. Andy was so awed by the bewildering scale and complexity of the Giant's Wall that he took full bivouac equipment and spent a night on the face on the first ascent with Brian Sprunt in 1980. Thus, the mountain's first grade VII, Die Reisenwand, was created.

The wall also sported two vertical clefts of truly Gothic scale and proportions. In 1983 and 1984 London-raiding parties led by the irrepressible adventurer Mick Fowler climbed them both. Gully of the Gods and Great Overhanging Gully are both intimidating grade VI routes. Beinn Bhan had attracted an illustrious list of pioneering climbers. Nevertheless, the great rock bastion in between Fowler's two clefts remained untouched. Far steeper than Die Reisenwand and described by the Scottish Mountaineering Club guidebook as the steepest mountain cliff in the country, this became the mountain's "last great problem". It was at this point that I dared to throw my hat in the ring.

My awareness of this face dated back to a teenage Scout trip in the summer of 1972. We camped by the sandy shores of Lochan Coire na Poite and next day we wandered up Coire an Fhamair and climbed the scree slopes to the right of the wall. I spent a long time gazing at the cliff, dreaming of future glories as I criss-crossed the face with a clutch of new routes. In particular, a soaring bottomless corner in the upper half of the wall fired my imagination. This would be the plum line, but entry was guarded by a series of turf-fringed overhangs. I could not have guessed that this cliff was far better suited to winter-climbing, or that twenty years later my home would be just seven miles away.

My trepidation over this route was such that I felt an abseil inspection of the corner was justified, even though this transgresses the ethical ideal of making a true on-sight ascent. On a fine October day in 2001 I took my black Labrador and a sackful of rope up the back side of the mountain. On finding the exit of the corner I tied Kyle to my belays and abseiled into the abyss. At the lip of the first overhang my stomach lurched at the sight of my rope swinging free above a 180m free fall to the corrie floor. However, I was heartened to see cracks and ledges choked with vegetation in the corner. I conveniently ignored intervening sections of primitive smooth rock and blithely scaled the prevailing features in feet rather than metres. After one full rope-length and the most cursory inspection I put prusik clamps on my rope and jumared out to rouse my sleeping dog.

The next problem was to find a suitable partner for this climb. A notoriously strong rock climber had become resident in Gairloch. Paul Tattersall was putting up dozens of desperate climbs on the local cliffs, routes that I couldn't even follow let alone lead! He was also a mountain lover with a twist of eccentricity. Much to the distaste of environmental purists he had taken a mountain bike to the top of all the Munros in a non-stop round of 81 days in 1989. This feat prompted Munro doyen Hamish Brown to comment "Anyone who takes a mountain bike up the Cuillin needs a psychiatrist!" Tatt wasn't known as a winter climber, but I heard through the grapevine that he had quietly soloed the grade VI Central Buttress on Beinn Eighe. Although he and wife Angela were busy with a newborn baby, Paul had never climbed on Beinn Bhan and was beguiled by my ingenuous promise of a grand day out that would take his mind off nappies and colic.

The final piece in the jigsaw was to pick a day of perfect weather with full winter conditions in the cliff. The wall is so steep that very little snow adheres. A long blast of north-westerly winds is required to blow snow into the face and to deposit rime ice on the steeper walls. One can wait years for this ripe juxtaposition of the elements, but 14 March 2002 was one such day. We left Tornapress bridge in a pink frosted dawn at 6.30 am and walked up the stalkers' path on to the north-east side of the mountain. The chain of corries came into view. Coire na Feola – *the flesh corrie*, Coire na Poite with its ice weeps and lattice of snow ledges, and finally the sheer profile of the wall we hoped to climb in Coire an Fhamair. We lingered in the sun at the lochan and tried to capture the morning's pristine beauty on camera, then pushed on up the bevelled bed of the Giant's Corrie, where the last glacier of the Lomond advance completed its work some 10,000 years ago.

We spent several minutes devising a route to get up the first hundred metres of compact cliff. Eventually, we chose the rightmost of two tiny snow-covered ramps that led through this barrier. 9.30 am was not an especially punctual starting time by winter standards but on this splendid March day we could count on ten hours of usable daylight. Immediately, the route was devious. The Torridonian sandstone was an unpredictable adversary, leading me along easy gangways and over big flakes, then suddenly closing its defences in rounded crackless bulges. The first pitch took me up left, then twenty metres horizontally right until I found a climbable crack to gain a stance under the ramp. Paul took over and made a hard pull up a vertical wall into the ramp. His progress was slow, as he linked tufts of heather and moss while bracing crampons on weathered sandstone ripples. Ingenuity and persistence were required to dig out decent protection placements. At forty metres his axe placement ripped and he fell two metres. Then, after nearly two hours of effort, he pulled through to the central depression of the wall where 60° snow slopes made a fair resemblance to the Eiger's White Spider.

An eight-metre tier of compact rock barred access to the tenuous ledge that girdles the face. I probed the band at several points but could find no cracks for protection. I contemplated a series of strenuous pulls on turf fringes, knowing that I would hit the terrace if I fell off. With no other options I summoned a new level of mental commitment. Thankfully, neither the turf nor my strength failed. Paul joined me and crawled along the tiny ledge sandwiched between large roofs and a hundred metres of fresh air. After fifteen metres he reached a point directly under the big corner and headed up and out of sight.

As I paid out the rope I gazed north and noted with rising alarm that the shadow of the Giant's Wall was rapidly creeping outwards while the distant Torridon peaks commenced their choral evensong. I had never imagined we would have to climb the big corner in the dark. Suddenly, the optimism engendered by my abseil inspection seemed presumptuous. I tried to second Paul's pitch quickly but was pegged back by a series of hard delicate mantleshelf moves between sloping ledges. What had started as a grade VI had quickly evolved into a grade VII, and, looking up at the blank corner, I realised that we were going to have to go one grade harder in order to succeed.

As night fell I bridged past Paul, set my headtorch and attacked a bulging crack-line just left of the main corner. The crack was verglassed. However hard I hammered my protection nuts, they could not be trusted to stay in place. In desperation I got a length of thin prusik cord and with a combination of fingers and teeth fed it through a small constriction to create a thread runner. With this in place I summoned extra reserves to power through to the top of the crack, where I found a tiny ledge for a belay. The corner continued to a large overhang. From my standpoint this seemed the ideal place for Tatt to display his legendary arm strength. Paul took a while to second the pitch, and reached the stance looking ashen, no longer seeming amused by my promise of a "grand day out".

"I'm knackered; I can't do any more leading. You'll have to go on."

My own arms and fingers were already suffering spasms of cramp and our fortunes dipped further when my headtorch commenced an intermittent flicker that warned of low battery power. I made a hard pull-up to the roof and bridged my feet out on the enclosing walls to take the strain off my arms while I placed a good cam for protection. I was still using wrist-loops on my axes. The advent of leash-free climbing and axes with handle-grips had not yet reached my corner of the Highlands. Wrist-loops prevent the dropping of axes and provide support to the grip of fingers, but pin the climber's arms above the head. Without the option of taking a hand off occasionally for a shake-out, the forearms slowly drain of blood and lactic acid engulfs the muscles.

Fighting this lactic pump, I stretched over the lip of the roof and scrabbled up on to a ledge. At this point my light completely failed. I lowered a rope loop to Paul and hauled up his torch which, by comparison, gave a surprisingly intense and brilliant light. This beam illuminated another overhanging joint, some five metres higher. There were no footholds on either wall. The only way to succeed would be to swing the axe picks into the corner, lock one arm and stretch the other into a higher part of the crack, then repeat the action several times. I placed two good runners at the bottom, but knew that I did not possess the strength to place any more once I was committed. Initially, I felt unequal to the task and spent several minutes in abject prevarication.

If I took a fall at the top it would be a big one with potential injury, and yet there was no choice other than to fail. I felt liberated the instant I made my commitment. The surge for an improbable glory is, after all, the stuff of climbers' dreams. The arm-locks worked and my strength held long enough to get my axes into the frozen grass at the top of the corner. Then one of the picks ripped out and I was left dangling on one arm. I thrashed the axe back in and hung limp for a few seconds. Unable to make a straight pull-up a radical solution was required. I swung my foot up to shoulder level and hooked the crampon points over a rock that protruded from the patch of grass, then hauled mightily until my body slumped on to the ledge. After two minutes of silent gasping I recovered sufficiently to place a couple of anchors for a belay. At that instant Paul's torchlight died with sudden and emphatic finality.

I was plunged into blackness. My pupils adjusted. There was a canopy of stars but not one sliver of moonlight. The brightest object in our Universe was the electric light of a salmon hatchery four miles away. Paul was stranded twenty metres below. Neither of us had spare clothes or an emergency bivouac sack.

"Fix a rope and I'll try to prusik up," he yelled.

I tied one of our ropes direct to the belay anchors with a clove hitch so that it would take Paul's weight and began a long vigil. He detached from his belays and swung out into space, then tried to slide his prusik cords up the fixed line. All the while I kept the other rope as tight as possible. He dropped a piton, then a karabiner, then an axe. Meanwhile, I took the batteries out of Paul's torch and stuffed them down my vest in hope that my body heat might generate a little residual power. After ten minutes I reconnected the torch and it produced a muted yellow glow, which I directed down the corner. This lasted long enough to allow Paul to make a couple of upward moves. The situation was perilous. Paul was gently spinning and had become enmeshed in a tangle of ropes. If he unclipped the wrong karabiner in the dark the consequences could be fatal. After more battery-warming antics he reached my stance, utterly spent. It was 11.30 pm.

"That's a halogen bulb on my torch," he said. "That's why it went out so quickly. I'm sure I've got a normal bulb somewhere as a spare. It draws less power and the batteries might still be strong enough."

The problem was that we had no light with which to locate the spare bulb and complete the delicate changing operation. An icy breeze, laden with spindrift, funnelled down the cliff. An exceedingly cold bivouac seemed likely, but then I had a brainwave.

"Paul, I'll put my mobile phone on; the screen gives off a light. It should be enough."

By the dimmest of margins the changeover was completed and true to prediction the new bulb emitted a life-saving light. Unfortunately, our ingenuity did not stretch to the realisation that we could also use the phone to call Angela and Joy to tell them that we were alive and still fighting. At around this time the two sleepless wives in

Lochcarron and Gairloch commenced frantic debate over whether a rescue should be initiated. Joy was inclined to wait but Angela had rarely been in this situation. One of my instructors was roused from his bed for arbitration.

"Don't worry," yawned Walter, "they'll get back whenever . . ." and dropped back to slumber.

I wondered what we had done to deserve this gift of light. Incompetence in provisioning vital pieces of kit is not usually so mercifully forgiven. With as much speed as my weary frame could muster I ploughed up the final section of the corner to meet a vertical wall of powder snow and a cornice. I took half an hour to dig a trench through this last impasse and at 2.30 am pulled on to Beinn Bhan's summit plateau. When Paul reached me the torch gave out its last feeble flickers of light. We lay contented under a vault of stars, an infinity broken only by the orange fringe of Broadford town and the white beam of North Rona lighthouse.

A pale reflection from the snow allowed us to pick a way over the plateau and down the descent gully back to our sacks. We slid down the slopes under the cliff and made good progress across the flat floor of the corrie. Then we passed the snowline and entered the black heather moor. We could have stopped and waited for daylight but were possessed by an illogical urgency to finish the job without a bivouac. For three kilometres we stumbled over peat hags, crashing headfirst across frozen ponds and disappearing down ditches at regular intervals, until the first glow of dawn showed to the south-east. At 6.00 am we hit the stalking path and hastened home to reassure our wives.

Paul was so concerned for Angela that he refused our offer of a bed and drove straight back to Gairloch after a quick cup of tea. Strange to say, he hasn't been seen out winter climbing much since that day, at least not with me! Joy roused me after one hour's sleep.

"Come on, you'll be late. You've promised to take Kyle to the vet." I writhed in an agony of metabolic dysfunction, and staggered up to face the day. In the constant flow of family life the last twenty-four hours might not have happened, but I walked on air for the next three weeks in the thrill of its remembrance.

We called the climb the Godfather in respect to the overpowering scale of the cliff and the divine providence which had allowed us to succeed. It became one of Scotland's most highly sought grade VIII routes. Five years later the second ascent was attempted by Pete Benson, Guy Robertson and Es Tresidder. They made a rapid ascent to the final corner, but they too were overtaken by darkness. Benson led the crux corner. Like me, he got his axes lodged in the turf at the top but ran out of strength and fell off. He was climbing leashless, so left both tools lodged in the grass, where they stayed for several months until they were retrieved on abseil. Benson sustained a badly sprained ankle in the impact and the party took ten hours to abseil off and then limp back to the road.

Subsequently, several parties have repeated the route in fast style and effectively demolished the aura, but for me the Godfather will always stand as a life-affirming event. Rarely in a climbing career does one embark on a route, long-cherished and much-feared, and succeed by such a slender margin.

Chapter 11

RUNNING THE RIDGE

The afternoon sun was beginning to wane but the rock remained warm to the touch as we scrambled to the summit of Sgurr a'Mhadaidh. Our day had commenced with an ascent of the Inaccessible Pinnacle and in the gentle warmth of a mid-May anticyclone we had extended our expedition across the three Munros of the central Cuillin. My clients were doubtless thinking of a relaxed descent back to Glen Brittle, but I was wearing my fell-running shoes and had another mission on my mind.

For years I had pondered on the speed record for traversing the Cuillin Ridge. As Britain's premier mountain traverse, the Cuillin record holds a distinctive cachet in the climbing world. The Ridge was first traversed by Alastair MacLaren and Leslie Shadbolt in June 1911, in 12 hours 18 minutes, peak to peak, a time that would be counted as very respectable in the modern era. Gradually the best time was reduced below six hours and in 1969 the legendary fell-runner Eric Beard set a truly modern record of 4 hours 9 minutes. Heads were turned. This record was a dual-test of extreme fell-running and solo climbing, a combination of talents possessed by only a few climbers. The Lakeland climber and runner, Andy Hyslop, reduced the mark to 4 hours 4 minutes in 1984 and established an "official" route for future record efforts, including all eleven Munro summits on the Ridge and all the difficult rock climbing sections, with no roped protection allowed. Respecting Andy's abilities I never imagined myself equal to such a feat. The speed seemed preposterous for a route that involves eleven kilometres of ground distance, 2200m of ascent, sustained scrambling on the roughest terrain imaginable, plus half a dozen graded rock climbs. In 1986 two little-known runners from North Wales, Del Davies and Paul Stott, lopped a massive fourteen minutes off the time to set 3 hours 50 minutes as the new target.

If an "impregnable" record could be so easily smashed, I began to wonder how I might fare.

So I stripped down to vest and shorts on Sgurr a'Mhadaidh that May afternoon and handed my sack to my clients.

"Do you think you could you take my kit down for me? I'm going to have a run along the Ridge to Sgurr nan Gillean and will meet you at Sligachan Hotel. In fact this will be fun. We'll see who is quicker. Take care, keep your helmets on till you're down in the corrie and here are the car keys . . ."

Abandonment of one's clients on top of a peak doesn't feature in the mountain guides' manual, but the temptation was just too great. Andy Hyslop's split time from Mhadaidh to Gillean was exactly a third of the total. To be anywhere near the Davies-Stott record I would need to run it in an hour and a quarter. The run was a joy. For every grinding ascent there was a compensating gallop along the knife-edged crest followed by a relaxing descent into the next bealach. The cardio-vascular system could recover on the rock climbing passages, where technical concentration took precedence. To my amazement I clambered on to the summit of Sgurr nan Gillean after just an hour and three minutes. I could barely credit the speed. I jogged down to Sligachan and had to wait half an hour for my team and transport to arrive. Even with allowance for an inevitable slowing after completing the first two-thirds of the traverse, I had the record "in the bag". That confidence gave me a tingle of excitement and I waited for a window of fine weather that coincided with a day off work.

The ideal day arrived on Saturday 2 June 1990. The forecast was dry with high cloud and a north-west breeze to keep the rock cool. I had no time to organise a support team. All I needed was a reliable watch and a vow of honesty in recording my performance. I planned to go for the whole traverse without carrying any liquid or food. I would stock up on honey sandwiches on the approach to Gars Bheinn and hoped I could finish the traverse before I "hit the wall". To show that I was treating the venture with appropriate athleticism I took a drink powder. Considering modern isotonic mixes to be ludicrously expensive I purchased a carton of Creamola foam crystals in our local Spar. My clothing comprised Walsh fell-running shoes, long johns, shorts and Helly Hansen vest, thin grippy gloves and a lightweight wind-smock that I could stuff into a tiny bum-bag on the run.

Leaving Glen Brittle campsite at 8.10 am I jogged across the four miles of moorland to the base of Gars Bheinn. I stopped twice at streams to mix a beaker of Creamola, which provided a sugar-rich stimulant for the grind up the scree-slopes of Gars Bheinn. This 500m-high slag-heap offers a warm-up that would intimidate any endurance athlete. A tenuous route linking strips of grass and larger rocks avoided the worst of the screes and I arrived on top at 10.20 am. I had hoped to find a walker who could verify my presence and record my starting time, but to my dismay there was no one within sight. After ten minutes of fruitless waiting I set my stopwatch, touched the cairn and sprang into action.

There was a surge of exhilaration to finally begin the traverse after the pensive approach. In lightweight shoes without a load I could skip along the crest, barely touching the rock at each springing step. How different from the heavy tread of a mountain boot and the drag of a ten-kilo sack on a normal traverse. I passed the first Munro, Sgurr nan Eag after seventeen minutes. This section usually takes an hour. The detour to Sgurr Dubh Mor crosses the bouldery wastes of the Garbh Choire. I had rehearsed my line over a dozen previous visits, and turned at the summit with just forty-four minutes on the clock.

The T-D Gap provides the technical crux of the traverse. There is no room for overtaking and the presence of other climbers could scupper the attempt. I clambered to the edge and was relieved to see that my way was clear. The descent into the gap is a ten-metre wall of Severe standard which is perched above a horrifying chasm. A slip here would be fatal. My fingers were warm and dry and they crimped firmly on the holds. Within two minutes I crossed the gap and wriggled up the polished chimney on the far side.

At Sgurr Alasdair, with one-third of the ridge complete, I was well within schedule with an elapsed time of 1 hour and 3 minutes. I scampered over Sgurr Thearlaich and down the weaving descent to the base of Sgurr Mhic Choinnich. Collie's Ledge offers a simple but circuitous route to the summit, but the official route climbs direct up the Very Difficult King's Chimney. With this despatched I faced a hard graft to the Inaccessible Pinnacle. I couldn't remember the target time for this section. Was I starting to drop precious minutes? That creeping doubt pushed me to raise my pace and take some risks. There is a steep downward step on the descent of Mhic Choinnich's

North Ridge, and a spectacular exposure into the base of Coire Lagan opens below. Normally, I would have faced in and back-climbed, but instead I tried a forward skip and a jump. My trailing foot snagged a rock edge and I pitched forwards, sprawling headlong down the ridge crest. I stopped a metre before the edge of the precipice but my shin banged hard on a fin of gabbro.

I got to my feet, tested that the leg could bear weight, and rolled up my leggings to reveal a superficial cut and a nascent white patch from the impact. The relief was enormous. Without a further second of delay I continued the run, but my confidence was knocked. A trickle of blood soaked into my sock and the bruise ached for a while, but by the time I reached the In Pinn the old rhythm was back. The descent of the short side of the pinnacle is another definite crux. The rock is highly polished and slopes outwards. I slowed my breathing and padded cautiously down from shelf to shelf until I could jump to the bottom.

At 1 hour 35 minutes my cumulative time was still good. The half-way point is passed at Sgurr nan Banachdich. Sgurr a'Ghreadaidh with its elegant curving arête was taken at a dash and I was on Sgurr a'Mhadaidh in 2 hours 20 minutes. With an hour and half to play with and a training time of an hour and three minutes, the record now looked assured, but there were two doubts. Would I take another tumble and would I get into glycogen deficit as the muscles expended their stores of energy? The notorious runner's "bonk" can reduce a record-breaker to a slow crawl in a matter of minutes. My endurance training would now meet its test. I thought myself to have enough reserves to manage but a cool drink would have been welcome.

Imperceptibly, my pace fell below the training time on the complex crenellations of Bidein Druim nan Ramh. Instinctive caution and natural depletion took their toll on the long ascent of Bruach na Frithe. From here Andy Hyslop had run to the finish in an amazing twenty-three minutes, including the ascent of the Severe Naismith's Route up the overhanging thumb of the Bhasteir Tooth. If a large roped party barred my way on the Tooth I could have been in trouble, but the rock was deserted. My intensity of concentration was such that I was unaffected by the huge exposure of the place. I knew every hold from memory and bounced over the exit mantleshelf with a quick forward thrust of the elbows. With the last major obstacle behind me I clambered on to the summit of Am Basteir to surprise a rotund check-shirted silver-haired gentleman who was admiring the panorama. He nearly jumped out of his skin.

"Who the bloody hell . . .!" he exclaimed as I brushed past. I gave him no time for further admonishment.

The strains of weariness slowed the final link to Sgurr nan Gillean. My hope of doing three and a half hours slipped away and I joined a group of happy scramblers on the summit plinth with my stop-watch at 3 hours and 33minutes[1].

"Where have you come from?" one of the group asked.

I pointed over to Gars Bheinn.

"How long has that taken you?"

"Just over three and a half hours," I replied.

Their gasps of amazement matched my own incredulity as I looked back along the switchback ridge to the hazy peaks at the southern end of the Ridge. Someone passed me a bottle of water and with my last Creamola crystals I concocted a Champagne-like celebration.

My route back to Glen Brittle took me across Coire a'Bhasteir and down the Fionn Choire. En-route I passed my silver-haired adversary from Am Basteir. He had just button-holed another walker.

"The lad came up out of nowhere; and the bugger had nowt on! Never seen anything like it in all my life."

I decided that the most diplomatic course would be to nip past unnoticed, and I kept my pleasure close to my chest. Few days would ever compare with the simple joy of running the Ridge.

Notes

1. In 1994 Andy Hyslop returned to the Cuillin and posted two record attempts. On the first he exactly equalled my time and in the second he knocked just one minute off it. It seemed as if a barrier had been reached, and the record lay untouched for another 13 years. Then, in 2007 Es Tresidder combined his climbing skills with a high-class running pedigree to smash the record in a time of 3 hours, 17 minutes and 28 seconds. This record was expected to last a good many years, but in June 2013, Finlay Wild, an elite fell-runner from Fort William, pushed the mark down to 3 hours 14 minutes and 58 seconds, and followed this up in October with an incredible time of 2 hours 59 minutes and 22 seconds.

Chapter 12

THE SAVING OF ANDY

A few climbs develop the status as classics of their region. In Torridon the one big ice route to which every visiting climber aspires is the Poachers Fall on the northern face of Liathach. The tiered Torridonian cliffs have a unique geological disposition for ice formation. The summit cap of Liathach is made of permeable quartzite, but at 900m this meets the banded cliffs of sandstone. All the drainage that filters through the quartz is forced outwards to form spring-lines over the sandstone cliffs. With progressive freezing during winter these form into trails of ice up to 150m high. Poachers Fall is the central spring-line in Coire Dubh Mor, forming a compelling plunge of silvery ice at the focal point of an amphitheatre of cliffs, and is a benchmark of grade V climbing.

The climb was first ascended by Andy Nisbet and Richard McHardy in 1978. Andy was then twenty-five years old, at the start of his prodigious climbing career, and beginning to venture out of Aberdonian homelands in search of new routes. Richard McHardy is one of climbing's most colourful characters, operating at the cutting edge of extreme climbing as part of the Alpha group in Manchester in the early 1970s. The story goes that Richard had agreed to do the climb with another partner but, presented with Andy's availability at short notice, broke his commitment; hence the guilt-tinged name. A winter classic has its attendant risks and challenges. The location is inspiringly remote; the climbing is sustained for four pitches at or near-vertical and the exit slopes are exposed and prone to avalanche. There have been serious accidents here, but Poachers Fall held a certain cachet for the more ambitious mountain guides.

The weather of February 2003 was impeccable. An anti-cyclone dominated, giving alpine warmth on southern slopes, but maintaining a hard frost in the snowy northern corries. Epics and accidents seemed far away. On the 18th only one of my instructors had gone high, the irrepressible Andy Nisbet. Andy had been one of my regular instructors for several years. As a living legend of winter climbing he was an immense asset to Moran Mountaineering. Andy didn't just play the part, he looked the part as well, with magnificent ginger beard, clothing that is best described as ancient-weathered and an iconic limp from a degenerate hip. He had led our clients up dozens of exploratory climbs in esoteric clefts all over Wester Ross, giving them the fleeting fame of appearances in climbing magazines and guidebooks.

While Andy went on to the north side of Liathach with two clients, the rest of us were happy to conduct a lazy coaching session on a sunny crag in Torridon. The phone rang just after I got back and the ominous words: "This is Dingwall Police . . ." changed my mellow mood. "There's been an accident on Liathach". It could only be Andy . . .

Ice conditions seemed good; there had been a thaw but now it was freezing again. Eddie and Julie were two of Martin's most experienced clients. The day before, on the 17th, we'd been sitting on the Beinn Bhan plateau in the early afternoon, enjoying the sun after finishing Mad Hatter's Gully. An easy day on the 18th was tempting. "But we've never sat around before on a Moran course", they said. "How about Poachers Fall tomorrow?" I asked. "We're up for that!" It was the route they'd come for.

Poachers Fall was complete. It's never easy but I'd done it many times before, and it was four days short of the 25th anniversary of the first ascent with Richard McHardy. The first two pitches went well and now I was on the third, an ice-filled groove. The ice was still wet after the thaw, but this gave first-time placements and I was running up it, with the aim to be back in time for tea at 5 o'clock. I put an ice-screw deep in the ice after 20m and continued to where the groove ended. Here you have to move out right over a bulge, and I placed another ice-screw here. That one wasn't so good, but never mind, it was easy today. Suddenly the ice became fresh and brittle, and my placement wasn't in far . . . End of memory!

I was hanging on the rope just above the clients. I had gone about 80 feet. "Lower me back down to the stance. Give me a couple of minutes and I'll go up again."

"No you won't," said Julie, "you've broken your leg".

There was no pain whatsoever and I was standing on the good leg.
"Are you sure?"

"Yes." Apparently, I'd been unconscious for a couple of minutes
with my leg tucked over my shoulder. It was the femur.

"You'd better abseil off and go for help; the helicopter will just
pick me up." The rucksacks with the mobile phone were down in
the corrie. They had climbed Grade V unguided, so were more than
competent to get off without me.

So I hung on the belay and waited; maybe four hours would do
it ...

Eddie and Julie took three hours to abseil off and walk out to
a point where there was a mobile signal. It was dusk by the time
Torridon rescue team gathered. Although I am a team member, I
would describe myself as a slightly begrudging mountain rescuer.
With a full-time job on the hill it is hard to work up enthusiasm
for late-night call-outs, and I can't deny a judgmental frustration
towards those who get into trouble through blatant incompetence,
all of which only raises my admiration of the other team members
who give their all to the service without condition or complaint. This
rescue was different, not just because it was Andy, but because the
stakes were so high. Bleeding from a femoral fracture can quickly
lead to fatal shock.

Rapid helicopter transit to the top of the route was vital. Maddening delays followed. The RAF helicopter was engaged on another
rescue, and then we heard it coming, only to be told that it was low
on fuel and needed a detour to fill up at Broadford. Then a decision
was made to go back to Inverness and collect the RAF Mountain
Rescue team who were driving over from Kinloss. We could have
walked in quicker!

As the only team member who knew the route I was given a pivotal role. The helicopter couldn't risk a winch on a big vertical cliff.
Instead, a manual lower and crag-snatch were planned.

"How long a rope do you want, Martin?" said team leader Neil.
"We've got 160 or 180 metres."

I knew the route involved 150m of climbing so played safe. "I'll
take the 180."

At 9.00 pm the helicopter reappeared, only for the pilot to decide that it was too windy to make a drop on the summit ridge. Well, at least we could get in to the base of the route, but no! Despite the clear night the cautious pilot put us down on the moors at 400m. To get to Andy we'd need to thrash uphill for an hour into Coire Dubh Mor, climb a 300m grade I gully and traverse across 40° névé slopes to the exit of the route.

Not knowing if he was alive or dead, we surmounted the corrie lip, and yelled at the icefalls, which glittered in the moonlight. There were a few seconds of fearful silence before we heard a hoarse cry.

"I'm really struggling . . . I can't hold on much longer . . . you'll need to be quick," – this from a man who had out-lasted most of Scotland's winter desperadoes in twenty-five years of pioneering climbs. He had survived but was clearly in severe stress.

There were some twenty rescuers, including a fit but youthful RAF contingent. In truth we were something of a rabble. Hurried preparations and hardware requisitions were now put to the test. At the snowline team doctor Gavin stopped and swore. "Shit, I've forgotten my crampons; I'll have to go back." He had been assigned to join me on the lower. Paramedic Mike was quickly commandeered to take his place, and we pushed on with unseemly haste.

In the gully I tied six RAF boys on to my rope, far in excess of a safe guiding ratio. The "seven-on-a-rope" scenario replicated Whymper's chosen roping system on the ill-fated first ascent of the Matterhorn and made an uncomfortable memory. The cream of the RAF was now dependent on my guiding ability. Was mass hysteria taking hold? With a silent prayer for the crampon skills of my young cohort I led them up bullet-hard snow to the top of Way Up gully. The traverse over to the route exit was especially scary. Strung out horizontally across the slope there was little chance of holding a slip. A new worry materialised. Which of several outcrops of rocks marked the exit gully from Poachers? All this is simple with the benefit of daylight. The neighbouring route, Salmon Leap, has similar topography. I made my guess and anchors were placed ready for a lower of 150m.

At the back of 1.00 am Mike and I went down together – the 180m 11mm static as the main line and dynamic 9mm ropes tied together as back-up. Andy's shouts had long-since subsided. Were we too late? Fifty metres down we swung over the void and front-pointed down the first vertical pillar of ice, but was it Poachers? A despairing cry echoed from the depths. "You're in the wrong gully."

Though relieved that Andy was still alive, we were now gently sliding down Salmon Leap a full ten metres left of Poachers. I was carrying a modest rack of gear. By placing ice screw runners and clipping the ropes to them we edged nearer to Poachers. I aid-climbed horizontally across the last five metres to reach Andy, who was standing on one leg on a ledge the size of a laptop, a pallid face shrunken behind his beard and jacket hood. There is no word other than heroic to describe the torment of standing for twelve hours at –5°C with a broken femur. Perhaps the cold had stemmed the bleeding and saved him.

Mike rummaged in his sack. "Where's the morphine? Oh shit . . ."

A crucial changeover of kit when Gavin dropped out had been forgotten in our rush. The medical bag was now sitting in Gavin's sack down in the corrie. In the ensuing silence I unscrewed my thermos flask. "I've got some paracetamol and herbal tea here for you Andy."

Being a gentleman he expressed thanks for these small mercies. Fortunately Mike did have a cylinder of Entonox, which could give real relief, and he rigged this up while I pondered the next moves. Our situation was decidedly precarious.

We were now ten metres off the natural line of the lower. If we simply detached from Andy's anchors we would make a massive pendule into the ice pillars of Salmon Leap and probably end up with three broken legs instead of one! Somehow, we had to minimise the swing. Mike and I strapped Andy horizontally in front of us and braced our feet on the ice. We were now a threesome, irrevocably linked by a web of slings. I placed my last two ice screws and we aid-climbed from one to the other, gaining a couple of metres. Then I made a daisy-chain with all our spare bits of tape down to my last prusik cord. We clipped one end to the last ice screw and I fed the chain slowly through my harnesses until the weight of three bodies was unbearable. We were still five metres off-line. There was no turning back. I fed out the last cord until I was clinging to it at arms-length. It was our Geronimo moment.

Gripping Andy tight into our stomachs and pedalling our feet we swooped across an ice chimney until a jarring shock on the static rope brought us to an instant stop. Andy was oblivious to the drama. Having pronounced ourselves unscathed we radioed for the lower to restart. We could see the gathered headlights of the Torridon boys down on the snow-slope at the base of the route, where they had prepared a stretcher. The lower continued. Guessing that we still had twenty metres to go my nerves jangled again. "How much rope?" I radioed.

"About twenty metres," came the reply.

The margins looked slim, but, lacking any alternative, the lower continued and we met the stretcher team with just three metres of rope left. Andy was transferred to the stretcher, strapped in, and lowered a further 120m down the snow slopes to a levelling.

This time the helicopter dared to land. Andy was packaged and lifted off to Raigmore Hospital at 4.00 am. Only with completion of the job did we feel the accumulated stress of the previous ten hours. I wandered back to the road and a peaceful dawn, pondering the mistakes made but immensely grateful that we'd got the vital judgements right, despite all the distractions of an unwieldy rescue effort. With luck we'd get Andy back in good shape come a few months . . .

The surgeon showed me the X-ray with seven breaks in my femur, one spiral, one horizontal and some smaller pieces. "Don't worry," he said, "femurs heal well and you'll be back on the hill; but you're lucky the breaks are high up, where they are less likely to cause fatal bleeding."

After 10 days he let me out with a femoral nail in place and instructions not to weight the leg. Back home and keen to regain arm-strength I tried a couple of pull-ups on a ladder into my attic, not realising that the hanging weight of my leg alone would cause the fractures to separate.

Back in the consulting room, the surgeon asked me if it was OK if they put me in traction for "a short while". This seemed a reasonable proposal. Nine weeks later they untied me from the bed. Another four months later he told me I could start putting gentle weight on the leg again. I decided it was better if didn't tell him I'd climbed a Corbett the previous day.

I had made some mistakes in my recovery but I still say that had I been over-cautious my leg might have healed safely but movement would have been so restricted as to end my mountaineering career. As to the accident I had learnt a few new lessons. Climbing ice routes quickly without placing too much gear is fun and speed can add to safety, but there are definite limits. Placing runners, even when finding the climbing easy, is wise. The hanger of one of my ice-screws broke in the fall. It was a Russian-made model, popular in its day, but clearly sub-standard. The freshly formed water ice must have failed when both my axes were in the same fragile plate. The change in ice quality was so sudden that I missed the risk.

All accidents are the result of misjudgements, most usually a series of misjudgements which accumulate to critical mass. Attention to detail is the key to safety.

Walking back to Glen Torridon, emotionally shaken by the rescue, I wished my life's trajectory to stray as far as possible from Poachers Fall in the coming weeks. Alas, a mountain guide has no choice in such matters. My next client, Mark Dixon, arrived with an enthusiasm for one route and one route only – Poachers Fall. So five days after the event I was back on the ice on the sharp end of the rope, reliving every minute of Andy's ordeal right up to the fatal swing of the axes into the brittle bulge at the top of the fall. Sadly, all of my abandoned kit had been snaffled by other climbers who doubtless must have wondered why such riches were left for their taking.

Someone with a mischievous sense of humour must have thought our efforts warranted wider recognition, for a few months later the Torridon team was nominated for the 2003 *Daily Express* "Life Savers" award. We duly assembled for publicity photos alongside Andy and his crutches. The prize was an invitation to a reception with the Prime Minister at 10 Downing Street but, perhaps to our relief, we missed out on the ultimate award.

Chapter 13

SEA STACK TOURS

The fact is little recognised that the finest summits in the British Isles are to be found scattered around our coasts. None of them exceeds 150m in altitude and none is likely to survive more than a few millennia. The sea stacks are our true inaccessible pinnacles, combining isolation with geological diversity and rich wildlife. In composition they are variously repulsive and forbidding. The fastidious climber should not apply. To climb the stacks you have to endure every insult to pretension as you get dirty, malodorous and frequently wet.

Tom Patey was the great pioneer of Scottish stacks. In the 1960s he made a trilogy of first ascents comprising The Old Man of Stoer off Assynt's north-west coast, Am Buachaille, "the Shepherd", by Sandwood Bay near Cape Wrath and, highest of them all, The Old Man of Hoy on Orkney, which acquired world renown after a ground-breaking live television broadcast by the BBC in 1967. The ascent of all three in a week is a challenge of tidal logistics and ferry timetables, in locations far removed from normal mountain trails.

I promoted my first Sea Stacks Tour in 1996 as much as a personal adventure as a means of enlarging my earnings. My first clients, Simon and Michael, were respectively reserved and taciturn. Six days of awkward silence is a long stretch when living cheek by jowl. An enquiry about jobs is usually an ice-breaking gambit but Michael's retort, "I'm a gasman", had a finality that brooked no further questions. For several days I believed that he installed central heating boilers until it dawned that he was an anaesthetist. Even the adrenalin-fuelled babble that is normal on completion of a climb was short-lived. Thankfully, both were able at the sharp end of business. The stacks demand good rope-work and reliable technical skills at Very Severe level with the ability to pull out the occasional harder move in scary situations.

The vertiginous bedlam of sea cliffs is an alarming experience for the uninitiated. On arrival at the brink of Stoer after a gentle moorland walk the senses are assaulted by the roar of waves, the screams of gulls and a giddy eighty-metre drop into the Atlantic. The Old Man sits opposite on a wave-cut plinth of Torridonian sandstone, separated from the land by an eight-metre sea channel. The phallic connotation of the title does this stack a disservice. Stoer is an elegant citadel, its landward face banded by bedding planes and its summit tapered to seaward.

On a damp morning my stomach tightened a notch when we stepped over the edge. An improbable muddy trod weaves down to the base, where we laid out kit and mentally rehearsed the procedure for getting over to the stack. I stripped down to shorts and helmet, tied a rope round my waist with a bowline and plunged into the channel. Sea temperatures hover around 10°C in spring but the swim is mercifully brief. As soon as I clambered out, the lads tied my rucksack to the rope and I pulled it across above the water. At the base of the landward face a cluster of corroded pegs and rotting slings form the anchors to tension the rope for a Tyrolean traverse. Once towelled and dressed I added an extra anchor point, then tensioned the rope horizontally using a Z-pulley system. My team could then slide over the water hanging in their harnesses from a karabiner on the rope. I had thought my rope tight but Michael plopped his bottom into the sea as he pulled himself across. In stormy weather people have drowned in this predicament. After readjustment and further tautening Simon made a dry crossing and we adjudged our line to be safe from any rise in the tide during our climb.

The first ten metres of the climb form a definite crux, making a hanging traverse on hand-jams across a break to gain good ledges on the south edge. The protection is plentiful, but the rock is habitually wet and slimy from sea spray. This despatched, we enjoyed two long pitches of Very Severe climbing on immaculate clean rock, spiralling rightwards up the face to finish at a razor-edged summit. The thrill was heightened by an audience of admiring walkers who watched the action from the cliff-top.

A single free-hanging fifty-five metre abseil took us back to our Tyrolean rope. I did not fancy a second swim, and worked out that if I doubled the Tyrolean rope back to the mainland anchor points we could re-tension the ropes to the landward side and then retrieve the rope by pulling one of doubled rope ends. I am easily flummoxed by complex rope manoeuvres and these re-arrangements proved tricky, but, with all of us safely back on shore, I felt a frisson of joy when the rope released as planned and splashed into the sea, leaving nothing behind on the stack. As a genuine mountaineering adventure, albeit one undertaken at sea level, Stoer has few equals.

If Stoer is a technical masterpiece Am Buachaille feels tenuous and committing. The stack sits sixty metres out from the mainland on a shallow platform that is only dry for two hours either side of low tide. The approach walk is six kilometres and the descent to the sea is difficult to find on first acquaintance. Calm seas and good timing are essential. We arrived in heatwave conditions, such that it was a relief to plunge into the six-metre tidal channel. Having fixed a rope for our return we tackled the frontal face of the stack. Whereas Stoer had been clean, the rock on Am Buachaille was sandy and brittle, and ledges were occupied by nesting fulmars. The first pitch was sparsely protected and a loud squawk almost threw me off-balance when making an ungainly belly-heave on to a rounded ledge. The female fulmar is cute and downy in nesting pose, but when threatened her retribution is swift. With a rapid reflux in the throat she loaded her gullet full of vomit and sprayed my face and chest. The treatment was preferable to falling off, but a sweet and penetrative stench lingered in my clothing for several weeks.

The route continued with an exposed struggle through brittle elephant-ears of sandstone. In grip factor I reckoned the grade to be harder than Stoer. Summit celebrations were brief. With the tide now on the rise we could brook no delays or tangles on the retreat. We knew of one party who had been trapped by tides and condemned to spend the night perched on the top. With the abseil safely completed we swung back over the Tyrolean crossing with a few minutes to spare before an all-out swim became necessary.

The drive along Scotland's north coast from Durness to Thurso is impressively bleak. The shapely peaks of the North-West Highlands are replaced by barren moors, which offer neither shelter nor succour. The state of the weather is the sole arbiter of mood. In sunshine these lands possess a lonely intense beauty, but on an overcast day, such as we endured on our journey to Orkney, an air of depression and foreboding descends. The tension was only increased with the sight of The Old Man of Hoy as we sailed past on the Scrabster to Stromness ferry.

While mainland Orkney is green, gentle and generously peopled, the island of Hoy is heather-clad and windswept. A single-track road runs west through sombre hills for four miles to the broad bay of Rackwick which is framed by towering cliffs of Old Red Sandstone. Surf-topped waves, propelled by the long reach of the Pentland Firth, roll gracefully up the beach in an unending succession. Behind a fringe of boulders and a strip of machair, there is a scattering of low-roofed cottages, including the former schoolhouse which is now a small hostel. The warden was an incomer from north London. Rackwick had provided his life's sanctuary.

We awoke to low cloud and idled over breakfast. Unwilling to prolong the suspense, I suggested that we get on with the climb. Thick mist shrouded the moors and the Old Man had vanished when we reached the cliff-edge. For several minutes we peered into the wall of fog feeling distinctly spooked. Then, with theatrical timing, the vapours parted to reveal the full length of the stack, steaming in the morning warmth. We needed no further encouragement and completed the climb in six hours. The main action focused on the second pitch which follows an impending shoulder-width crack through two sizeable roofs at E1, 5b standard. The mood of apprehension that had dogged our steps was finally nailed.

My next sea stack clients were Dave, a chartered surveyor and keen club climber, and Carlos, a professional masseur with an unhealthy obsession for vertical lingams of rock. Both could climb E-grades with ease and surprisingly they bonded well. Rackwick Hostel promised a haven of peace after a tiring day of travel from the mainland, but we were dismayed to find the place crammed with camera equipment. The warden directed us to alternative accommodation and told us that a film team was operating on the stack all week with a famous French climber. Carlos's ears pricked up when we divined that this was none other than Catherine Destivelle, at that time the pin-up girl of climbing thanks to her bare-footed soloing video on the desert cliffs of Mali. We would be unwelcome guests if we tried to climb The Old Man during normal working hours. I checked my watch; it was already 5.30 pm.

"Guys, I think we should pack the kit and get straight out to the stack tonight. It's light until eleven."

We walked over to the viewpoint where a gaggle of cameramen and safety crew were assembled, plus a features photographer from

Paris Match magazine. At 7.00 pm they declared filming over for the day so we got to work. Dressed in bright yellow Destivelle flitted about the stack like a canary as she fixed her lines. She abseiled down as we started the second pitch and requested that we didn't move any of her ropes or anchors. In response Carlos merely whimpered in rapture. We climbed the rest of the stack with ferocious efficiency and sat atop in the gloaming at 10.15 pm, just eight hours after sailing past on the ferry. Our satisfaction only increased when we awoke to heavy rain next morning. We departed swiftly, leaving the celebrity entourage to endure an Orkney deluge.

The long journey to reach Hoy raises the spectre of an expensive failure. In 1999 high winds curtailed our activities in the early part of the sea stacks week. With a team of four eager clients I felt no little pressure to succeed on Hoy. On arrival in Orkney the cobbled wynds of Stromness were bathed in midsummer sunlight, but tomorrow's forecast promised the return of high winds accompanied by rain. I wished us on The Old Man there and then.

At Rackwick we rose at 5.00 am in hope of beating the elements, but a heavy drizzle had already commenced. On any other day we would have gone back to bed. I weighed the trials and risks of attempting the stack against the gloom that would descend on the party should I decline the challenge, and decided that a wetting was to be preferred. We carried a double rack of hardware to provide the necessary protection to protect our elongated crocodile of four ropes, one for each client. Normally, the East Face is sheltered from the weather but today's wind cut in from the north and blasted every belay ledge. The rock on the second pitch was the consistency of a sand castle, such that I left my fingerprints on every hold. Were anyone to swing off here the options were limited. Either the hanging climber could prusik up the rope or else be lowered fifty metres to the base of the stack. In light of such conjectures I decided to belay all four climbers up to the hanging belay before I continued. One of the team, Simon, had not brought waterproof shell-trousers and bailed out after the first pitch. I dangled motionless under a curtain of drips for two full hours while bringing up the other three, by which time I had shivered myself into a state of mild hypothermia.

The next two pitches are usually the easiest on the climb, but today they were covered in an evil mix of sea lichen and slimy guano. I climbed with numbed white claws in place of fingers. Each pitch took an hour and a half. Relief was only gained in the steeper final corner where I could make use of hand-jams. We raised heads above the summit parapet for a few seconds then turned tail. After nearly nine hours pinned to the mast we touched the base of the stack at 6.30 pm, and, as we dragged saturated ropes through the last abseil anchor, Simon appeared with sandwiches and flasks of hot tea. Rather than brood in disappointment he had returned to Rackwick, prepared our victuals and walked back in the rain to wait for us. His gallantry counted more than our success.

In 2002 another four able climbers signed up for the tour, all of them capable of leading Very Severe standard. Gill was a particularly enthusiastic lady, and on successful completion of each climb her delight encompassed an open-armed exchange of kisses. On a day at Rhiconich outcrops none of the climbs exceeded ten metres in length and after six routes the cheek-pecking was becoming more than a trifle irksome.

Come our visit to Hoy I was happy to let the team lead all the pitches except the E1 crux. After each pitch I pulled my rope up, leaving them to clip their own rope to my runners. Derek led the final corner and brought up Gill. The summit was just a few metres above and I knew that Gill would be thrilled to be first on top. I motioned her to lead through. She squeezed past us but instead of taking the easy corner, swung up a wall directly above me.

The words "go right" had barely left my lips when Gill pulled out a loose block and flew off backwards. She knocked me off my stance, and plunged past Derek, who heroically jammed his belay plate and held the factor-two fall[1]. We were, all three, left hanging inverted in space with a bird's-eye view of the crashing waves and bobbing seals 140m below. Our collective injuries were no worse than a squashed thumb and bruised ribs, but to my relief, Gill was so shaken that she forgot to dispense the ritual summit kisses.

Rock climbing is a tactile sport, as much to do with geological sensibility and athletic intuition as with the wider view. In 2013, I was contacted by Redmond Szell who suffered a degenerative eye condition known as *retinitis pigmentosa*. His remaining vision was, he said, akin to looking through a pinhole into a smoke-filled room. He was intent on attempting The Old Man of Hoy even though his recent experience was confined to London climbing walls. With an

agreement to provide two guides and three-days of prior outdoor
training I accepted the assignment. Fears of tortuous days and ultimate failure were quickly dispelled when he arrived in Lochcarron.
Red dispatched sport climbs up to 6b standard with such speed that
it was hard to keep abreast pointing out the holds. A nine-hour day
on the Applecross Cioch Nose tested his stamina and scrambling
ability and he made the E1 grade at Diabaig crags with no more
than an occasional tug on the rope. Under his charming exterior Red
occasionally evinced the anger and frustration that had attended a
condition first diagnosed at the age of nineteen. He admitted that the
onset of each winter was a particularly depressing time, but the Hoy
project had given him new purpose.

On 19 June our team of six took residence in Rackwick Hostel
– including Red's friends and supporters Matthew and Andres,
adventure-film cameraman Keith Partridge, and my guiding colleague, Nick Carter from Inverness. First Nick and I took Matthew
and Andres up the Old Man visualising the technical challenges for
Red, while Keith checked camera positions and shot the incidental
footage.

The day of Red's climb was dry but overcast. For a second time we
led him over the two-mile approach track. We tied Red on to a short
rope, and descended the muddy track down the tumbling slopes of
bladder campion and sea thrift to the bridge of fallen blocks that lead
out to the stack. In the late eighteenth century a huge sea arch collapsed to leave the Old Man as an erosional remnant and the bridge
gives non-tidal access. Red scrambled over the barrier with complete
trust in our directions and we reached the base two and half hours
after leaving Rackwick.

Nick is effectively laid-back in coaching style while I can bark a
bit when stressed, so we agreed that I would lead the climb while
Nick mentored Red. Keith gave Nick a "handycam" to do the
close-up action filming then retreated to the cliff-top to work his
long lens on the big crack. The crux pitch begins with a five-metre
descent followed by the sandy traverse to gain the crack. I belayed
Red on two ropes, keeping one direct to him so that he wouldn't
swing too far if he slipped. Meanwhile Nick attached jumar clamps
to a third rope which I had fixed to my anchors. From my belay I
could see nothing of Red's progress and the enveloping tumult of
sea and wind prevented verbal contact. I kept the ropes a little slack

fearing that I would pull Red off if I hauled tight as he traversed. Finally his red shirt appeared under the crack and he climbed into the bottomless chimney known as "the coffin". The crux lies in making three-dimensional calculus to quit the coffin on to a tiny sloping ledge on its left face. Even for the sighted these moves are distinctly tricky and strenuous. Go too high and you get horribly jammed in the roof of the chimney, come out too soon and you can slip off into space.

Nick simultaneously worked his camera, moved his jumars and gave Red directions. I saw Red's hands feverishly sweeping the left wall until he felt the ledge. Then he made a contorted Egyptian bridge across the coffin and swung out. I pulled in, fearing he would lose grip, but Red used brute strength to yard his left arm up to a higher flake hold. Panting furiously he stepped up on the ledge. With the crux surmounted Red had nought to fear on the upper pitches. Two hours later he bridged up the final corner and felt the cold sea breeze blowing through the crack that splits the twin summit blocks, then scrambled to the top. He was probably right in his claim that fewer people have sat here than have reached the summit of Everest. The three abseils were dream-like in their simplicity. Red slid down the final free-hanging abseil so fast that it was well that Nick was holding the ropes from below to slow him before touchdown.

Wearily, we reversed the long scramble back to the cliff-top where Keith conducted a triumphant interview and Matthew and Andres hugged him in celebration. Red admitted he was mentally shattered and I felt pretty worn as we trudged back to Rackwick. Keith is a consummate professional and was busily sorting video and audio content before the first cup of tea was brewed. Nick proudly handed over his camera.

"It's so easy this camera," he said. "You just open the viewer and away you go. Brilliant."

Keith looked quizzical as he opened the list of clips, ready for download. The film was empty.

"You mean you didn't press the red record button?" he asked politely. For a couple of minutes Keith scrolled through his own footage, gently shaking his head.

Nick sidled off towards the shower, while the all-conquering "blind man of Hoy" sat dumbfounded, clutching his celebratory can of beer.

"I am sorry, chaps; we've only got half a programme here; we really need to go back tomorrow and do it again."

Few are the climbers who get the chance to realise their life's dream twice in two days.

Notes

1. "Factor two" falls occur when there is no protection runner between belayer and leader, so that the length of fall is double the length of rope paid out. This places the maximum shock load on the main belay.

Part Three

ALPINE ADVENTURES

Chapter 14

MONT BLANC DREAMS

Above me are the Alps,
The palaces of Nature, whose vast walls
Have pinnacled in clouds their snowy scalps
And throned Eternity in icy halls
Of cold sublimity
                    Byron (*Childe Harold's Pilgrimage*)

Pick a fine day and look out from any point of vantage above the Chamonix valley. You will see Western Europe's highest summit, Mont Blanc – the monarch, without doubt the most beautiful and dominant mountain of our continent – besieged by sprawling chalet developments, high-rise apartments, four-lane highways, cable car stations and snaking paths that are bleached white by erosion. The skies are speckled with paragliders, the air vibrates with the constant drone of helicopters. Mont Blanc has been blighted by everybody else's dreams. Is there any room for your own?

I first climbed the mountain alone and on foot in winter in a two-day escape from a ski holiday in 1981. Under such conditions Mont Blanc repaid my every expectation. The only deflation came on the final ridge, where I was passed by a group of ski mountaineers. At the summit they clipped their bindings into downhill mode and skied through the séracs of the north face with infinite grace and ease, leaving me to a day-long trudge back down the Goûter Ridge. Clearly I was missing a trick somewhere, but when I guided Mont Blanc for the first time with my own clients I wanted to recapture the essence of my solo adventure.

Over six days I prepared my team. Neil Lindsey was a running friend from time we shared in Sheffield and he brought along his sixteen-year-old stepson, Jim. The third member was a young blond lad, Chris, who was possessed of that other-worldliness that spoke of a loving but cosseted upbringing. My final training mission was to walk the Vallée Blanche route, starting from Montenvers station at 1910m, then climbing up the Mer de Glace and through its icefalls to finish at the Aiguille du Midi at 3842m altitude, an itinerary that most would consider wiser to take in the opposite direction and preferably on skis. Chris displayed increasing fatigue and recalcitrance as this day proceeded to a faintly epic conclusion. His sack looked enormous, so I demanded the complete disgorgement of its contents on the glacier. Below the necessities of helmet and crampons I pulled out a five-hundred-page paperback thriller, a wash-kit complete with deodorant spray, a full change of clothing including spare underpants and a set of striped pyjamas. At the bottom my searching hands stuck into a glutinous mass, and I extracted the squashed remains of a month's worth of packed lunches, a composite of mouldy sandwiches, melted Mars Bars and rotten fruit, all fused into further surplus items of apparel. If only his mother had known!

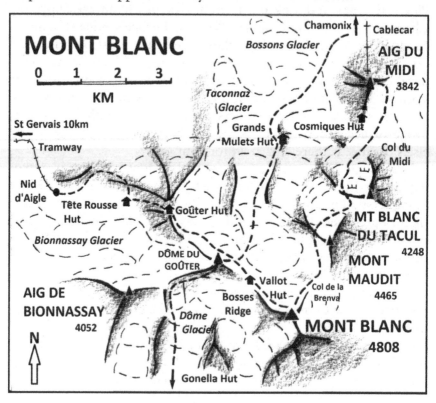

My lecture on the lightweight ethic was tempered with a warning that strong winds and low temperatures were to be anticipated. Knowing that the huts on the Goûter Ridge become desperately crowded in settled weather, I gambled on departure as soon as a major frontal storm cleared the massif. We took the morning tramway to its terminus at Nid d'Aigle and disembarked into a chill drizzle. Our mood was apprehensive. I prayed for the revelation that would lend my troops some stomach for the fight and just above the Tête Rousse hut we pierced through the fog into clear blue skies. Nothing compares to the clarity and joy of climbing on to the back of a mountain immediately after a storm. The Grand Couloir and rock rib leading up to the Goûter Hut were firmly frozen and plastered in new snow. Far from enduring the lottery of falling stones that is usual here in hot weather, we enjoyed an exhilarating mixed climb in crampons.

Arriving in early afternoon we found the Goûter deserted but the cabin can quickly be transformed into a black hole of despair when the crowds arrive. We cooked a meal and I judged spirits sufficiently buoyant to suggest an evening departure towards the summit. We left at 6.30 pm and zigzagged up the long slopes of the Dôme du Goûter, the 4304m forepeak of Mont Blanc. Fresh snow-drifts squeaked under our boots as the air temperatures plunged far below freezing. The Dôme hid all sight of the greater goal until, on rounding its shoulder, the summit shrine of Mont Blanc was revealed. Spindrift streamers whipped off her crown and the sinuous crest of the Bosses Ridge was bathed in golden evening sunlight. At its base the aluminium shell of the Vallot bivouac hut made a point of blinding white light.

I had promised the boys shelter and sleep at the Vallot, but my ulterior motive was to scale the summit that very night. We stopped outside the Vallot and I ordered the team to muffle up in mitts and balaclavas. Chris shivered helplessly. I took charge and stuffed his icy hands into my armpits for a minute, then got out his mittens and retied his harness over his overcoat. The treatment was meted with scant mercy. Would this make the man or be consigned as one of his life's most bitter memories? I could not tell but thought it worth the test.

The wind rose on the Bosses, but the ridge was swept clear of fresh snow and firm to climb. Our lengthy acclimatisation now paid its dividend. We romped from the Vallot at 4362m to the 4810m summit in an hour and a quarter, accompanied by a blood-red sunset. When we stood atop at 10.05 pm only a lurid fringe of mauve lingered above a blanket of grey cloud which covered every surrounding range.

We thought ourselves alone, but stumbled against the wall of a tiny dome tent that was dug into the summit crest and half-buried by drifts. The occupants responded heartily to my shout of greeting. The year was 1986, the two-hundredth anniversary of Mont Blanc's first ascent by Jacques Balmat and Michel-Gabriel Paccard. The campers were attempting to set a record for the longest sojourn on the summit, their target an unbroken stay of thirty-five nights.

Five minutes was the most we could manage before the cold sent us scurrying down to the Vallot Hut. We squeezed into its inner sanctum, a rancid straw-laid cell three metres square, and found a bench where we could sit and doze with our heads slumped forwards against our knees. By 4.00 am the cold had seeped through our every bone and we made our escape. Scattered groups of climbers were already approaching from the Goûter Hut as we turned off the trail and headed down the Grands Mulets glacier descent.

This was the standard route of early ascents of Mont Blanc, until it was superseded with the opening of the Goûter Ridge in 1861. Glacial retreat has made the Grands Mulets route increasingly problematic and there are objective dangers, but in early July the crevasses were still closed. With the assurance of frozen snow, we lost a thousand metres of height in little more than an hour. Under a cool canopy of morning shade we passed under the Grands Mulets Hut and traversed a wonderland of glacial brickwork across the Bossons Glacier and over to the Plan de l'Aiguille cablecar station. By 10.45 am we were back in Chamonix. I felt fit, fresh and tactically vindicated, but the puffed red sacks that ringed young Jim's eyes told another story.

Since the 1980s Mont Blanc has become a target for media stunts and charitable fundraising. I maintained lofty detachment from such events until, in 2006, I was approached by Roger Owen, one of my regular clients. Roger had commenced a personnel job in a large wealth management company, which ran a charitable foundation. Company partners, staff and friends took part in fundraising efforts each year. Roger was a man of "can-do" conviction, his face permanently fixed in a beam of positivity. Would I be able to organise guides, training and support to get a party of fifteen up Mont Blanc to celebrate the company's fifteenth anniversary? This company did not talk small. It could afford to book Bill Clinton to speak at its annual conference. The fundraising target was £250,000.

High mountains are a questionable arena for corporate events, but Roger's enthusiasm proved irresistible. In February, after running a selection process worthy of his Royal Marine training, he presented fifteen successful candidates for a winter training weekend in Scotland. Some were already consummate mountain scramblers, others could barely stand up in crampons; but we were sufficiently reassured to rent a luxury chalet in Chamonix for a fortnight in June, complete with outdoor hot-tub.

The team duly assembled. They were a perfectly normal and entirely affable bunch, except for an obsessive attachment to Blackberry phone devices. Without these, it seemed their financial world would fall apart. The mechanics of wealth management appeared to be a dark art. I could elicit no clear answer as to what they actually did. After consultation of clients and an inordinate amount of conferencing, they spent most time pondering their forthcoming Caribbean cruise or ski holiday. Resourceful personal assistants seemed to organise everything from their business diaries to their next change of socks. Nonetheless, I was impressed by how well they worked as a team. They clearly loved the competitive edge of their challenge but this was no "dog eat dog" mission. They were unstintingly supportive of each other and quick on the uptake of new techniques, coping with an ice école on the Mer de Glace, and then scaling the Aiguille du Tour and the 4017m Weissmies in the first week.

Storms arrived on the day before the scheduled Mont Blanc attempt and lasted for forty-eight hours. Some played golf, others gourmandised in Italy. As the days slipped by the pressure mounted. We missed our hut reservations and, when the weather cleared, temperatures of –20°C were predicted at 4000m. On Wednesday morning our group of fifteen climbers and seven guides set forth. We had forty-eight hours in which to succeed. Immediately, we were thrown on the defensive. The tramway was closed, so we had to walk from the Bellevue cablecar terminus at 1750m to the Tête Rousse hut at 3170m. A clear and bitterly cold evening set in. Mayhem reigned in the hut. There were well over a hundred climbers in competition for seventy-four beds. Despairing of getting any rest, five of our guides made off for the Goûter Hut in full knowledge that similar chaos would prevail up there.

Dave Hollinger and I decided to stay put until midnight and we made our beds on the dining room floor. We had care of one of the top company executives Steve; Lisa, who was Roger's partner; Clare; Mike; and Roger himself, who professed considerable satisfaction at the way arrangements were turning out, blissfully unaware of the distant sound of a helicopter hovering over the Goûter Hut, where one of our star members, Richard, had just slipped and dislocated his shoulder.

At 11.30 pm I attempted to extricate myself. Random bodies were strewn in every available nook and cranny. I brushed against a two-metre stack of tables and chairs, which tottered perilously over a line of sleeping bodies. The results of collapse would have been catastrophic. Desperately, I palmed my hands to hold the stack until someone came to my aid. An hour later, with thermos flasks filled, we stepped into the sharp night air. Although he was the boss, Steve was as modest and good-natured as any in our group, but he was far out of his comfort zone by the time we had crossed the Grand Couloir. It became imperative to have a prolonged stop at the Goûter Hut. We arrived at 4.00 am and tumbled into the annexe dormitory. An overpowering stench of garlic assailed our nostrils. Many occupants had already left so we grabbed bunks and tried to sleep. Even with four blankets each the cold was penetrating, and we were forced out again at 6.00 am.

The morning was fine but windy, survival weather at its best. I felt for each and every torment of my team. On breasting the Dôme du Goûter we were fully exposed to the gale and here the team suffered a collective loss of resolve. While Roger indulged some blue-skies thinking with a group hug and pep talk, I felt that hot coffee better served the needs of the moment. Roger subsequently suggested that somewhere around this point Steve experienced a moment of epiphany and vowed to throw in the wealth management game for a more exciting life. In the event he did retire a year later, not to mountaineering, but to the more lucrative pursuit of racehorse ownership. At the Vallot we met our first descending teams who had succeeded. This gave a huge fillip to our own spirits, but the next team down, guide Neil Johnson, Shauna and Nigel, had just turned back. Shauna looked pale and distraught. They planned a long stop at the Goûter Hut.

Through our two and half hour crawl up the Bosses Ridge there was only one spot where we could escape the 60km/hr wind. In its lee I saw that Clare was shivering and lent her my down jacket. Deprived of my own warmth layer, I now depended on the glow of Samaritan zeal for my insulation. We got to the top half an hour after midday. The surrounding views, from Monte Rosa, to the Oberland peaks, west to the Jura and down south to the Barre des Ecrins were stunningly sharp. Planned telephone calls and radio phone-ins were forgotten. It was enough to unfurl the foundation flag for some photos before we turned tail. Roger possessed a happy "what could go wrong now" grin. I wondered how on earth we were going to get back down.

Meanwhile, a second helicopter was being scrambled to the Goûter Hut. Shauna had failed to disclose a recurrent susceptibility to anaphylactic shock on her medical declaration.

Extreme allergic reaction, whether it is to nuts or trauma, is quickly fatal. While resting in the dormitory shock set in and she began a descent into a coma. Only Neil was there. Shauna stammered that she needed Nigel, but he had just left with another guide. Neil ran out to the hut balcony and yelled for them to come back. At first they petulantly refused to retrace their steps, but when Neil became frantic, Nigel realised the problem. He was the only person she had told.

"She's got an Epipen," he shouted. Neil rushed back in, rifled through her possessions until he found the syringe and rammed the life-saving shot of adrenalin into her thigh.

The stress of several hours' exposure to a searing wind is impossible to explain until experienced. My own team teetered on the edge of control. I did not think them capable of withstanding many more hours of this beating, nor of being able to safely descend the rock face under the Goûter Hut. The Grands Mulets glacier descent promised escape from the wind and a rapid loss of height, but there were no tracks visible on the route. If we ventured down it would be a one-way ticket. We could become hopelessly trapped in a crevasse maze. We approached the Vallot Hut with the moment of decision just minutes away, yet I was still in a quandary. Then, with spectacular timing, a line of ascending figures appeared from the brow of the Mulets route. With a proven trail I needed no further thought.

We got out ski sticks for balance and plunged down the trail until, at 3450m, we encountered bottomless slopes of sugary crystals criss-crossed by crevasses. Progress stopped. Steve and the girls could barely lift their legs to make downhill steps. As a last resort Dave and I ordered the team to sit on their backsides and we slid down the slopes in roped file.

At 6.00 pm, nearly eighteen hours after leaving the Tête Rousse, the remnants of wealth management reached the base of the rock *rognon*, upon which stands the Grands Mulets Hut. A line of ladders and chains ascended fifty metres to the hut. The building looked deserted and shuttered. We tried to coax the team upwards but the mood of some was of wanton abandonment. The protestations were many and voluble.

"That hut is definitely closed." "There's no way I'm taking another uphill step." "Just leave us alone. We'll sit here for the night."

Finally, I despatched Dave to scramble up to the hut. He opened the door, and summoned the guardian to come out and wave. With some residual reluctance the team picked themselves up and staggered to the door. Our escape from the madding Goûter crowds was complete and instant. We entered a sanctuary of peace. There were only three other occupants and fifty empty beds. Shafts of evening sun lighted the interior and there were little vases of flowers on every table. Only Dave and I managed dinner. Even Roger succumbed to the charms of slumber. Twelve out of fifteen on top and £268,000 raised for charity; in the circumstances I think he could count that as success.

When your daughter, who has been averse to exercise throughout her teenage years, declares that she intends to climb Mont Blanc, a father's reaction might be that of incredulity. My Hazel was both blithely confident and deadly serious when she stated her plan in the autumn of 2012. This was no occasion for scorn. I booked her on to one of our Mont Blanc Ascent courses, while she proved her intent by jogging a half-marathon and acquiring some snow skills. That still left a massive leap of faith to the scenario at 2.00 am on 15 July 2013 when she stepped out of the Tête Rousse hut.

With guide Euan Whittaker, John Flood and Dan Davies, Hazel had already traversed the Pigne d'Arolla and climbed the 4206m Alphubel, and yet, faced with the scale of the 1650m Mont Blanc summit climb her confidence seemed to desert her. From the moment we left the hut she dragged her heels. Gone were the verve and sense of fun that had carried her over the training climbs. We crossed the Grand Couloir in the safety of night, but the intermittent rumble of ice avalanches from the Bionnassay Glacier exacerbated the air of tension. The scramble up to the Goûter Hut seemed never-ending.

Behind her, Dan was an exemplary rope-mate and mentor, crying "wonderful" at every completed move and responding with a cheery but intensely irritating "okley dokley" to every guide-command. Excessive optimism often serves to intensify the pessimist's gloom. Dreams are easily sacrificed when the spirit wavers and, inwardly, I'd abandoned hope for Hazel when we pulled on to the old hut railings at 4.45 am. Our two-hour schedule had long-passed.

I switched Dan over to Euan and John's rope and they disappeared at a lick while Hazel and I reorganised ourselves. We donned down jackets and crampons and supped from a flask of hot coffee. The dawn was perfectly still and clear. I prayed that the transition to snow would revive her, and, indeed, we moved over the crest of the Aiguille du Goûter with some purpose. Far from agonising over every difficulty, Hazel was now wondering what was up ahead, and seemed to relish the long drag up the Dôme du Goûter. My faith was restored.

Mont Blanc is a terrain for all-comers. Hardened alpinists and record-breakers mix with showmen, eccentrics and those who should never be let loose on a big hill. Today the mountain was relatively quiet, the climate tolerable and the social atmosphere mellow and accommodating. At the shoulder of the Dôme the unforgettable view of the Bosses Ridge and the summit cap appeared. We were passed by three of our course clients from the previous week who had climbed the mountain on their own. All this stimulation kept Hazel keen to the task. We edged up the Bosses Ridge in stints of forty or fifty paces, and reached the top at 10.40 am.

I turned away and choked back several sobs while Hazel herself had a little cry. Then we hugged. It was an "only a hill but all of life to me" moment. While we busied ourselves taking photos for Hazel's charity, the Aberlour Child Care Trust, a team from a well-known competitor guiding company turned up. Their guide immediately straddled the summit crest, pulled out his radio and called his colleague, who, it seemed, was operating on the Gran Paradiso sixty kilometres away.

"Mont Blanc John calling Paradiso Jim, do you read, over . . ." After a crackle, Paradiso Jim reported in to say he was waiting in a queue to get to the summit Madonna. "And where are you?" Jim asked.

"Well, if you look hard over at Mont Blanc you'll see me standing on the top," he proudly announced.

After this particularly vacuous display of communications expertise, Mont Blanc John recognised me and, after the usual guides' handshakes, he took a photo of Hazel and me together. Then he headed back down the ridge with his clients. Within minutes a helicopter appeared close by. This was to be no fly-past. With a hurricane blast the helicopter landed ten metres away. Perhaps Mont Blanc John had more power than we thought. A quick call to the high mountain *gendarmerie* and his competition could be effectively blown off the mountain. We dived to hold down rucksacks and each other. Two policemen jumped out, strolled about the summit for a couple of minutes, then jumped back in. When the chopper took off I stood up, forgetting that I'd been pinning my water-bottle between my legs. My one-euro bottle of mineral water slid off down the north face with distressing ease. We would have to survive the descent on the half-litre that Hazel had left.

Our plan was to complete the classic traverse down the Three Monts route to the Aiguille du Midi. Euan and team were already somewhere down there. In choosing this route I had reasoned that we would walk quicker on snow, save punishment to the knees and would avoid re-crossing the Grand Couloir at the most dangerous time of the day. That logic was to ignore the seriousness of the glacial slopes on Mont Maudit and Mont Blanc du Tacul, as well as the 300m of re-ascent needed to reach the cable car station. Initially, the descent is fast and simple. We stopped on the Col de la Brenva for a snack. Time spent here is precious. There are few wilder spots in the Alps.

Arrival at the brink of Mont Maudit's north-west face gave me a reality check. I peered down the 55° ice slope. How could I have thought to send my little girl down there? This was some way beyond her past experience. A nearby party was abseiling but our rope wasn't long enough to do the same. I cajoled Hazel to back-climb to a rock anchor fifteen metres down. Then I lowered her to the ledge at the bottom, and climbed down after her. Having failed to credit her with technical sagacity I was dumbfounded to find that she had neatly coiled the rope ready for my arrival.

We continued to a steep lip with an enormous crevasse below. Hazel bottled up her fears and made a five-foot jump to clear the chasm, while I belayed hopefully on a wobbly boot-axe belay. This is a dangerous spot with steep slope facets broken by little ice séracs. Hazel remembered last year's Mont Blanc tragedy.

"Did your friend Roger die somewhere around here?" she asked.

A year previous, almost to the day, Roger Payne, former president of the British Mountain Guides, had perished here in an ice avalanche along with his two clients and six others. I hadn't wanted to touch her sensibilities by this remembrance. A father imagines his daughter to be forever young, but now she had asked.

"Well, it was just about here actually, Haze," I replied. We hurried on to the safer inclines of the Col Maudit.

By now the sun was burning our necks and we were reduced to stuffing Hazel's bottle full of slush in hope of further drink. We breasted the Tacul shoulder and at last could see the Midi, but Hazel was not to be fooled. I sensed the despair she felt at seeing the vast snowfields and the terminal climb that still separated us from the journey's end. Still there was danger. The tracks down the Tacul face crossed jumbled ice blocks from an old sérac collapse, and then veered across another huge chasm. Having resigned ourselves to the risk there was no point in panic. I hurried Hazel as best she could manage, and by 4.00 pm we were sat on the Col du Midi, safe from avalanche but still three kilometres from the station.

I knew that I'd already taken Hazel well beyond her limits. We were both parched. Now I had to push her still harder, for there was risk that we might miss the last cable car down to Chamonix if we didn't get a move on. When necessary, I can force my clients along on a rope with cheerful dispassion, but it wasn't easy to make my daughter suffer so. She responded positively, but her legs were all but gone. As the slope under the Midi took hold our pace count dropped from twenty to ten and then five. A string of late parties passed us.

Would we miss the cabin? The sight of a gaggle of tourists still lingering on the viewing platforms calmed my fears. There was a backlog of visitors to be shuttled off the mountain. We would make it. We inched our way up the final arête, and fifteen hours after tying to the rope at the Tête Rousse, lurched through the safety gate into the throngs.

Immediately, we were accosted by a silver-haired moustached American and his perfectly permed wife.

"I know that look anywhere," he said. "That's the Mont Blanc stare." It was slightly discomforting to realise that it was not Hazel he was looking at but me!

Chapter 15

THE MATTERHORN WORLD

Climb if you will, but remember that courage and strength are nought without prudence; and that a momentary negligence may destroy the happiness of a lifetime. Do nothing in haste; look well to each step; and from the beginning think what may be the end.

These sombre but wise words conclude Edward Whymper's *Scrambles amongst the Alps*. His victory in achieving the first ascent of the Matterhorn capped a mercurial and joyous young career. For five summers he strode through alpine passes and valleys with his guides, scoring brilliant climbs and taming virgin peaks. Yet within two hours of his crowning glory at the Matterhorn summit on 14 July 1865 his life was shattered as four of his companions plunged to their deaths. The inexperienced Douglas Hadow slipped, pulling off Lord Francis-Douglas and Charles Hudson. The rope broke under the load and together with guide Michel Croz they slid down the north face.

The most famous accident in mountaineering history served only to enhance the magnetic appeal of Europe's most iconic peak. Zermatt became a major tourist resort and a mountain guiding industry grew on the Matterhorn's back that has flourished for 150 years. The vast majority of tourist-climbers are guided up the quickest and easiest route, the Hörnli Ridge. The local guides' bureau handles many thousands of requests each summer. The deal is simple. After a couple days' training and acclimatising the prospective client is sent up to the Hörnli Hut to meet a guide whose task is to get the client up and down again, preferably in the quickest possible time and by whatever means are expedient. The brave questing days of Whymper are long gone.

I stayed away from the Matterhorn for several years, but the longer I put it off the more I was intrigued. Was it as frenetic as people said? Would I fall in love with the Matterhorn in the way I romanced with graceful peaks like the Aiguille Verte. In 1991 I received a specific request and could no longer equivocate. I had never set foot on the peak. Many would argue that a guide should not undertake a climb as serious as the Matterhorn without prior personal acquaintance, but the joy of adventure is, for me, an essence of the job. I know that I am a better guide and stronger climber when I am motivated by doing something new. There may be occasional route-finding errors and the route may take a bit longer, but it's safer to be "switched-on" than to climb with jaded complacency on a route you know only too well.

My client was Mike Holt, a diminutive builder from Burnley with sunken eyes and a haggard complexion that betrayed a lifetime of chain-smoking and physical labour. Mountaineering was helping to heal the wound of losing his wife two years earlier, and to cope with a daughter who had been diagnosed with schizophrenia. There was every reason to forgive his taciturnity. He said nothing he didn't mean, and sometimes nothing at all. I couldn't help but like him.

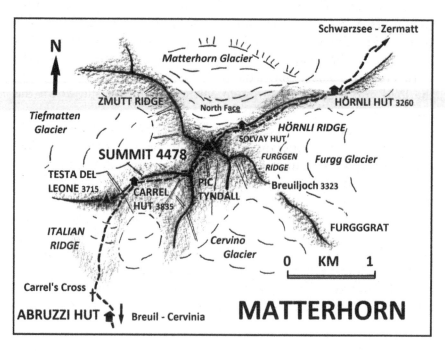

Mike drove me up the Rhône valley at an unedifying speed in his open-topped Honda sports car. We performed the Matterhorn approach ritual, a transfer by taxi to Zermatt, followed by a voyeuristic hike through the crowds on the main street and a cable car ride up to 2580m at Schwarzsee. In the afternoon the Hörnli flanks of the mountain are in shade. As you walk up the approach path the Matterhorn towers 1500m overhead without a visible chink of weakness, and the sense of vertical improbability only increases the nearer you get.

Even in 1991 the twin Hörnli and Belvedere Huts were in a shabby state. The atmosphere was more akin to an army barracks than one of Switzerland's premier tourist destinations. We queued to register at a single serving hatch, which serviced both check-in and drinks orders for up to 120 guests. The day-trippers had all descended and groups of pensive climbers were gathered on the terrace, warily eyeing their competition. Indoors, prospective clients of multifarious nationalities nervously awaited an audience with their guide. Leaving Mike to these comforts I set out to reconnoitre the lower section of the climb before dinner.

After a steep initial wall the route makes two successive loops on the East Face, crossing couloirs and then zigzagging up steep buttresses to regain the crest at 3600m. Cairns, paint-marks and several iron stanchions marked the way. The terrain is never more than a hard scramble but the route is fiendishly complex and all this section has to be done in the dark. I consigned every twist to memory and rejoined Mike in the hut.

Vegetarian dinner delights encompassed reconstituted mashed potato, tinned green beans and a slice of cheese, not quite what might be expected in an establishment that is owned by the five-star Matterhorn Hotels group.[1] Only after the meal did the Zermatt guides emerge from their private dining area, looking like a bunch of desperadoes from a spaghetti western, an assortment of handlebar moustaches among the older specimens and thousand-yard blue-eyed stares among the young. The clients were paired off. A bespectacled Japanese businessman was briefed.

"You have helmet." "Yes." "You have harness?" "Yes." "You have crampons?" "Yes."

"Good; I see you at 4.00 am after breakfast and we go."

With these curt preliminaries guide and client would bind their lives together for nine hours on four thousand feet of roof tiles.

At the stroke of 04.00 hours the Zermatt guides and clients marched out of the hut in roped file ready to do battle. A rendition of Wagner's *Ride of the Valkyries* would have made a suitable accompaniment. We finished our breakfast and left at 4.15 am. Crossing the First Couloir Mike dislodged his head-torch and it tumbled down the gully in cartwheels of light.

We decided to press on by my light alone. Mike was galvanised by his mishap. We passed numerous parties and continued above the high point of my reconnaissance. Almost immediately, the polished dusty rock of the lower section was replaced by a ridge of shattered flakes. We heard warning shouts from below and saw the torchlights of all the other parties heading out left. Not only were we off-route but we were also threatening the teams below if we dislodged any of the debris. The Hörnli Ridge route avoids the risk of man-made rock fall by cleverly making a series of detours out on the East Face, but this only works if you keep to the route.

We had lost our advantage but at least could see our way in the twilight. The upper prow of the mountain changed from looming silhouette to a spearhead of rosy rock. We spotted a string of parties snaking up the slabs hundreds of metres above us. The scale of the Matterhorn was revealed. I began to like the climb even more when a warm sun lit our backs as we approached the steeper ramp of the Moseley Slab. The scrambling was solid and of pleasant if unmemorable quality, but the exposure demanded constant vigilance. The Solvay bivouac hut at 4000m marks the halfway point of the climb in time, and is best quickly passed due to the foul reek of its open toilet. Mike was going well and we established the easy rhythm that can make alpine climbing so pleasurable when a well-drilled team moves together on a short rope.

The rock was dry up to The Shoulder at 4250m, where the ridge kinks leftwards and steepens to an imposing buttress. To avoid this obstacle, the 1865 Whymper party made a bold and delicate detour out right on to the icy North Face, and it was at this crux section on descent that the accident occurred. A series of three-inch diameter hawser-laid ropes has since been fixed down the buttress to allow a direct ascent. As we fixed our crampons we were assailed by a long chain of descending parties. The Zermatt guides lowered their clients direct down the ropes, irrespective of who was below. Each client, preceded by his twenty-four crampon points, landed on the ledge in a heap. We had to jump clear to avoid impalement. The guide then swooped down, his face twisted in a grimace of stress, and smartly planted his rope on top of ours on the stanchion belay so that we were trapped. The client was then ordered to jump off again, and given a timely prod of the guide's boot if he failed to comply.

The Swiss, for all their reputation for efficiency, haven't thought to install a second line of ropes for descent. Barked orders, shouts and even screams resonated as a mood of mass hysteria took hold. We could have been stuck motionless for half-an-hour. I battled hand-over-hand up the ropes and through each belay mêleé, terrified I would be knocked off.

The fixed lines ended abruptly at the summit ice slope. We reverted to short-roping, took our axes in our hands and zigzagged up the 40° ice. The crowds disappeared and the aesthetics of the enterprise returned as we mounted a final arête to the summit, the piled snow peaks of Monte Rosa behind us and the distant dome of Mont Blanc ahead. We had been slow, something over five hours, but we extended the precious minutes by continuing to the cross on the Italian top. There is no summit which offers a comparable roof-top perch. On all sides the mountain shears away into overhangs, leaving one doubtful that there could be any way down. We descended at a brisk tempo in a little over four hours. By way of reply Mike drove me home so fast that I pleaded for him to slow up on the hairpins of the Col de Forclaz. He dropped the speed to 70mph and the wryest of smiles puckered his lips. He was a happy man.[2]

For many climbers the Matterhorn becomes an obsession. In 1996 I faced a tricky assignment in the shape of a car assembly worker from North Wales called Bernard. Not only had Bernard tried the mountain twice before but he was also highly aggrieved that his previous guide had retreated. So as not be outfoxed again he had booked a second Matterhorn course with a rival company the week immediately after his stay with us. The plot was further complicated by the addition of a second client, Roy from Aberdeen. By the 1990s most guides were complying with local practice that the Matterhorn is guided on a 1:1 ratio. On this week I lacked staff to employ a second guide. So long as I had personally trained my clients and knew them to be competent I felt it was reasonable to take two, and would never countenance the Zermatt bureau's "off the street" method of recruitment. Happily, Roy proved to be a natural rock climber, so nimble and sure-footed that we nicknamed him the Mountain Goat.

"I'm not going home until I've done the Matterhorn," announced Bernard before we left our base. When we arrived in Zermatt this declaration took on a new complexion. The mountain was plastered from head to toe in fresh snow.

In such conditions the Zermatt guides quit the mountain and their absence puts any visiting guide under psychological stress to justify making an attempt. Should anything go wrong the implications are potentially serious. British climbers are normally used to snowed-up rock from their Scottish experiences, and when conditions are frozen in the night the Matterhorn ascent can be accomplished efficiently in crampons. The problem comes in descent. The Hörnli Ridge gets the full blast of the morning sun and within a couple of hours firm safe snow deteriorates to sloppy mush with no dependable adhesion to the rock underneath. Conditions are then highly treacherous. My foreboding only deepened when we met a retreating team on the hut path. They had only managed the first four hundred metres of the route but Bernard's countenance remained expectant. We had to give it a go.

By skipping breakfast we got off half an hour earlier than normal. We followed yesterday's tracks for an hour before putting on crampons and striking out on our own. I kept Bernard under close supervision while the Mountain Goat ambled behind. Roy was diabetic but so long as he grazed on a large bag of Opal Fruits he was unstoppable. The mountain was deserted, the weather magnificent and we enjoyed a marvellous climb of five-and-a-quarter hours. As expected, the descent became highly delicate below the Solvay Hut where the melting snow revealed an undercoat of sheet ice. I belayed from bolt rings and spikes wherever possible. Time threatened to run away from us, but we held our concentration and triumphantly entered the Hörnli Hut at 4.10 pm. Large beers were ordered and the absence of nutrition forgotten.

Swaying euphorically, we walked three-abreast down the Schwarzsee path. At 200m above the lift station the Mountain Goat was just explaining his family holiday plans for the following week when he stumbled over a boulder and fell sideways off the path down a grassy scarp. We found him ten metres down clutching his lower leg and groaning in pain.

From its alarming angulation we diagnosed that the ankle was fractured. The combination of alcohol and lack of sugar had felled my best-ever Matterhorn client. The irony was delightful, but Roy's wife would not necessarily share in the amusement.

A fog had gathered, so there could be no rapid helicopter evacuation, and the last cable car was due to leave in twenty minutes. There was no point performing extended first aid, and a climbing boot is as good a splint as ever devised. I raced down and raised the alarm whereupon the Zermatt lift system was put on hold. I dashed back up and Bernard and I shoulder-carried Roy to the station. By 9.00 pm he was getting plastered in Sion hospital and next day he was shipped back to Aberdeen. Sadly, the Mountain Goat has never been seen again, and, mercifully, neither has Bernard.

As years passed the daily scrummage on the Matterhorn became increasingly tiresome. I would try to leave just before or alongside the Zermatt guides if my client was fit. One day I set off just behind the lead *führer*. He was towing a waddling client who looked ready to expire after the First Couloir. I was stunned when he stopped and gestured with outstretched arm for me to pass. "This way please," he said. Such co-operation is quite beyond the Matterhorn norms. For a moment I truly believed that courtesy was returning to the mountain, but after half a dozen paces I realised that he had deliberately sent me off-route. When I turned round a phalanx of his compatriots were streaming through and we regained the route at the back of the queue. Visiting guides eventually have to respect that the locals take a proprietorial attitude to their mountain and are best given precedence.

Their harsh treatment of clients sometimes goes beyond the humane. One legendary tale recalls an unfit client who begged to stop for a drink on the first part of the climb. The guide promised that they would stop at the Solvay Hut. When the hut was reached the guide continued without a pause tugging the rope with the usual impatience. The client was by now utterly demoralised and beside himself with exhaustion.

"But you said that we could stop at the Solvay Hut," he pleaded.

"Yah, but we only stop there on the way down, not on the way up!"

On 15 August Zermatt holds its annual summer festival and all local guides are expected to don lederhosen and join the street parade. This is a good day for a crowd-free ascent. On the festival day in 1997 I left a deserted hut with my client, an exceptionally fit detective from the London Met. With dry conditions and an empty mountain we climbed on cruise control. However, we noticed a pursuing party as we approached the Shoulder and a zealous young Zermatt guide materialised, dragging a perspiring Korean client at an immodest rate. He was desperate to get ahead, so we played the game and subtly raised our pace. We were on the summit, munching flapjacks, when he caught us, and he was clearly miffed. I made the error of proffering a piece of chocolate.

"We do not eat on the top; we eat down at the hut," he admonished.

"You seem in an awful hurry," I ventured with affected charm.

"I have to be in Zermatt at midday for the parade," and with that riposte and a single photograph his client was about-turned and quick-marched down the ice slope. Choking on our biscuit crumbs we followed as best we could to complete a six-and-a-half hour round trip, the fastest I've ever managed.

The alpine regimen whereby everyone leaves the hut at exactly the same time is maddening and frustrating on a mountain as busy as the Matterhorn. With stable weather an ascent from valley to summit in a single push is an intriguing possibility. One August we had four Matterhorn candidates, only two guides and a forecast that offered just thirty-six hours of settled weather before the arrival of a major snow storm. We were now committed to work a 1:1 ratio on the mountain. Some bold action was required.

I rang my aspirant guide. "Jonny, we are going to do the Matterhorn tomorrow afternoon, and then we'll do it again the next morning. I need you over here at 5.30 am ready to go."

I registered several moments of speechless consternation before he acceded to the plan. As an aspirant training under my tutelage he had little choice in the matter, but the promise of an extra day's wage for "doing the double" sweetened the pill.

With the plan hatched my excitement mounted. We drove to Zermatt with the first two clients to catch the first lift to Schwarzsee at 8.00 am. We hiked up to the Hörnli Hut and savoured a midmorning coffee before starting the climb. Exhausted parties streamed past us on their final descent. Spared the stress of route-finding in the dark we romped to the top in four hours and descended as swiftly to get back in time for dinner.

However, we were only halfway there. Our other two candidates were already ensconced in the hut, primed for action. I felt my knee-joints creak. In eight hours we'd have to get up and do it all again. Bleary-eyed, we tottered off to bed. Strangely, the climb seemed easier the second time around. Every rock and piton was now familiar. The only anxiety was to complete the return journey before the storms arrived. The delight of our clients compensated for the pounding of joints on the second 1200m descent.

The Italian Ridge of the Matterhorn or Cresta del Leone (Lion's Ridge) is an altogether trickier proposition. The ridge is technically more difficult and prone to icing due to its shaded westerly aspect. For those wearied of the Hörnli circus, a visit to the Italian flank is a delightful antidote. Most early attempts on the Matterhorn focused on the Italian Ridge, the Hörnli being generally ignored despite its gentler profile. Between 1858 and 1865 local guide Jean-Antoine Carrel, Irish physicist John Tyndall and Whymper led over a dozen attempts. The Italian Ridge became the first-ever siege climb. Progress was laborious. After overcoming a series of difficult rock steps Tyndall established a high point on the prominent shoulder at 4241m in 1862.

There the matter rested until the dramas of 1865 when Carrel assigned his services to Italian politician Signor Quintino Sella, abandoning Whymper in favour of a sponsored nationalistic enterprise. The piqued Whymper hastened to Zermatt to assemble his ill-fated Hörnli Ridge party. Carrel was beaten to the first ascent, but conquered the Italian Ridge three days later, making a desperate traverse, the *Galerie Carrel,* to outwit the final tower. In 1867 the Maquignaz brothers made a direct ascent of the final bastion to complete the modern route. Despite the provision of fixed ropes, chains and a ladder at the hardest sections, the Italian Ridge remains a sensational undertaking.

Climbers based in Switzerland can make a wonderful traverse of the Matterhorn by travelling round to the Italian flank and ascending to the Carrel bivouac hut at 3825m, a journey from Zermatt of some nine hours. The summit can then be traversed with a descent by the Hörnli Ridge back to Zermatt. In July 2008 Neil Johnson and I had care of two able clients, Martyn and Ed. Eager for a change from the Hörnli pistes I persuaded my team to invest in this venture. The cable car ascent from Zermatt to Klein Matterhorn set Martyn and Ed back sixty francs apiece so it was concerning to see cloud banks boiling up from the Italian valleys. The lady in the coffee shop at Plan Maison only added to my discomfiture by predicting "you will be back".

We traversed to the Abruzzi Hut at 2800m and commenced the climb towards the Carrel Hut. The *Croce di Carrel* sits on the first outcrop, marking the spot where Jean-Antoine Carrel perished in August 1890. After spending two nights on the mountain with his client in a tempest, he directed an epic retreat. Within a stone's throw of safety, the party stopped to imbibe some brandy. Immediately Carrel became disoriented and collapsed. More cognac was applied. His companions asked whether he wished to commend his soul to God whereupon the great guide and cragsman nodded in assent and expired.[3] Intake of alcohol has a disastrous effect on hypothermic patients by stimulating circulation and diminishing the heat reserves of the core organs. This was not understood in the nineteenth century. Carrel was sixty-one years old, and the manner of his death serves a warning to ageing mountain guides.

At 3500m the route makes a traverse across loose ribs and snow patches under the vertical wall of the Testa del Leone. In icy conditions this is a treacherous passage. Whymper fell trying to cross without an ice axe while descending from a solo attempt in 1862. He tumbled sixty metres and fortuitously stopped at the brink of a terminal precipice. The Italian Ridge properly starts at the Colle del Leone. After a hundred metres of loose ground smooth steps of rock are encountered, each adorned with a fixed rope or chain. The steepest of these is plumb vertical for fifteen metres. I pulled vigorously on the rope, with feet braced on the face. Suddenly the rope lurched outwards, leaving me hanging free with no protection. One of the intermediate anchor pins had pulled out. I hauled frantically and reached the top gasping in shock.

The Carrel Hut is perched on the ridge a few metres higher. There were only four other climbers in residence. This bivouac hut is run by the Cervinia guides' company and is an aging relict of post-war austerity, the dormitory stuffed with unwashed blankets and the kitchen area stacked with dirty pans. A couple of reluctant gas burners are provided for cooking. The hut commands a magnificent westward view over the Dent d'Hérens and its primitive seclusion is infinitely preferable to the crowded Hörnli refuge.

At dawn the sky was clear overhead but cloud-masses shifted uneasily on the western horizon, spitting shafts of lightning. The others left for the summit, but we deferred departure until the weather portents were positive. At 7.00 am a light snow shower caressed the ridge and the sky remained troubled. I lay in an agony of prevarication. It is the guide's nightmare to commit to a climb and find conditions in such marginal mood. The likelihood was that we would succeed, but at such times we have to ask ourselves if we could justify our decision in a cold court of law against the given probabilities. With even a twenty per cent chance of a thunderstorm we couldn't take the risk of getting trapped on the summit tower. The logic was simple in theory but it was a different matter breaking the news to eager clients.

"Does that mean we won't climb the Matterhorn then?" they asked.

I squirmed uneasily, thinking of their precious holiday plans being ruined by my impetuous promotion of the Italian route. I had no choice but to be magnanimous, whatever the resultant physical torment.

"OK, guys; I suppose we could descend and walk back round to Switzerland then go to the Hörnli Hut this evening. That means we can have a crack from that side tomorrow."

Ed and Martyn brightened. I was reprieved. We descended to Plan Maison, where the *barista* delivered the withering judgement that we should have checked the forecast before going up. All afternoon we trudged over the slush-covered glaciers under the eastern ramparts of the Matterhorn and reached the Hörnli Hut just in time for dinner. In the preceding nine hours we had walked 13km, descended 2000m and ascended 600. You pay dearly for an abortive attempt on the Italian Ridge. Thankfully, the weather was fine enough next day to grant us an untroubled ascent of the Hörnli Ridge.

I returned to the Italian Ridge with Martin Bewsher in 2012. We enjoyed a superb climb from the Carrel Hut up round the side of the Great Tower, across the Crête du Coq and along the tiptoe traverse above the Cravate. The rock was dry, we had the ridge to ourselves and I gloried in the pleasure of guiding. As we climbed we noticed a team far below us climbing at breakneck speed. They caught us at 4200m on the Corde Tyndall. The leader, an Italian guide, looked strained. He paused to belay his client.

"I didn't see you at the Carrel Hut," I said.

"No, we have come up this morning. I took my jeep from Cervinia to the Abruzzi Hut and we started from there at 4.00 am." They had ascended 1400m in two and a half hours![4]

"That's impressive," I said.

"Yes, but you know I have climbed this route 120 times and it only gets harder. So I have to do it quickly."

He gave me a melancholic glance, and I sensed his sadness to be treating his beloved mountain as a racetrack in order to make a living.

Martin and I continued at our more modest pace, revelling in the exposures of the level shoulder at the Pic Tyndall and the athletic swings up the Echelle Jordan on the summit tower. We timed our descent of the Hörnli Ridge to perfection, completing our Matterhorn traverse at the Schwarzsee cable car station ten minutes before it closed.

There can be few job satisfactions to equal the afterglow of guiding the Matterhorn. The trick is to keep the experience sufficiently fresh to sustain the spirit of the venture. For all its desiccated crumbling rock and despite the collective madness of the multitudes that climb it, I retain a perverse affection for the Matterhorn. It is a mountain that needs to be loved more and conquered less.

Notes

1. A complete renovation of the Hörnli and Belvedere Huts commenced in 2013.
2. Mike Holt climbed with me and other guides in the Alps for many years after his Matterhorn ascent. He became known as "Slabman" on account of his predilection for the extreme slab climbs of Eldorado cliff in central Switzerland. Mike died of lung cancer in 2012.
3. The death of Carrel is described in detail in Appendix E of Whymper's *Scrambles amongst the Alps*.
4. In August 2013 Spanish mountain runner, Kilian Jornet, broke the record for ascent of the Italian Ridge. He took 2hr 52min for the return trip from Cervinia church to the summit and back.

Chapter 16

TWO NIGHTS ON THE GRANDES JORASSES

Courage is grace under pressure
Ernest Hemingway

When a long-sought mountaineering goal draws near, there is a pressure to hurry to claim the prize, especially when the project has occupied twelve years and the sands of time start to slip. Of the eighty-two 4000m peaks and tops of the Alps listed by the UIAA, David Litherland had fourteen left to climb by the summer of 1998. As his guide and friend for half his ascents I didn't need reminding which they were.

Mont Blanc and the Breithorn, as the easy summits, would complete his ascent of all fifty-one major 4000m mountains and posed few technical problems, but in alpine peak-bagging the subsidiary tops are the hardest propositions. To climb them you must enjoy sensational ridge terrain a full grade harder than any of the normal routes on the main peaks. Seven on David's "list to do" ranked among the hardest and most committing of the collection. Three – Punta Baretti, Mont Brouillard and the Pic Luigi Amadeo – are located on the precipitous Italian side of Mont Blanc. Twice, we had been rebuffed by bad weather in trying to reach these. Four – Pointes Whymper, Croz, Hélène and Marguerite – are located on the summit ridge of the Grandes Jorasses. On the Jorasses, it was the Marguerite that really counted, a precocious fin of granite sticking out of the West Ridge at 4061m. David and I had attempted a full ascent of the *difficile* West Ridge a decade earlier. As a slightly easier alternative, I devised a way to reach the Marguerite by a detour from the normal route from the Boccalatte Hut. From Pointe Marguerite we could double-back along the easier upper crest of the West Ridge to the 4184m Pointe Whymper.

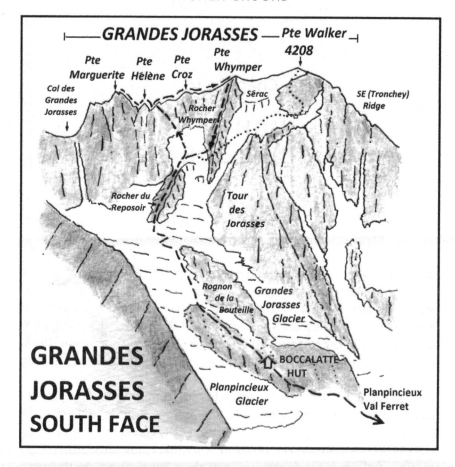

GRANDES JORASSES — Pte Walker
4208

Pte Walker

Pte Whymper

Pte Croz

Pte Hélène

Pte Marguerite

Col des Grandes Jorasses

Rocher Whymper

Sérac

SE (Tronchey) Ridge

Rocher du Reposoir

Tour des Jorasses

Rognon de la Bouteille

Grandes Jorasses Glacier

GRANDES JORASSES SOUTH FACE

BOCCALATTE HUT

Planpincieux Glacier

Planpincieux Val Ferret

On 24 June 1865 Edward Whymper made the first ascent of his eponymous point with guides Croz, Almer and Biner in a continuous ascent from Courmayeur, starting at midnight and arriving at the summit at 1.00 pm. This was a *tour de force* of route-finding skill. Surprisingly, the party did not make the thirty-minute stroll across to the crowning summit, which was claimed by Horace Walker and party three years later, but to all intents and purposes the Grandes Jorasses was climbed that day. David had already climbed the 4204m Pointe Walker with Simon Jenkins in 1995 in a fast return time of under nine hours.

Looking back 130 years, a considerably greater depth of glacier and snow covered the mountain, giving easier passage to the pioneering parties. Today, the South Face of the Jorasses is a mass of hanging séracs and crumpled icefalls, split by steep rock ribs – *rog-nons* – that provide the only islands of safety in the wilderness. The little Boccalatte Hut sits low on one rognon at 2804m, while 600m higher the slim ridge of the Rocher du Reposoir is the key passage on the normal route to the summit. Although it is the north face of the Jorasses that gets all the media attention, no mountaineer should forget the complexity of the Italian flank, and the guidebook grades understate of the seriousness of its routes.

At midday on 27 August we parked in the pastoral tranquility of Planpincieux. The old village sits in stands of resinous pinewood. In nearby restaurants happy Italian families sat down to lunch, enjoying the magnificent late summer sunshine. A sudden and severe storm front had passed three days earlier, enveloping the Alps with cold and brilliantly clear air. The open beauty of the Val Ferret contrasted with the dizzy pinnacles of Mont Blanc's Peuterey Ridge and the Rochefort Arêtes which pierced an unblemished blue sky. This was the last chance of the season for an attempt on the Jorasses.

It was that pristine-perfect sort of day which makes you glad to be alive, yet leaves you sad that it can never again be grasped. My peace might have been complete but for the fact that I had booked a Channel ferry forty-eight hours hence. At the end of a long season I wanted to be home. The schedule was tight. I needed to get back to the hut the next evening to be on the road the following day. We bent our backs to the 1300m climb to the hut and slowly cast off the languor of the valley. From forest to open meadow, across ravine, rock bluffs, moraine and finally up rock slabs alongside a hanging glacier, the walk took us from rural idyll to savage wilderness in three and a half hours.

The Boccalatte is *par excellence* a climber's hut, musty, traditional in atmosphere, and with a young guardian who was genuinely interested in what we were doing. You feel the hut is there to serve rather than exploit you; a far cry from the commercial imperative that often sours the atmosphere of larger alpine refuges. Reveille was to be the ungodly hour of 1.00 am, the guardian explaining that two parties setting out an hour later that morning had been forced to retreat when caught by the sun on the steep snow traverses high on the mountain. We warned him by return that we expected to be sixteen hours on our tour of the tops.

Our only companions at dinner that evening were a venerable silver-haired Italian guide and client who could have been contemporaries of Boccalatte[1] himself! We could hardly expect them to lead the way next day, so I spent an hour above the hut scanning the Planpincieux Glacier for tracks. Those that were visible were faint and discontinuous and after a dry summer the glacier was badly mangled. We would need sharp wits to find a line.

After a spartan breakfast of a stale bun and a bowl of lemon tea, we set forth into a moonless night at 1.30 am, aware that five hours of darkness lay ahead of us. After a straightforward climb up moraines and dry ice, we sneaked along some narrow wafers of ice at the edge of the glacier under the rognon of Pt 3301, then made a decisive traverse left into the sea of ice, but in so doing lost all trace of former tracks.

Out in the open we could dimly decipher waves of séracs rising with menace up to our right towards Pointe Walker. My stomach tightened. At 4.30 am on 2 August 1993 a huge section of this sérac had broken away under the summit of Pointe Walker and obliterated all in its path down the lower glacier over the place where we now stood. Eight climbers were killed. Simon Jenkins and I witnessed the aftermath of this catastrophe from the Jorasses West Ridge that morning. As recently as spring 1998, further massive avalanches had swept the glacier. We were charming fate for as long as we lingered.

Challenged to find a passable route, we threaded in and out of bulging ice walls and crossed several major crevasses and bergschrunds, always tending towards the looming black mass of the Rocher du Reposoir. On my reconnoitre I had spotted from afar a snow slope with a line of tracks leading to the rocks. When the desired slope and trail took tangible form in our torch beams, I began to feel that oneness with the terrain which breeds a conviction of success.

The initial ice-smoothed rocks of the Rocher du Reposoir were delicate. We took belays and climbed several short pitches of Grade III to get established on the easier crest of the rib. Now we had the joy of a sure line and easy terrain, and pushed on to the point where the normal route to Pointe Walker traverses right. The West Ridge lay three hundred metres directly above. Brim full of confidence I led us direct through a short but complicated band of ice bulges, and a vivid dawn captured us on the névé slopes above. The light over Mont Blanc had a precious green tinge, the air was sharp, and the snows cemented by frost. Every omen suggested a great day to come.

Some 150m of dirty mixed climbing brought us to the crest of the West Ridge, where one's thresholds of vertigo must be instantly revised. Apart from the plunge of the North Face over the edge, the pinnacled terrain to our left, though relatively small in scale, held the prospects of healthy terror – first a couple of gendarmes, then the spear tip of the 4045m Pointe Hélène, a narrow brèche and finally a slender knife-edge which climbed fifty metres to the Marguerite. This is truly a stupendous spot.

Ensconced on the south side of the ridge for our second breakfast, and seeing the sunlight just a few minutes away, we decided to travel light on the detour out to Pointe Marguerite. We anchored David's sack, which contained spare warm clothing, axes and crampons, for later collection, and set forth in shell jackets and base-layer thermals. Our first northward exposure came as we squeezed through the gap between the two gendarmes. The plated slabs of the north face sheared a thousand metres down to the Leschaux Glacier and a searing north wind cut through the brèche.

The degree of cold only became apparent as we clambered over the top of Pointe Hélène. The wind blew at a constant 60km/hr and the air temperature was well below zero. This was not a temporary dawn wind but a pressure-driven arctic blast that might not relent for days. We might have gone back to get axes and extra clothing, but such delay could be critical to our chances of success. Many guides would have abandoned the day altogether but, having come so far, I was now more determined than David to capture the prize of Pointe Marguerite. Supporting a client's goals is admirable, but adopting them for personal gratification is perhaps less healthy, yet I loved to bask in the reflected glow of my clients' successes and loathed the spectre of failure. I swopped thin gloves for fleece-lined mittens, more as a means of staving off frostbite than achieving any real warmth. The rocks on the windward north face were coated in an inch of dry glassy ice. With vigorous kicks great plates of it would shatter en-masse, allowing us to get to grips with the rock holds underneath.

We abseiled into the gap beyond Pointe Hélène and crawled up a slender arête towards Marguerite. Here the exposures on the South Face become more pronounced than those to the north. A memorable pitch took me out over the lip of a great overhang leaving naught but air for two hundred metres below my heels; yet I perched happily

on this brink for half a minute to gain relief from the piercing chill
of the northerly wind.

"These conditions are horrendous. Do you think we should bin
it?" yelled David when we were thirty metres from the top of Pointe
Marguerite.

"David, I haven't come all this way just to turn back now; just get
on with it!" I snapped back. My blood was up. I knew that David
might never again get so close.

We tapped the top of Pointe Marguerite and turned tail. The
return journey repeated the excitements of the outward leg, constantly nudging the border between exhilaration and terror. The
re-ascent of Hélène was a blur of flying ice shards and skating boots.
We regained the sack after taking five hours for what should have
taken two and a half, then scrambled along the onward ridge over
the Pointe Croz towards the Pointe Whymper. Faster travel brought
a return of warmth, but every little difficulty brought added delay.
I was already resigned to finishing our descent in darkness, but the
sight of white clouds boiling up the south face brought a real prospect
of benightment. A thick fog enveloped the rock spur dropping from
Pointe Whymper. Twelve years had passed since I had last descended
these rocks and I held little hope that I could find the correct line in
mist. I silently cursed this cruel twist of fate. We had climbed so well.
Surely we deserved better.

We reached Pointe Whymper at 4.40 pm, thoroughly drained after
eight hours in the gale. Within minutes the cloudbanks immersed us
in chilling white vapours. The tops were vanquished, but our day
was barely half-done. We heard the faint sound of voices from the
mists below. We had seen the guide and client from the hut turn
back, so the voices were those of another team. If we could find their
tracks lower on the spur we might yet be saved a bivouac.

Attempts to hurry faltered. We put crampons on when the terrain
became icy, only to be forced to take them off five minutes later
when rock became bare. We faced in to the rock and down-climbed
much of the ground, yet our energies for this fluid style of progress
soon waned. At a steeper Grade III crack I decided we should abseil
and we got out our second rope. We slid down smoothly but when I
tried to retrieve the ropes they jammed in a crack. I abhor profanities
in the mountains, but self-control snapped at this misfortune and I
swore into the mist with all my vocal power.

There are three golden rules in the etiquette of a guide: never lose your temper in front of your client; never blame your client for the circumstances that have led to the loss of temper; and finally, avoid any discussion of financial issues once an engagement is commenced.

Having shattered the first rule I hung my head and simultaneously broke rules two and three.

"I could have walked up the Pigne d'Arolla for the same money as I'm getting today," I moaned.

I felt ashamed the instant the words were out. David was always a scrupulously fair paymaster, although our agreed Grandes Jorasses bonus did look rather meagre at this particular juncture[2]. He stood beside me, impassively silent. What could he be feeling: fear that his guide might have lost all control, abject misery at the thought of a bivouac or plain regret at getting into this predicament? Words of comfort or encouragement might have appeared trite in the circumstances, so he wisely withheld his thoughts and let my frustration subside.

At least the air was cleared and I forgot my personal scruples. My desire to get home was irrelevant and most certainly wasn't David's fault. There would be no tomorrows to worry over if we didn't get ourselves safely off this hill so I duly climbed back up and freed the snag. Then we roped up and continued as before. We found a few footprints of the party ahead of us on the odd snow-patch, but the voices had disappeared. The ledge where the normal route to Pointe Walker crosses the spur was probably close, but in the fog we could only see fifty metres. The ridge was getting steeper and smoother. Abseiling seemed safer than blindly moving together on this terrain, and from the first available anchor we launched down vertical walls of granite towards the glacier. After the second abseil the ropes again got jammed, but this time I climbed back up to free them without a word.

We'd been out for eighteen hours and the light was now fading. Others must have abseiled this line recently for we found a camming device, slings and karabiners on one of the anchors. The surplus ironmongery was gratefully pocketed. A third abseil gained the steep glacier slopes under the spur. The ground shelved steeply below us and we had to traverse several hundred metres to reach the top of the Reposoir. Our crampons clogged with the soggy snow[3], and we couldn't risk a slip. Going out in front David immediately found tracks. I followed three metres behind, digging my feet and axe hard into the snow, ready to stop any slide. The boot-prints were vague but David wove a line through a narrow corridor between séracs, across an awesome crevasse and down to a rock terrace which we remembered from the morning as the top of the Reposoir.

Having reached what felt like "home ground" I pulled out my mobile phone and rang the hut to foreclose any premature worry about our predicament.

"So I think you will make the twenty-four hours!" said a cheery guardian when I told him where we were. This was not an accolade I especially welcomed – eighteen hours was my previous record on a route with David!

Darkness fell but the mist cleared from time to time, and we looked down with longing on the floodlit sports pitches eight thousand feet below at Courmayeur. At 10.00 pm I was hanging on the abseil ropes at the foot of the Reposoir fumbling with a horrible tangle of knots. Waves of sleepiness confused my logic.

"Damn!" I gave up and went back to the ends to start again. A single coiling operation took twenty minutes.

We could have bivouacked safely up on the rocks but, driven by the thought of warm hut blankets, I never thought to stop so long as we were on the right route and able to move. The glacier could yet outfox us. We started down tracks, but lost them when we dropped into a zone of yawning black crevasses which split a 35° slope of glassy ice. There was limited chance of holding a fall here. I was anxious to get out in front and find the way, but on this angle I needed to be at the back ready to check a slip. If we stayed too close and both slipped, we would end up at the bottom of the nearest chasm. Wherever possible, I positioned myself above David on the lip of a higher crevasse. If he slipped I could jump into the higher slot so that we would hang by counterweight!

On many occasions I could find no protection and trusted solely to David's ability, as he did to mine. We went ahead alternately, each ready to take the lead when one of us reached an impasse. In clear spells the black outline of the rognon of Pt 3301 could be made out, growing ever larger with its promise of an end to our meanderings. After an hour we reached the side of its rocks and picked up our line of the previous morning. Snow slopes gave way to dry glacier, the crevasses thinned and finally closed up, and two hundred metres lower we met the rocks of the lower rognon. The way was clear back to the hut.

Light-headed with dehydration and relief we pulled off our gear. Life suddenly seemed immeasurably sweet; cool drinks and a bed were now in immediate prospect and tomorrow, after a gentle return to the valley, I would, after all, be homeward bound. My watch showed 1.00 am, half an hour short of twenty-four. Thanks to fumbling in the fog we took another full hour to find the hut.

Meanwhile, David's goal of completing the 4000m summits was significantly nearer to completion, but I had played my part to a wise conclusion and it was time to step back from the quest for the remainder. The climb reminded me that one can push too hard. I invested all of my own emotions on the Jorasses. While sharing the passions and thrill of the climb, a guide must keep a slight objective detachment from the client's ambitions. The balance is finely struck.

David turned fifty-nine years old in 2001 and I arranged for him to make a third attempt on the Brouillard tops of Mont Blanc in company of guide Jonathan Preston and aspirant Rick Marchant. After traversing across the upper Brouillard Glacier from the Eccles Hut they were caught in warm conditions halfway up the approach couloir to the Col Emile Rey. When stones began to rattle down from the Brouillard pillars the attempt was called off. David made no further attempts. He might have become one of the first British climbers to have completed all eighty-two 4000ers[4], but he didn't let regrets sour his love of the mountains and continued to climb all over Europe, the USA and New Zealand. There is more to life than lists.

Notes

1. Gabriele Boccalatte was a leading pre-war Italian alpinist, killed on the South Face of the Aiguille de Triolet in 1938 at the age of thirty-one.
2. The traverse of the Pigne d'Arolla is a popular beginner's climb of *facile* standard in the Swiss Valais Alps. David offered an appropriate fee enhancement on completion of the Jorasses climb!
3. Anti-balling plates – rubber or plastic attachments fitted under the crampons to avoid adhesion of snow – did not become widely used until after the year 2000. They are now considered essential to safety on snow.
4. At the end of his 4000m peaks campaign David had climbed seventy-four out of the UIAA 82. The missing summits were Punta Baretti, Mont Brouillard, Pic Luigi Amadeo, Corne du Diable, Grand Pilier d'Angle, Mont Blanc de Courmayeur, Dôme du Goûter and Combin de Tsessette.

Chapter 17

PIZ BADILE

The mountains are a deep source of happiness. They dispense a lion's share of sorrow too, but it's the joy that always wins out.

George Lowe

Every climber holds a special place in the heart for a mountain that combines sweet memory and delectable beauty. Of all the alpine peaks the Piz Badile was my fond favourite, despite its modest altitude of 3308m. The Badile is the presiding summit of the Val Bregaglia, a deep, forested valley tucked into a corner of south-east Switzerland. Here an indigenous culture is preserved in a string of clustered medieval villages, a far cry from the commercial depravity of Chamonix. However, the mountain chain on the south Bregaglia skyline is built from a similar grain of granite to that of Mont Blanc and forms a series of eye-catching blades with slabby faces in between remnant glaciers. The North-East Face of Piz Badile is the finest of the range and its scalloped profile bears resemblance to the inner face of a shovel, from which the mountain is named. The first ascent was made in 1937 by a party led by Italian climber Riccardo Cassin, and was a milestone in alpine climbing history. When designated as one of the six premier north faces of the Alps the climb became a classic, a status confirmed when Hermann Buhl made a solo ascent in 1952. For Buhl the Badile was a dream mountain.

Its faces and ridges swing upwards in clean-cut lines to a comb, crowned by the glittering white rim of the summit cornice.

The Bregaglia was the place of my first alpine climbing holiday. Joy and I spent two weeks camped at Bondo village in 1979. We trekked the mountain trails, supped in shaded cafes and lazed by limpid pools in the Bondasca gorge. Every two or three days I stole away to make a solo climb, in imitation of my hero Buhl. I climbed the Cassin Route in four-and-a-half hours, and then got benighted high on the British Route on the North-East Pillar. Through a long icy night my torchlight was the sole proof of life up on the face. Down at the Sciora Hut the guardians looked after Joy with kindness, ministering lemon tea along with words of comfort while I completed the climb and crossed back over the range on the following day. Bregaglia would evermore be in my heart, but, fearful that I'd break the magical spell of first love, I did not go back for twenty-five years.

In June 2004 I promoted a two-week climbing holiday for experienced clients in Bregaglia and the nearby Bernina Alps. Although we received only two bookings I took on an aspirant guide, Jules Cartwright, as my assistant. With a 1:1 ratio we could achieve some good climbs. The aspirant apprenticeship has become an integral, and many say the most valuable, part of the British Mountain Guides training scheme. For two summers the aspirant works under supervision of a full guide, leading a separate rope but gaining the benefit of the guide's logistical and technical experience, particularly in the softer skills of handling clients.

I was especially lucky to have Jules, for he had built a reputation as a brilliant alpinist through a series of swift climbs that culminated with a daring first ascent of the huge North-West Ridge of Ama Dablam in Nepal Himalaya in 2001. He had achieved this ten-day climb with Rich Cross carrying just two ice screws, one snow stake and "two anorexic ropes" for protection or retreat. Though lean in build Jules was a happy antidote to the ascetic image of the extreme climber. I first met him during an avalanche course at Glenmore Lodge, where he was perched on a bar stool eating a fat-drenched bar meal simultaneous with drinking Guinness and smoking. We quickly became engaged in animated chat.

Julie Colverd had been one of our regular guiding clients for ten years. She was a firearms officer in the Metropolitan Police and, having started with our basic Winter Munros course, she had worked through the alpine levels to become a competent *difficile* climber. In contrast to Julie's neat efficiency Neil Lindsey possessed a bear-like shambling gait, and a gentle persona that was instantly disarming. Back in 1986 I had guided him and his stepson up Mont Blanc. Since then he had made several trips to the Greater Ranges and maintained his rock climbing skills to Very Severe level.

With a good forecast the four of us set our sights on the Piz Badile, either by the Cassin Route or the easier but equally classic North Ridge. That decision would be decided through a couple of training climbs and for this we took a tiny cable car to the Albigna valley a few miles east of the Badile. We first ascended the 2487m Spazzacaldeira by its North-East Ridge. The peak is topped by a remarkable fifteen-metre blade of granite, called the Fiamma. Jules obliged photographic demands with a smooth lead of the pinnacle at grade V+ standard, whereupon we retired to the Albigna Hut for beer and apple strudel. Next morning we did the longer and more serious Steiger Route on the Punta Albigna, a *difficile* climb with thirteen pitches of grade IV and V.

Over a dinner of trout and *frites* down at Castasegna village we reviewed plans and pondered an attempt on the Badile. We had gelled as a team, and had not yet reached that point where progress is outweighed by cumulative fatigue. I thought it time to strike, and we all harboured a particular fancy for the *très difficile* Cassin Route. Even Neil was persuaded that his extra bodyweight would not be an impediment on the slabs and grooves of the face.

The following afternoon we drove to the road-end of the Bondasca valley and climbed the steep winding forest path to the Sasc Fura Hut, which was deserted save for the guardian.

This hut stands at only 1904m and nestles in pinewood. The weather was peerless and the air mint clear. The Sciora, Cengalo, Badile and Trubinasca peaks were arrayed above the treeline like a miniature Patagonia. The sight of their sweeping ice-scraped slabs conspired to give us all yearnings and conjectures for future climbs. Over a beer Jules outlined a madcap scheme to take his dad up all six classic north faces of the Alps. We couldn't guess whether his father was yet aware of the plan, but concluded that with his vigour and bright-eyed optimism Jules could persuade anyone to a cause.

Maybe it was the effect of drinking two wheat beers, but during the night I had a terrible nightmare and awoke to find myself hammering against the hut window. A sense of calm was restored during a silent dawn ascent through stunted pines and up firm snowfields to a shoulder at the base of the North Ridge at 2590m. A golden dawn flooded down the North-East Face as we approached the notch. We were decided on the Cassin Route. We could enjoy the climb without the pressure of following parties. That evening we planned a descent of the Italian flank of the Badile to the Gianetti Hut.

At the notch my mood swung to one of apprehension. We had to descend a hundred metres down a ramp, then traverse a series of shelves and terraces across the lower slabs to gain the base of the route. The ledges were all covered in substantial snow-banks, complicating what becomes a simple scramble later in the summer. I asked Jules and Julie to go first, while I minded the more cumbersome style of Neil. Initially, we all put on crampons, but I saw that the others were having difficulty getting a grip on sections of slabby rocks so I told Neil to take his crampons off. We then descended lower down the ramp until I could lead a pitch up dry slabs back to the traverse line. We caught the others just before a second snow-band. This was barred by a three-metre vertical wall of snow, but Jules burrowed behind this and found a cave which avoided the obstacle. The delays and diversions were frustrating, and we all longed to get over to the route which was now just sixty metres away. Neil and I had to put crampons back on so we nestled in the cave while Jules and Julie set off across the traverse.

The snow was firm and secure at an angle of 50°, but was exposed above a hundred metres of steep slabs. When we started we couldn't see the others, but assumed they had dropped into another cavity. I cautioned Neil to hold his axe low and dagger his pick. I kicked my toes several times to improve each step and we edged across just a metre apart. After thirty metres the steps stopped. We exchanged quizzical looks. Had they gone down on the rocks or up to a trough at the top of the snow? We shouted, but there was no response. I looked down and saw scuff marks beneath my feet, and then a yellow stuff sack down on the slabs. My throat tightened. I said nothing, but Neil knew as well. We scanned the glacier until we saw two shapes side-by-side in the snow, then yelled and yelled to no avail.

"They've gone." My throat was so dry that I could barely gasp the words. Then, with instant transfer of my emotions to the practical I told Neil. "Drive your axe in the snow and clip it to your harness."

With fevered haste I chopped a ledge in the snow in which we could stand safely. Action brought hope. I got out my phone and called the REGA rescue service, then pondered what to do. I couldn't contemplate reversing the unprotected traverse in our emotional state, but spotted a bolt four metres down the slab. This was the line of a modern rock route called Another Day in Paradise. I asked Neil to belay me and precariously climbed down the slab until I could clip the anchor. Neil teetered across to join me and we prepared a series of short abseils using our single fifty-metre rope.

After half an hour two helicopters flew in. We saw Jules and Julie being loaded into one of them, but it didn't take off, and with that severance of hope, I was momentarily overcome with nausea. Neil stayed silent while I gathered my wits sufficiently to continue the tricky series of abseils. Our rope was not long enough to reach the main belay points, so we had to use single bolts on the smooth slabs as intermediate stanchions. On reaching the snow we wandered over the slopes collecting scattered pieces of equipment. My throat was scorched dry. Finally, we walked down to the helicopters, our arms full of climbing accoutrements. The moment I saw the pilot's face I turned away and sobbed.

"It happens every year," was all he said. He had coiled their rope.

Twenty minutes later we were dropped back in the Val Bondasca close to our parked car, while the other helicopter headed to Samedan hospital. The morning was still young with the peaks impeccably sharp against an azure sky, and here in the cool confines of the valley the river danced joyously while the great old pines maintained their stately gaze. A trough of loneliness devoured me. Nobody knew. For a second I felt an urge to disappear, to be back in the Bregaglia of dreams, but then I slumped against Neil and cried.

"I just don't know where to begin."

Where many clients might not have coped, Neil stayed and supported me through the traumatic days that followed. Hans and Marco, the helicopter crew, met the Cartwright family and graciously recounted every detail of the rescue. Jules' vibrant life was celebrated with a wake at his family's Herefordshire home and the family set up The Cartwright Trust to give financial assistance to trainees going through the Guides' training scheme. Four months later I helped Julie's mother and brother to scatter her ashes at the Bealach na Ba in Applecross, a place Julie had visited many times on our courses. There was grateful consolation that we had not seen them fall. There could be no blame and there was no point in conjecture. They were roped in close file as is correct. One had slipped; the other had followed.

For seven years the Piz Badile hovered uneasily in my memory. Only by going back could I find true closure and the chance came in a heatwave in August 2011. With freezing levels soaring to 5000m the solid granite of Bregaglia beckoned. Andy Teasdale and I guided the North Ridge, up and down, with Bill Shaw and Des Winterbone, who shared 134 years between them, Irishman Aidan Roe and Glaswegian Roy Fitzsimmons. Quite apart from the magnificence of the climb, the hospitality of the Sasc Fura Hut combined with high-spirited clients to produce a lively social occasion that bordered on the raucous. As the beer, wine and banter flowed, I felt a pang of guilt to be participating in such merriment in a place of sombre recollection. I stepped outside on the terrace, felt the mellow warmth of the evening air and watched the jagged skyline of Trubinasca, Badile and Cengalo fade to silhouette. From within, the hubbub of the hut kitchen combined with crescendos of laughter. I smiled to imagine how Jules would have revelled in this outpouring of mountain camaraderie, and how Julie would have delighted in putting the men in their place in the verbal joust. At that moment and in that place, I could not have remembered two lives in a more fitting way, but I also knew that for those who were closest the pain of loss will never disappear.

Chapter 18

THE GRÉPON TRAVERSE

An inaccessible peak – the most difficult climb in the Alps – an easy day for a lady.
Albert Mummery (*My Climbs in the Alps and Caucasus*)

One Saturday night in winter 1997 I was giving my welcome speech to our new course clients when my attention was drawn to an elfin bearded chap who kept grinning and winking at me throughout my brief. Whether this was an involuntary reflex action, an expression of unwonted enthusiasm for the tasks ahead or some hidden invitation to a tryst, I couldn't at first divine. Happily, further acquaintance proved the former conjectures to be true and Des Winterbone became a regular on our courses and expeditions. A rapier-sharp wit betrayed an intellectual brilliance. He was professor of engineering at Manchester University and a world-expert on diesel engines, but beneath his formidable exterior was hidden a vulnerable and ever-changing persona. Des the Red Devil, dressed in scarlet pants, could climb fast and fearlessly, achieving remarkable performances on big routes well into his dotage, but he could also be ribald, mischievous or needy, exercising our virtues of compassion. We guides never knew which version of Des was going to turn up on a climb, but concluded that every scoundrel must be treasured.

The ascent of the 3482m Aiguille du Grépon above Chamonix by Albert Mummery with guides Alexandre Burgener and Benedikt Venetz in 1881 was a seminal feat in the development of alpine climbing. The Golden Age of Alpinism, during which first ascents of the major peaks were accomplished, was over. Mummery sought new challenge in the rock pinnacles of the Chamonix Aiguilles which had previously been regarded as inaccessible. To the consternation of many in the Alpine Club he promoted the virtues of technical rock climbing, claiming:

The aesthetic value of an ascent generally varies with its difficulty.

For a short while the Grépon was indeed the hardest route in the Alps, thanks in particular to the desperate crack by which the crenellated summit ridge was gained. In 1893 Mummery repeated the route with a highly able female climber, Miss Lily Bristow, and he wrote the immortal epitaph that the Grépon was now an easy day for a lady.

In the twentieth century, Chamonix guides made the Grépon one of their favourite courses and Gaston Rébuffat posted the route in his famous guide *The Hundred Finest Routes in the Mont Blanc Range* with the advice that the climb should be accomplished in an eleven-hour round trip from Plan de l'Aiguille. However, in recent decades the retreat of the Nantillons Glacier, by which the climb is approached, has caused increasing problems of access. As the glacier shrank and steepened, large séracs produced regular avalanche activity. The route became distinctly more serious and fell into relative disuse.

In July 2007 I had charge of Des for a week and he was partnered by a self-effacing but likeable chap from Bolton. Allan Isherwood made his living constructing and installing electronic scoreboards in sports grounds. The digital age had relegated his technology from Premier to Conference league status but he was happy to admit that he was managing a business in decline. I warmed to his realism. Allan had proved himself a talented rock climber. A heatwave had commenced, putting most snow and ice routes out of condition. A rock route beckoned. The boys were keen and I had never climbed to the Grépon summit, but could we chance the Nantillons Glacier? Guides based in Chamonix told me that the ice cliffs which threatened the glacier were temporarily rounded and relatively benign.

At 3.30 am on 15 July we left the Plan de l'Aiguille refuge and headed into the clutches of a warm muggy night. I had reconnoitred the complex approach to the Nantillons the previous afternoon, and it was with some pride that I remembered all the twists of the tiny path as it crossed the boulder-strewn remnants of the Blaitière Glacier before climbing a sharp lateral moraine crest to the edge of the Nantillons. As is his wont Des was carrying a voluminous rucksack filled with imponderables. I made a final plea for all unnecessary equipment to be stowed and ceremoniously added my headtorch to the pile, as it was already light. Our tactics were geared to speed. On strenuous rock pitches every extra ounce in the sack counts as a pound. We carried only one fifty-metre rope, lightweight clothing and a nylon group shelter was our only concession to an emergency.

With strict orders to quick-march we traversed the lower glacier under a series of couloirs on the north flank of the Aiguille de Blaitière, each scarred by a deep avalanche runnel.

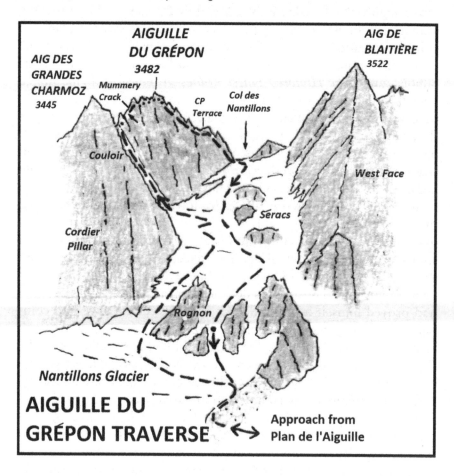

Halfway to the safety of a rock rognon a rumble sounded from above, accompanied by a cartwheel of sparks. A large boulder tumbled out of a couloir and smashed into several pieces. Its offspring ricocheted in oblique trajectories, and a stray fragment bounced towards our middleman Des, who scampered one way then the other until it rolled by. The incident persuaded me not to dally anywhere near the Blaitière and we took a direct line up steep glacier slopes left of the rognon. With a single axe apiece and just one ice screw in the party the 50° ice slopes tested our lightweight ethic to its limit.

After a tense hour jinking from one crevasse to another we gained névé snows and traversed swiftly beyond the reach of the séracs of the upper glacier and over to the base of the couloir that drops from the col between the Aiguille des Grands Charmoz and the Grépon. We were already over an hour behind Rébuffat time, but were relieved to find firm snow in the couloir. At the exit the couloir bent right and narrowed into a gully. On its right side we could see the infamous Mummery Crack, smooth, shaded and repellent. Our route went left, surmounted a short slab to gain the main ridge, then traversed round the east side to the head of the gully. We took our second breakfast in the sunshine enjoying a splendid view over the Mer de Glace, Les Drus and the Aiguille Verte.

"What a place to be celebrating your twenty-fifth wedding anniversary," I said to Allan with a hint of irony.

The previous evening in the hut Allan had divulged that the Grépon day marked an important milestone in what was clearly a long-suffering marriage.

"But what will your wife think?" I asked. "Would you not like to borrow my phone to give her a call?"

"Don't worry," he replied. "We'll be doing something when I get back."

Phlegmatic would be the best adjective to describe some of these Lancastrians.

The time was nigh to make the acquaintance of the Mummery Crack. On the first ascent Venetz led the crack without aid. Mummery himself took the lead on a guideless repeat in 1892. From the head of the gully we had to descend and traverse slabs to the base of the crack. Despite the hot weather this passage was sheathed in ice. The moves were patently desperate with high probability that even if I got across, Allan or Des would peel off and making a bone-crunching swing into the right wall of the crack. Instead, I tried a higher line where old pegs offered initial protection. With some delicate hooking with my axe and palming with my gloved hand I climbed diagonally down to reach the crack three metres above its base. The crack itself is an off-width, in other words too wide for secure hand-jams but too narrow to admit the whole body. To add to my concerns I could not clip my rope to any protection for at least six metres to avert the danger of my seconds swinging into the wall. With a succession of knee and elbow jams I struggled up the crack, which would have rated Hard Very Severe or even E1 on Derbyshire gritstone. My respect for Venetz and Mummery rose with every upward thrutch. I was at last able to place a good sling for a runner round a chockstone in the crack, and then found a finger crack within the main cleft to assist progress on the final moves to a platform.

I had used twenty-five metres of rope and now dropped the spare end back to the lads to haul up our bags. Allan seconded the pitch with aplomb whereas Des had a gruelling wrestle and only made it after several hanging rests. He arrived ashen-faced, looking like Mummery's ghost. I regretted that we hadn't thought to provision ourselves like the first ascensionists who, having conquered the crack, partook of *libations duly poured from a bottle of Bouvier*.

After a minute's recovery Des struck an aloof posture and excused his struggles:

"This isn't really my style of climbing."

The plaint was to be heard on many occasions in the ensuing hours. Mont Blanc granite is the most beautiful of all rock, richly burnished and sharply chiselled into sheer cracks and flakes. Grade IV is now thought to be a level for beginners, but on Chamonix granite is to be respected, demanding athletic laybacks and graceful technique. The onward crest to the Grépon's summit offered several such passages. I led through the *Trou à Canon* and up a chimney to gain the *Boîte aux Lettres*, which led back to the Nantillons flank. The *Rateau de Chèvre* came next, a smooth gently angled flake crack – a hardish grade IV in boots. A further flake led to a hanging stance off a spike under the North Summit, from which I lowered Allan and Des down a chimney into a brèche. The chimney did its best to spit me out when I slithered down after them. After a short delicate step up, we reached an abseil point, from which the Grépon's crowning pinnacles were displayed in full.

The summit was little more than a hundred metres distant, but first we had to make an awkward diagonal abseil into another gap. As the abseil anchors were old pegs of Rébuffat vintage I clipped the ropes into an extra piton as a back-up to the load[1]. As Des was the lightest of the party he was assigned to abseil last.

"Bring the back-up sling with you, Des," I shouted as he slid over the edge.

Des arrived minus my sling and karabiners and was summarily admonished.

"But it got jammed," he grumbled.

"You should have sorted it," I retorted.

"I couldn't; I was hanging from it," he complained. "Yer bugger, you're never satisfied."

The loss of a quick-draw[2] was not critical but reduced my already sparse rack of hardware. At least Des and I now had a bone of contention, which rankled pleasantly through the rest of the day.

Beyond the gap we discovered the famous *Vire aux Bicyclettes*, a remarkable horizontal ledge, which circumvents some awkward intermediate pinnacles and was named after Mummery optimistically described it as *a broad road suitable for carriages, bicycles or similar conveyances*. In fact, the terrace is never more than a metre wide but took us easily to the summit block. Venetz had led this direct by a desperate crack and only with aid of a human pyramid provided by his companions. A slightly easier crackline is found further right, the *Fissure en Z*. Here, Des ran out of jamming power and I gave him a quick hoist to the top.

A metal Madonna now sits bolted to the summit plinth. In blasphemous contrast, the first adornment here was an empty bottle of champagne left by Mummery as proof of his ascent. French climbers spent the next four years in vain attempts to remove the blatant taunt of this Englishman and his Swiss guides. Not until September 1885 was a second ascent made, but via the easier southern arête which we now hoped to descend. Despite the glorious weather the summit was a sequestered spot. We looked down seven thousand feet to Chamonix town, where the municipal swimming pool shone with turquoise allure. Hundreds of trekkers and tourists were doubtless plying the ice trails down on the Mer de Glace or milling around Montenvers station. They might have been a hundred miles away, for all they mattered in our world. We perched in lonely but kingly isolation.

We fixed our slings round the Madonna's foundation bolts for the crucial abseil down the overhanging Mer de Glace face. Our ascent had already brought us many thrills of exposure but the abseil raised the bar to a new extreme. Suspecting a conspiracy after the quick-draw incident Des whimpered sundry protests at being left to come down last.

We returned through a gap to the sunny south side and made an awkward descent towards a massive jammed boulder which spanned a cleft in the ridge. The rock was continuously uncooperative and we struggled to find the easiest route. Finally, we gave in and I made a difficult diagonal abseil to land precariously on the sloping spine of the boulder, which bridged a drop of several hundred metres. On the east side of this chasm a fantastic needle of granite soared skyward, the Aiguille de Roc. No painter or writer could ever be accused of hyperbole in depicting such a wonder of erosion. Happily it lay off our route. Once Allan and Des joined my hanging stance we straddled the boulder's smooth edge *à cheval* like three petrified monkeys. The complexities of rearranging our positions so that I could belay them as they slid down the spine into the gap took half-an-hour. Having two on my rope had proved more than sociable, but for speed and efficiency a 1:1 ratio is to be preferred on such a route. I slithered down after them, bereft of protection, adhesion or style.

To quit the abyss we climbed a short steep wall on to a spacious platform, named the CP Terrace after the rock scratching made in the 1870s by one early suitor to the peak. At this point the exigencies of the route substantially diminished, but we still faced an hour of awkward down-climbing to reach the 3292m Col des Nantillons at the head of the glacier. The day had sailed by leaving us far adrift of the Rébuffat timings, but our lateness gave the blessing that the perilous glacier was now in shade and less liable to avalanche.

We marched down slopes of wet snow until level with the leaning sérac that guards the lower glacier. I decided we would make a rapid traverse under the ice-cliff towards open slopes on the far side and commanded the troops to proceed at a canter. We ploughed across steep slopes above the rock rognon. The snow had taken the full brunt of ten hours' sunlight and was deeply rotted into masses of sugary granules. I feared that the whole slope could slide under our weight, so we dug into firmer snow a metre down and made ice axe belays. In several successive pitches I lowered Allan and Des down the slope towards a couloir just left of the rognon. At the brink of the couloir I dug out a buried boulder and we fixed a sling for an abseil. Instead of doing short twenty-five-metre abseils I fixed the whole fifty-metre length of the rope so that Allan and Des could get down this dangerous gully as quickly as possible. Des had moaned quite enough about coming last on abseils, so this time I let him go first. Unfortunately, the rope was horribly tangled in the jaws of the gully under a sizeable cascade of melt-water and Des got a well-earned drenching while he sorted the mess. I ordered the boys to continue unroped, while I rearranged the rope, abseiled twenty-five metres and back-climbed the rest.

Throughout this passage we were totally exposed to any stonefall that might be triggered up on the Blaitière. Safety was just a minute or two away when Allan plunged up to his thigh in a hidden crevasse. His knee had twisted and his foot was completely jammed by the weight of overlying snow. His repeated attempts to wrench free failed, so Des and I set to work to dig him out with our axes. Climbers experience a strange serenity when their lives are irrevocably committed to the hands of God. Even Des became mildly beatific, dare I say solicitous, during the ten minutes it took to free Allan from the trap.

We reached our ski poles and torches at the glacier edge in the last glimmers of twilight, a mere eight hours behind the exacting Rébuffat schedule. We possessed one trashed rope, one knackered knee and a collective happiness that we had quitted the mountain safely. I relaxed too early and somehow lost the path back to Plan de l'Aiguille. For an hour we blundered through a maze of boulders traversing towards the dim night-light of the cablecar station. Des padded behind like a faithful terrier. His remarkable endurance totally belied his sixty-five years and was the fruit of a fanatical fitness regime, which still included hundred-mile cycle rides. Allan limped gamely in the rear, his anniversary waltz over. The quick-draw dispute rumbled on. Des finally conceded that he would replace the lost items, and so it was with the added piquancy of victory that I stumbled upon the hut at 11.45 pm. For twenty hours we had each survived on a pint of liquid, a single sandwich and a bar of chocolate. A drink would have been welcome but the kitchen was closed, so we found spare bunks and crashed out.

Down in Chamonix next morning we breakfasted magnificently on coffee and fresh quiche, but I choked on my chocolate croissant when Des declared that he had an old quick-draw in his garage at home in Stockport, which he could post to me. The skinflint was promptly frogmarched into the nearest gear shop where the contents of his red trouser pockets were emptied in purchase of a brand new replacement. Justice was finally done.

Notes

1. It is standard procedure to place a back-up anchor to protect the first person down an abseil. The back-up is arranged so that the full load comes on the main anchor. If this fails then the back-up comes into play. If the main anchor is successfully tested the last person down can remove the back-up before abseiling.
2. A quick-draw consists of two karabiners linked by a stitched sling and is also known as an "extender", enabling the climbing ropes to be clipped to anchor points without creating drag.

Part Four

NORWEGIAN LIGHTS

Chapter 19

IN THE HALL OF THE MOUNTAIN KING

To write of matters Norwegian admits a guilt of disloyalty to my home country; yet those whose hearts are moved by Scotland's wildlands cannot but be impressed by Norway's ice-scraped vastness. The country has 130 mountains in excess of 2000m in altitude, the biggest ice cap in mainland Europe, and hundreds of mountainous islands along its prodigious western seaboard.

In winter the volume and scale of Norway's frozen waterfalls is astounding. Courtesy of an hour's flight from Aberdeen to Bergen they can be reached in the same time it takes to get to the bottom of Ben Nevis. My first sight of these ephemeral wonders left me breathless, agitated, infused with the urgency of living and the need to do. I started running Norwegian ice courses in 2005 in the eastern valley of Hemsedal, a sweeping vale draining the Reinskardet plateau. The centrepiece for ice climbers is the 160m Hydnefossen, which sits at 1000m altitude in the eastern cleft of Veslehødn and exudes its menace over the forested flats of Hemsedal. The top is rimmed by cornices; the approach couloir an avalanche trap. Hydnefossen only succumbed to us after two attempts and an orgy of trepidation.

Successive years of ice homage barely dented my excitement. We had heard of yet-greater falls in the western valleys that drain into the Sognefjord. One misty morning Jon Bracey and I braved the lonely drive over the drifted plateau, steered down the hairpins into the trench of Lærdal and beheld a brave new world. Every bend of the E16 highway brought astonishing lines of ice into view. Oblivious, the truckers rumbled through the sombre walls on the Oslo-Bergen run. The side valley of Råsdalen holds the greatest wonders, a series of canyons called *gjeli*, so steep that one cannot give glaciers the credit for their creation. After an hour of drop-jawed cruising we picked a line. Eight pitches and ten hours later we completed the Kjorlifossen, then swooped back to the base in a series of huge abseils. Nothing was written or signposted here, no expectations, only the climactic joy of discovery. Next year we made Lærdal our exclusive base and began a running record of ascents.

Pure ice is one of the most challenging styles of climbing for a guide. Big leads on vertical ice require complete commitment. There are few resting places, protection possibilities are intermittent, and ice quality can vary from bullet-proof screens to honeycombed pillars. Yet there are many clients who possess the strength to second such pitches. Steep ice is "out there" and guides can be pushed to their psychological limits to provide their clients' thrills.

Ice climbers are a particular breed. Many are ambivalent about summer rock or alpine terrain. They thirst only for the pure rush that comes from ice, and spend autumnal evenings sharpening tools in readiness for their February fix. Girls can make excellent ice climbers by virtue of their footwork skills and ingenuity, but alpha-males are more often to be encountered. Those of rugby-playing weight struggle horribly on fingery rock climbs or crusted snow slopes but can apply their upper arm and shoulder power to swing for glory on steep ice.

Russ Chapman epitomised the male stereotype, a burly heating engineer who drove a van to work with livery proclaiming the size of his tool. He turned up on ice courses with a rack of massive tubular ice-screws which he called his "big Berthas". He could lead grade V with attitude and seconded anything else with trademark ferocity, yelling "Gerr in there!" with each thrust of his axe. Back at our cabins when the day's climbing was over, Russ displayed his feminine side, donning apron and chopping herbs as he indulged his other passion of cookery. We coached Russ from training falls of twenty metres in height to the ultimate level of traditional Norwegian ice. The hallowed Grade VI denotes a waterfall both long and serious with several pitches of unrelenting steepness. On his fourth season we deemed him ready to tackle mighty Thorfossen, which traces a white thread down Klypegjeli canyon in Lærdal. The total drop is five hundred metres with a lower fall attractively offset from a stupendous upper cascade. Russ was just the man I needed for the task and I drafted in Dave Hollinger as a second guide to bolster the squad.

By early afternoon, six hours into the climb, a precious shaft of sunshine crept into our canyon and the improbability of our situation became evident. We were trapped within concave shields of rock 800m above our car, which was parked by the raspberry canes of Råsdalen's summer orchards. A series of convex snow-caked bulwarks framed either side of Lærdal, each the size of Ben Nevis. White clouds and blowing spindrift shrouded the high plateaux. Above lay our final obstacle, a colonnaded curtain of ice, eighty metres high. Dave led up perpendicular grooves and found a tiny cave. Russ and I seconded simultaneously climbing a few metres apart. While Russ and Dave crouched in the cave I squeezed past to claim the finale. Already the sun had slipped behind the clouds and the pinch of frost returned. I pulled over a bulge into a tight funnel and bridged up to a terminal umbrella where winds had drawn the icicles into outward-pointing fangs. I smashed these aside to create an escape hatch and wriggled through. The fall ended quite suddenly at a measly spring of water surrounded by moss, with nought but scattered birch trees and a grey sky above. Our altitude was 1150m.

A thread of old rope through a jammed rock flake gave a sure start for descent and we abseiled into the night from six millimetre cords threaded through the ice[1], way down the pillars, then out and over a twenty metre stalactite of ice to reach the canyon floor. After each abseil the ropes followed with terrifying whiplash. Thorfossen was the zenith of Russ's ice career and I think he knew the game was up. He would never do a greater climb than this and so he never came back.

There remained one ice climb which drove my dreams and resisted the years, a route that I feared to tread with paying clients. At the very head of the Sognefjord, a hundred kilometres inland from the Norwegian Sea is the industrial town of Øvre Ardal, a smoking agglomeration of aluminium smelters and metal-plating plants enclosed by sombre valley walls rising to 1400m in altitude. Fort William on a wet day is an Arcadia by compare. Innumerable pencils of ice tumble down the valley sides, but these are accessory to the greatest treasure. From Øvre Ardal the valley trench of Utladalen cuts north-eastwards into the Jotunheimen massif. Eight kilometres upstream and sequestered from the casual view, a vertical side-canyon drops into the valley. Here lies Vettisfossen – a vertical plunge of 275m, which is claimed as Northern Europe's highest single-drop waterfall.

When Vettisfossen was first-climbed in 1978 the feat overshadowed all contemporary developments. Less than a decade had passed since the "front-point revolution". With front-pointed crampons and a pair of ice axes with dropped picks steep ice could be climbed in an uninterrupted run without the need to chop a single step. Scottish climbers were justly proud of their front-point innovations on Ben Nevis, where the Orion Face was criss-crossed with new climbs bearing hallucinogenic names like Galactic Hitch-hiker and Journey into Space, but Vettisfossen was in a different league. Americans "Hot" Henry Barber and Rob Taylor found a tunnel in the ice by which they overcame the crux fringe of hanging icicles, then jammed the organ-pipe columns of the upper fall wearing leather gloves. Their climb took eighteen hours. The second ascent was filmed for television and was screened on BBC's *Blue Peter*, by which Vettisfossen was registered on my conscience at an early age.

Vettisfossen has the added enigma that it takes an exceptionally long and cold winter to form. A substantial river flows over the lip. The base ice cone must build to a height of eighty metres, while the water spray freezes on to the sidewalls. These wings slowly thicken and coalesce, eventually covering the central flow of residual water. Finally, giant tentacles of ice reach down to touch the bottom cone and complete the symphony. A time-lapse web-cam would give a fascinating record. Give or take a week, it takes three sub-zero months for this to happen. The last time was 2006, when several ascents were made to take the recorded total into the teens.

Any aficionado of ice might guess that Europe's record-breaking winter of 2010 would produce a repeat performance, but it was impossible to be sure without taking a two and a half hour hike up Utladalen to inspect the fall. On a day off from guiding I buckled to that task. A mile beyond Vetti farm the canyon opened to my right and in its deepest recess a pearl-white plunge of ice emerged. The connecting tendrils of ice were in place. Timorously, I crept around a sea of ice blocks, fallen from periodic collapses of overburdened icicles, and gazed in awe, piecing together a feasible line though creaking, dripping overhangs at one-third height. The "kark, kark, kark" of the resident raven echoed round the enclosing walls. Otherwise there was a terrifying silence. Truly, this is the hall of the mountain king.

I jogged back and consulted Martin Welch – for twenty years my best instructor, a soul mate in passion for wild places, yet often wanting of direction to harness his talents. His life was a charismatic tangle and I suspected that he saw its affirmation through combat with the great ice wall. What of me? If I ducked this challenge, on the eve of my fifty-fifth birthday, I feared the slow descent of old age would be my only comfort. We would take our chance together.

We checked that the weather outlook was favourable for our next day off. A temperature in the range from –5°C to –10°C was crucial. Any warming above zero and the fall would become dangerously wet. Any cooling below minus ten and the ice would be hard and dangerously brittle, fracturing into giant dinner-plates at each swing of the axe. We set the alarm for 2.30 am, left our course students to their sleep, and drove the empty highways back to Utladalen. The public road ended in darkness at the gate of Hjelle. We put on crampons and trudged up the icy vehicle track to Vetti farm. Dawn was breaking as we clambered up into the amphitheatre under Vettisfossen. Then came the shock. I peered up to the overhang through the morning murk and saw a gap. Most of the crucial linking icicles had disappeared in the five days since my recce. We were now standing in the debris of the collapse. I was spooked. I had been sure that the ice curtain was solid and would grow with time.

Thankfully, Martin got the bit between his teeth. We soloed thirty metres up the base cone and I belayed under the shelter of an ice umbrella while Martin forged ahead to escape an imminent threat from the remaining daggers that were still stuck to the overhang. His lead took us into a massive cavern behind the cone. The upward view was sobering. Water poured from two circular drainage chutes which looked like the thrust cones of a space rocket. There was no chance that we could climb direct, but there was a possibility that we could by-pass the overhang using ledges on the rock walls to its right side. A long ramp of glass ice led to a point level with the roof. Along its lip a series of snow-covered ramps and ledges led back to regain the ice.

Martin stepped into the breach and led a hair-raising pitch across the rock wall, linking blobs of snow-ice with scanty protection. Our climb was back on track. I led a fifty-metre pitch of green ice towards a cave on the right edge of the fall, hoping to escape the threat of a gigantic claw of ice that hung overhead. This appendage was attached to the icefall by a slender horizontal arm and had no right to resist gravity. Far from offering sanctuary, the cave stance was sited directly under the claw. I cowered at the back in the recess and commenced a two-hour vigil under the finger of doom.

From here the sole line of weakness led leftward up ramps and through a squeeze-box behind an icicle to gain the centre of the upper fall, where the ice narrowed and steepened into an eighty metre series of columns and grooves, split here and there by overhangs. I guessed this was where "Hot" Henry reputedly hand-jammed up the icicles. As Martin wound in his ice screws at the next belay, the icefall emanated an alarming cracking sound that reverberated thirty metres down to my stance. It was as if Vettisfossen had shifted an inch. His stance had a hanging bosse of ice fangs as a canopy and sported a glass window, through which we could see the water flowing down the central drainpipe of the fall. As I climbed to him he swung his video camera across the lifeless ranks of ice spears then down the sweep of the fall to the crumbs of its debris, and murmured in deadpan Glaswegian: "it's f**kin spooky, I'm tellin ye".

The next pitch above overhung about three metres but sported grooves and lips that allowed for funky bridging. Any ice splinters that I kicked off fell uninterrupted for 150m to hit the bottom cone. The Vetti raven wheeled overhead then settled on a pine tree at the lip of the fall to watch the outcome. After twenty-five metres I reached a tight pill-box stance, belayed tight to three screws and relieved Martin of his miseries under the fangs.

We reckoned there were seventy metres to go, and the threat of being wiped out from falling ice was steadily diminishing. I relaxed enough to enjoy the abyss and the outward views over to the snow-smothered Hurrungane mountains. The chance to briefly stand in such a place is reason enough for me to go on climbing. Martin's next lead sported a ten-metre wall that overhung gently. He was on fire. His diet of protein milk shakes and malt whisky seemed to be working.

The light was fading as I swung to the final pillar on the left of the icefall. The angle stayed plumb vertical but the ice was solid, the climbing simple but stressful. Every six metres I stopped to place a screw, at which point fall potential is twelve metres plus the stretch of the rope. Standing motionless on the tips of my front-points while fighting calf-burn, I tried not to think of the consequences of a slip. After fifty metres I pulled up to the very lip of the fall. I paused for minute and felt a pang of reluctance to leave the vertical world. For years I had dreamt of climbing Vettisfossen and now the deed was all but done. Then, carefully, I stepped on to the level river-bed and lashed myself to the biggest birch tree within reach.

Any thoughts of abseiling the icefall in darkness were quickly quelled. However long it took we would walk down. After a few hundred metres of wading in the snow we struck a trail, and skipped down its zigzags back to Vetti farm, floating in euphoric relief. Through the ten kilometre slog back to the base of the fall and then out to the road I felt boundlessly strong. My world fitted to perfection, and I loved everything in it. We regained the car at 9.30 pm, fuelled up in Ardal garage and switched the radio to familiar tunes, then rode the shoreline roads and empty tunnels back to our cabin at Aurland. Seven hours later we crawled out from bed, two empty shells – cramp-ridden and crusty-eyed – to face another day of guiding work; but what the matter? The battle was won.

Notes

1. Ice threads were invented by the Russian climber, Vitali Abalakov, and are constructed by drilling a pair of joining diagonal holes with ice screws. Cord is then threaded through the holes to create the rope anchor. In good ice the threads are extremely strong.

Chapter 20

THE ROUGHEST BOUND

The tremendous two-eared Rulten, lifted up against the alpenglow above a score of lesser spires and bastions; Rulten, that kept you and me hard at work for nineteen hours climbing your paltry three thousand feet.

Eric Rücker Eddison

The Magic Isles, they are called, flung out a hundred miles into the Norwegian Sea in waves of ice-sculpted granite. The Lofoten are inspiration for saga and fantasy, their peaks an innumerable array of Arctic gems, washed by summer rains and dried by the midnight sun. No mountain in the archipelago exceeds 1200m in altitude, but the rock walls and castellated summits are as fierce and as beautiful as any mountains of the world. The toughest of all are the chain of peaks bounding the west side of Raftsund on the Lofoten's largest island, Austvågøya.

In 2008 we drove into this paradise for the first time, fresh from a successful ascent of the chisel-head of Norway's national mountain, the iconic Stetind. The Lofoten islands are now linked by a remarkable series of tunnels, causeways and bridges, built on the back of Norway's oil and gas wealth. From the ferry terminal at Lodingen we joined the E10 highway, sped through a ten-kilometre tunnel and emerged into an enchanted world of savage summits, rushing cascades and emerald green drapery, all lit by the lush evening light of the summer Arctic. A dozen miles short of the island capital Svolvær we pulled up at the sight of a peak we knew by reputation, Rulten. Across the fjord a pile of granite bulwarks, streaked here and there by winter snow fields but without a chink of grassy weakness, led through interlocking ridges to twin summits.

The east-most and highest top is 1062m in height, and was first climbed in 1903 by the father of Norwegian mountaineering, William Cecil Slingsby, with Geoffrey Hastings and the eminent scientist and Cuillin pioneer, John Norman Collie. Their East Ridge route was described in our *Lofoten Rock* guide, but the vagueness of the text suggested that the author had never been anywhere near the mountain. More helpful was the account of a later luminary of Scottish mountaineering, Tom Weir, who climbed Rulten in the Coronation year and recorded a round-trip time of fifteen hours from the Raftsund shore[1].

After climbing Stetind our confidence was buoyant and the weather outlook was settled so we were propelled into a flurry of preparation. First we needed a boat to cross the Raftsund. After phoning several of Svolvær's boat operators we chose Gunnar and his high-powered "jet boat", which promised a transit time of just thirty-five minutes for the fifteen-kilometre crossing.

We were a somewhat weathered band of brothers. Richard Hampshire was my first-remembered guiding client in the Ecrins in 1982, nicknamed Winthrop after his predilection for traditional tweed garb. He was still the airy academic, with an added dash of Yorkshire grit. Although he wrote safety manuals for nuclear power plants, he found boiling an egg a major logistical challenge. His gait was a fusion of prancing and prowling, and his stamina was sustained by a love of the hills that found its natural home in Norway. Richard was one of those rare specimens of humanity in whom there was no trace of malice, only a goodness of heart that defied any temptation to mockery.

Vic Williams hailed from East Lothian, and was a successful chartered surveyor and aspiring virtuoso on the mouth organ. Having tried and failed to function at Himalayan altitudes Vic too found a hearth for his mountain love in Norwegian climes. Bill Shaw was a Glaswegian dental surgeon whose precocious climbing talent surprised him as much as it did us. When he wasn't forging new developments in cleft-palate surgery Bill spent his time composing excruciating verse, to be set to music and inflicted on any unwary social gathering.

My fellow guide, Jonathan Preston, was a man of impeccable manners and southern English charm, yet possessed of an edge that could cut the fumbling client to size with a single stab of rebuke. Together our team mustered an aggregate of 293 years. Gunnar must have wondered at our sanity as he sped us over the water to the jetty at the summer farm of Reknes. The step off the boat took us into a primeval world of rampant vegetation and glacial rules. We requested a pick-up for twenty-four hours hence, and ploughed off through knolls of springy heather to a clearing where we pitched tents in readiness for our evening return. Knowing Weir as the loveable naturalist and broadcaster of his later life we felt we could use his fifteen-hour time as the upper limit of likelihood.

We set out at 9.30 am. Rulten towered overhead, the scoop of its north-east wall filled with snow from which a waterfall spouted several hundred metres over pristine granite slabs. We aimed left of the cascade towards the foot of the ridge, wading through cushions of blaeberry and bearberry, bedecked with white dwarf cornel and the nests of willow grouse. We dodged through rock bluffs, stands of dense birchwood and rank pools, ripe with mosquitos. Finally we scrambled up a scree gully to a col under the triple-hatted forepeak of Trehakkatinden. For all this we gained a measly three hundred metres in height. The feather-strewn perch of a sea eagle seemed a good place to take second breakfast. Rulten's ridge looked easy-angled to begin. I roped with Bill and Vic while Jonathan took Richard. We expected a fast scramble in Cuillin mode, but were quickly forced into detours by smooth slabs. Any vegetation was just inches thick and of mossy texture that simply peeled off the rock under the pressure of the boot. We weaved through grass ledges to a series of small but abrupt steps, which demanded committing friction moves on sloping granite. Already, I regretted wearing my stiff mountain boots. On this terrain we needed footwear with bend and sole grip.

I clambered behind a huge detached block and flailed ineffectually in a flared chimney. Jonathan arrived, took a cursory look at my predicament, then stepped on top of the block and, to my astonishment, made a five-foot leap over my head on to the face above. Richard baulked at the jump.

"Are you sure I'm going to make this?" he asked nervously, Jonathan's response a sharp tug on the rope and the abrupt retort "you won't know till you try".

The slabs tapered into a more pronounced ridge where real exposure hit. An elephant's back of holdless rock, devoid of belays, barred the way. Jonathan forged ahead, and leapt boldly on to the arête, then tiptoed to its farther end. Come my turn, I failed to lock my elbows on the initial mantleshelf move. My feet slipped, my body lurched left over a sizeable void and I ended hanging by my arms from the rounded ridge, all but off. Vic held my slack rope with his usual couthy grin, oblivious to potential consequences. With a desperate scrabble I got back into balance.

We lunched at an easement before Rulten's second big step. The mood was a trifle tense so Bill told his story about the death of his grandfather who fell into the whisky vat at Glenlivet distillery.

"He climbed out three times to go to the toilet before he succumbed," said Bill.

We chuckled politely and rolled our eyes skywards, but Richard was horror struck. "That's terrible; couldn't anybody stop him going back in?"

A snow gully offered easy progress for fifty metres, and then we climbed under a huge jammed chockstone and out right on to a line of off-width cracks, which were choked with moss, and therefore unprotectable. The terrain was virgin, without a single peg or scratch to evidence previous passage, and we were continually delayed in sniffing out the best of a multitude of possible lines. I thought ruefully how wonderful this route would be in winter condition when the caterpillars of grass would offer perfect axe and crampon placements.

Vic and Bill were still smiling, just. Below us the blue waters of the Raftsund sparkled in sunlight but mists were now licking the summit towers of Rulten adding a tension to the climb. At 940m altitude we encountered a short level section of conventional scrambling.

"For goodness sake," I thought, "the top is only 120m above; it can't take much longer."

Then we were forced into a flanking movement down and across narrow ledges on the left side. These ended at an abrupt downfall. We knew from Weir's account that there was a gap before the summit, but were not prepared for a chasm one hundred metres deep. A vertiginous series of mud and grass shelves dropped into a Y-shaped snow couloir. Beyond and above, the true summit of Rulten smoked in defiance. We had been seven hours on the climb and the team were visibly tiring. Even Jonathan, leader of our assault, was wavering. The safe option was retreat, but I spun a narrative of persuasion.

"So much effort spent, guys . . . the descent won't be as bad as it looks . . . Slingsby, Collie and Weir kept going . . . it might yet clear up and we'll see the midnight sun."

Even so, the hairs on the nape of my neck were tingling with fear as we stepped over the brink. A series of short slithering pitches deposited us on 55° snow in the right branch. We had ice axes but no crampons. The edge of the snowfield bordering the rocks was icy, so I chopped steps into the centre where the snow was granular and yielding. From ice axe belays Bill and Vic climbed down to the join of the Y. Jonathan forged his own line, preferring to use the rocks where possible.

After five full rope-lengths of step-kicking in the mush our feet were swimming in our boots. Rulten's crowning turret glowered through the mists. I steered into a subsidiary snow runnel and aimed for two parallel chimneys. Jonathan took Richard out on to the rocky crest to our right. Occasionally, we heard his barks of command followed by Richard's strangled cries of "That's me!"

The chimneys were monolithic and oozed streaks of slime. I chose the left-hand and after a dynamic entry, got myself wedged in its cleft and back-and-footed to the top, where there was an old abseil sling and, just above, a tiny summit cairn. Jonathan arrived seconds before us. This was as joyless a summit as I have known. We had spent ten hours in the climb, there was no view, and now we had to reverse each and every step without the surety of regular belays. Three men in their sixties, and two guides in their fifties, all stranded in a dank evening chill – this was some boys' outing. I envisaged the media uproar should we need to be rescued, but realised that we were beyond help while the mountain remained clamped in fog. When spirits droop, a team is prone to mistakes and prey to hypothermia. We needed to gather our remaining courage.

An efficient descent of the Y-gully was essential. We abseiled down the chimneys, and plugged steps back down the snowfields, re-using each belay stance. Pitch after pitch, I gave Bill and Vic a tight rope to speed their descent. Then we climbed back up the right branch and up the vegetated face to regain the shoulder. There was a palpable rise in spirits on quitting the trap of the chasm, but as we slithered down the mossy grooves of the second step the mist thickened and squeezed out a mournful drizzle. We had entered that zone of exhaustion, where latent endurance must be displayed or else the ship will sink. Our three wise men drank deep of their summer wine while Jonathan made no visible concession to fatigue.

The back-climbing became increasingly precarious and at around midnight Jonathan and I spotted a big rock spike at the brink of an overhanging wall and decided to make an abseil. Half an hour was spent manoeuvring everyone across to the spike, and spinning our fifty metre ropes into the void. There was no ledge for our feet. All five of us hung in a web of slings, occasionally slipping and squashing into each other. Having achieved this remarkable counterbalance Richard thought it the right time to ask:

"Are you sure this spike is safe?"

On the lower ridge I abandoned any pretence to controlled down-climbing. If there was a ledge to land on, I simply lowered Bill and Vic down, then slid after them jumping the last couple of metres. The light was poor. Jonathan and Richard drew ahead and I missed the best line. My exasperation was near-complete. A twenty-five metre abseil and a rope-grinding fifty metre lower took Bill and Vic to easier ground. I soloed behind without any belay, clawing at clumps of vegetation, close to my limits of adhesion. The sight of my brand new rope, horribly chewed and abraded to its core strands, completed my misery. We were getting spanked, yet I was strangely intrigued by the sheer awfulness of it all. How could a mountain be so cruel?

At 4.20 am we reached the Trehakkatinden col and staggered down to the swamplands. We had yearned for the moment we could lay down our sacks, stretch out on the heather and savour a brew. Perhaps Vic would give us some sylvan airs on his "moothie", Bill a joke and a song or two. When we finally arrived we found Jonathan crouching over our stove, cloaked and hooded, and swathed by a swarm of midges, gnats and mosquitos. While we scratched, fidgeted and walked round in imbecilic circles he bravely completed the task and handed round cups of tomato soup peppered with flies. Barely had we slurped the contents than we dived into the our airless tents, zipped up and struggled into sleeping bags, our bodies soaked in sweat, grime and insect repellent; thus ended our nineteen-hour day.

For three hours we writhed in exhausted turmoil, then made a break for freedom half-an-hour before our pick-up time. The sound of Gunnar's engine out in the fjord was as sweet as a symphony. Meanwhile, Rulten temporarily emerged from the mists to bid us farewell.

"So you climbed Rulten?" exclaimed Gunnar in some disbelief. "You must tell the newspapers. Nobody had been up there for twenty years. It is Norway's hardest mountain[2]."

These were facts he had omitted to tell us on the ride over, but we were grateful for consolatory words, and with a vestige of pride restored we returned to the living world.

Notes

1. *Camps and Climbs in Arctic Norway* Tom Weir (Cassell, 1953).
2. The true grade of Rulten is unpronounceable, but a guidebook should assign it an alpine *Difficile* with many moves of Grades III and IV.

Chapter 21

MIDNIGHT MOUNTAINS

I will go up, up to the highest mountain tops;
I'll see the sun rise once again, and gaze upon the promised land
Henrik Ibsen (*Peer Gynt*)

At first sight there is nothing that special about the Lyngen Alps. Flying in to Tromsø airport they appear as a barrier wall on the eastern skyline, part of the interminable shield of crystalline rock that forms the barren plateaux of northern Norway. There is no indication of the savage glacial erosion which has isolated Lyngen as a slender peninsula, protruding for sixty kilometres and pointing direct towards Ultima Thule. Nowhere is Lyngen more than fifteen kilometres in breadth yet the peninsula possesses sixty-three separate peaks over a thousand metres in altitude, of which over half pose difficulties of technical stature. The highest is 1834m Jiehkkevárri, an ice cap defended by sérac walls and rock scarps, which was described by Slingsby as "the Mont Blanc of the North". The interior of Lyngen has been designated a wilderness zone and is spared the usual DNT huts[1] and sign-posted trails. In May and June the peaks are a jumbled mix of white glaciers, rime-caked towers, heady ridges and fluted cornices, complemented by verdant dales with rivers brimful of meltwater. Here, at 71°N, is a playground for skiers, fishermen and climbers but, remarkably, the whole place is utterly and gloriously empty!

The first impression on disembarking at Tromsø airport is an atmospheric purity that makes one's nose tingle. In spring the climate can veer from bitter to torrid according to the airstream, but the blanket humidity of the Gulf Stream is usually muted. The capital of Arctic Norway is a city in flux with wood-panelled stores and chandlers' yards mixing with glass-fronted boutiques and high-tech oil-support vessels. In late May the social scene is cosmopolitan. A mix of Nordic, black and Asian residents enjoy street music and shirt-sleeved promenades in the balmy summer respite between the grim months of rain and darkness. The momentous days of Nansen's northward journeys and the sinking of the Tirpitz are lost in the distant past. A sprawl of chain stores and supermarkets surrounds the city, erasing some of its individual charm. Take a drive and the country's road culture is likewise crushingly monotonous. Container lorries drive prodigious distances up the E-roads, their drivers sustained by hot-dogs and Coke from soulless truck stops. Yet there is always a skyline mirage of moor and mountain to sustain the Nordic fantasy.

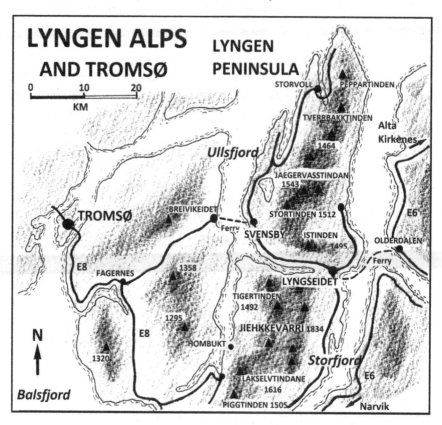

The approach to Lyngen leaves the E8 and barrels twenty kilometres down the pine-clad strath of Stordal. Concave slopes sweep up to 1200m ridges on both sides. The uniformity and scale of this scenery can be depressing, even to one used to Scotland's bleaker spaces.

The road ends at Breivikeidet jetty. From here a car ferry crosses the Ullsfjord to Lyngen. On a sunny afternoon in late May 2010 we stood here and marvelled at the array of peaks on the far side of the Ullsfjord. Colossal wedges of mountain, 1500m in height, filled the horizon. Their snowy flanks plunged unceremoniously to a fringe of forest, beneath which a strip of bare grassland sloped gently to a pebbled littoral. A scattering of farmhouses, painted in Norway's traditional burnt-red, clung to the shoreline. Our stomachs churned with the knowledge that in fifteen hours the current heatwave was due to be replaced by a series of rain fronts that would last all week. We had to strike fast and skip the usual training route.

While the others cooked dinner at Svensby campsite I took a drive ten kilometres north to Jægervatnet, a remarkable diamond-shaped freshwater lake dammed by a rock bar just a few metres above sea level. On the far side a ridge formed low down on screes, then narrowed to a rock crest and rose over a sharp forepeak to an alpine summit, crisply etched in snow. Though I knew nothing of its difficulty I could see the quality. The North-West Ridge of 1512m Stortinden became our first objective. We ate, then dozed until midnight and commenced our expedition at the north end of Jægervatnet at 1.30 am.

Richard Hampshire was with us again, as eager as ever, plus another Richard, a retiring accountant who lived in Australia, and Keith, a landscape architect from Edinburgh. My assistant in the venture was Robin Thomas. Wide-eyed and disarmingly honest, Robin ranks as the best guide I never had. Despite undisputed brilliance as a climber and exceptional coaching skills Robin always found a way of side-stepping training courses, until he finally rejected the professional route altogether. For a man who abhorred the strictures of assessment, Robin was a handy companion for a big day out.

To approach the base of the ridge we followed trails for four kilometres along the east shore of the lake, passing a number of summer cabins, each with a chimney, jetty and boat that suggested the joys of the simple life. The lake itself was still largely frozen despite two weeks of fine weather. We broke away uphill, exiting the birch-woods on a clear lateral moraine crest, fording the Forholtelva river and working up through gravel slopes on the lower ridge. For four hundred metres the climb was a pleasant amble, but a pronounced notch signalled a change in geology from crumbly agglomerate to the aggressive black gabbro that forms the core of the Lyngen peaks. The climbing started at once.

For the next four hours we picked our way up the ridge, straddling cracked slabs and creeping round abrupt outcrops. With every hundred metres the standard of climbing rose until we were taking belays and doing pitches at several junctures. The upper atmosphere gradually acquired a milky hue, although we could still see across the Ullsfjord to the islands north of Tromsø. Then, with a magical delicacy, thin smudges of cloud began to form beneath us. The veils spread and thickened and finally rose to envelop us. Nearing the forepeak we encountered sections of snow and the holiday atmosphere of the lower ridge vanished.

The forepeak represented a watershed in commitment. A fifty-metre vertical buttress barred access to the saddle before the true summit. We searched out a descent on the east flank, and abseiled an overhanging wall to gain a snowshelf which led round to the col. I was confident that we could scout out an easier way back up this step on our return. Snowfields predominated on the final climb and we reached the top at 2.00 pm. By now the mist was thickset, and a damp chill harried our steps back to the saddle. There was a temptation to descend steep snow slopes into the glacier bowl on the east side of the ridge and thus avoid the ridge altogether, but with visibility less than fifty metres we couldn't be sure of the outcome.

Still confident we could find an easier way back over the forepeak we went up to the rock step. Everywhere we looked the angles were fierce. Finally, we found ourselves back at the line of our abseil. An impending wall of splintery white rock barred our way. A free ascent was out of the question. We would have to use aid[2]. Robin and I pooled our hardware and surveyed a pathetic collection of wired nuts and a couple of cams. We had come equipped for a fast alpine scramble, not a big-wall siege.

Although Robin could have scampered up the wall faster than me, I felt it my duty to lead the escape. The first gear placements were critical. If they failed under my bodyweight I would hit my belayers and bounce on to the snow-slopes below. With every move I had to visualise how three aid-climbing novices might manage. I couldn't leave every piece of kit in place, for fear that I'd run short of gear higher up. After fifteen metres the angle eased back under the vertical and, on reaching a ledge, I gratefully draped my last sling around a solid anchor block. Robin organised foot-slings and cows'-tails[3] for the team, while I rigged our second rope as a safety line. One-by-one they climbed through the overhang while I hauled on the safety line. Finally, Robin seconded the pitch and cleaned the equipment. The impasse had swallowed two precious hours and the forecast rain commenced as we began the 1400m descent.

Although the rocks turned slippery and our fingers became wooden with cold, we now had some downward momentum, and in three more hours we regained the notch at the end of the difficulties. We dropped under the cloud to a monochrome landscape. By texting our other group down at Svensby we allayed any worries for our safety and freed ourselves of the tyranny of the clock. There was no wind, only a continuing muted drizzle. We sidestepped softly down the lower slopes and forded the riverbed back to the woods.

Denied any distant sights I felt a feline awareness for the surrounding terrain. Every change in texture, climate and smell of the ground layers, from the gravelled chill of the riverbank to the lush scents of the woods, was impregnated on my memory, to resonate thereafter in my affections. Such connections, once established, are never broken. For the rest of life I would recall Lyngen with a single sniff of a springtime birchwood.

The road was a long time coming and midnight already gone when we laid our sacks aside and peeled our feet out of saturated boots.

"Thank you, that was a grand day," said Richard H, with a sincerity that would melt the heart of the hardest guide.

A meal, a sleep, sauna, another meal; for the next thirty-six hours we could do whatsoever we wanted, until the next climb beckoned.

A few kilometres north of Stortinden lies another peak with instant impact and alpine challenge, the 1543m Store Jægervasstinden. Lyngen weather windows can arrive with startling speed. After two wet days the clouds roll back, leaving a scattering of residual showers, and the sun shafts dispense a host of rainbows. In such atmospheric splendour we hiked up the broad flats of Strupskardet one evening in 2011. Our trod was bordered by a pinky carpet of spring saxifrage, creeping azalea and moss campion. A moraine of giant boulders drew us into the high *fjell*. As we passed the frozen sheet of Blåvatnet, the spires and glaciers of Jægervasstindane and Lenangstindane slowly emerged from the receding clouds and the sky settled to the six-hour sunset that is the polar night in June. Then we kicked steps up long snow-slopes round the tongue of the Lenangs glacier and pondered our objective.

The north face of Store Jægervasstinden sported an unbroken ramp of untouched snow which led direct to the summit, a line so pure that we could overcome all apprehension as to its angle. The old névé snow was superceded by thick fresh drifts in which we sunk to our knees. Midnight brought a rising wreath of mist up from the glacier to enhance the virginal splendour of our surrounds. The sunlight was blinding. Every rock above us was thickly caked with winter rime. There was not a single scar on the landscape apart from the trail we made. It seemed sacrilegious to leave our cake-crumbs behind. The ramp gradually steepened to 55°, and we dug out belays for the last hundred metres. We reached the summit ridge at 3.00 am and shuffled à cheval along the final arête. For brief minutes a multitude of snow-wrapped peaks lined the horizon, and in the mêleé we spotted a pink-tipped spire, Stortinden, where we'd suffered for our art just one year before. Then grey mists lapped up from the southern face and closed the show.

This brief taste of nirvana gave every incentive to return to the midnight heights, and, besides, after four visits to Lyngen none of our groups had yet managed to scale Jiehkkevárri. An attempt in 2011 took us up the wooded dells of Lyngsdalen to a chill bivouac under the 800m south wall. All evening we were blattered by squalls of rain and we retreated empty-handed. The mountain has assiduously prepared its defences. Jiehkkevárri is the culminating point of an ice cap thirty square kilometres in extent, and spawns a multitude of glaciers which flow off the plateau into deep concave valleys and thence to the sea. The name is the Sámi for "peak of the glaciers". As a bulwark against the cool maritime air of the Arctic Ocean, Jiehkkevárri is a magnet for cloud and storms. In four trips to Lyngen I had rarely even seen it. While surrounding ranges remained clear Jiehkkevárri would stubbornly wear its cap of mist. This would be a frightful place in a blizzard. Multiply the worst winter offerings of the Cairngorms two or three times and you'll get the picture.

In 2012 I was determined to put the hurt to rights. My team of four – George Burgess, Martin Hulme, Andy Matthews, and Alan Renville – were not blessed with the beauty of youth, but possessed of fortitude and strong heart. Politically, we had High Tories and card-carrying Labourites in the team. Discussion of politics is usually taboo in the smalltalk of the guide-client fraternity, but this bunch could remain amicable so long as discussions were lubricated by a decent single malt. The week had started in booming Foehn winds and bottomless corn snow. Then a cold front swung the airflow to the north-west and within twenty-four hours winter conditions returned to Lyngen with fresh snowfall down to two hundred metres altitude. Fresh drifts were thigh-deep in the higher hollows. On Thursday a lull was forecast with summit temperatures of –8°C. In full knowledge that we would face tough trailbreaking I dared to suggest an attempt, and the team responded with near-fanatical enthusiasm. Whisky glasses were discarded and we tumbled out of Larsvoll cabin with large sandwich stacks and down jackets packed.

We discarded the eastern approach from Lyngsdalen and drove round the southern end of the peninsula to tackle the shorter western route from Hombukt village on Ullsfjord. It was one of those rare days when Norwegian car hire charges are worth every *krone*. As the clouds cleared the plum peaks of Arctic Norway emerged in sumptuous white raiment. Otertinden – the otter peak – looked ready to give Cerro Torre a run for supremacy while the 1500m wedge of Piggtinden made a breathtaking simulation of Alpamayo. We left Hombukt at 2.15 pm. The forepeak of Hombuktinden (1666m) presents a sheer craggy face to the sea and guards access to the Jiehk-kevárri plateau. In stints of a hundred metres we broke tracks up a long couloir that runs left under the face and curves round to the easier north ridge. Sloppy slush gave way to a frozen crust at 1200m and when we stopped to eat at 6.45 pm we felt the nip of a hardening frost.

Residual mist still clung to our ridge but brightened in the embrace of the evening sun. A delicate cornice edge led us to Hombuktind summit where the final vapours parted. The slumbering fjords and ice-clad giants of Troms county were laid out at our feet. A small cornice guarded a steep descent to a sinuous ridge of pristine snow, which led across to the summit dome of Jiehkkevárri, a distance of four kilometres. My heart recoiled. Would the whole slope avalanche as we applied our weight? Without testing I couldn't be sure so I made a tentative jump off the lip and tested the snow for any inherent windslab formation. Suitably reassured, the others followed and we plunged down for one hundred metres in knee-deep powder, then ploughed a trench of steps along the ridge to a vertical notch. We cut down to its left and waded up a 60° slope on the far side to regain the crest. The colours deepened as the arctic night commenced.

The sun hovered over the northern horizon in a golden glare. We passed an enormous cornice meringue, under which an eddying stream of ice particles threw the sunlight into spectral arrays. The swell of Jiehkkevárri's forepeak, Pt 1738m, brought welcome relief from the drifts. Here the snow had blown clear and a rime crust had formed. Although only a stroll, the final mile to the main summit felt serious and committing. We were pushing into the zone where survival would be short-lived in a storm. With a sense of privilege we gained the top at 11.00 pm. The midnight sun threw our shadows twenty metres across the ice. Alpenglow lit up every summit above 1500m in altitude and the mountains feigned levity, in deceit to their true geologic indifference. We had climbed nothing of technical difficulty, had nothing to report that would excite the public, and yet, looking in the frost-pinched faces of my companions, I sensed the joy of catharsis.

After fifteen minutes of reverie the cold drove us downwards. As we left, a bank of grey cloud spread from the east. The cap of Jiehk-kevárri glowed lilac against this menace, soon to be swallowed in the fog. From Hombuktinden the snow couloir swept five thousand feet down to the sunlit farm roofs down by the fjord. We followed the trajectory and at 4.00 am reached the road to surprise our companions, Jonathan Preston and Ian Lancaster, who, reading our summit text of success, had decided to make their own attempt and were just booting up. Alas, they hit the cloudbanks on the linking ridge and turned back in a white-out just two kilometres from the top at 10.00 am. We had indeed been fortunate.

Then the shine disappeared from the venture. An overwhelming sleepiness and a series of potholes in the road plagued the seventy-kilometre drive back to Larsvoll. Twice I drifted off into the verge to be nudged back to consciousness by Andy. At 6.00 am the shore of the Storfjord was alive with eider ducks and oystercatchers. Clutching mugs of tea we watched the scene and then turned into our beds. The "Mont Blanc of the North" had proven a worthy match for her greater cousin in the Alps. Mountains exert their greatest emotive power when they are lonely and unblemished. One of the great nights of our lives was done.

Notes

1. Den Norsk Turistforening. The Norwegian touring association runs a network of huts across most of the country's wilderness areas.
2. Aid climbing requires the use of hardware (wires, nuts, cams or pegs) for direct assistance, using foot slings for support.
3. A "cow's-tail" is a knotted sling attached to the waist of the harness for clipping in to belay anchors for safety and support.

Part Five

INDIAN PIONEER: THE HIMALAYA

Vettisfossen – Norway's most-prized icefall

Russ Chapman topping out on Thorfossen 900 metres above our car

Martin Welch geared up for Vettisfossen

Martin Welch leads the traverse on pitch four of Vettisfossen

Lofoten's lost citadel – Rulten from the Raftsund

Our 2010 Lyngen team prepare for battle: left to right: Robin Thomas, Neil Lindsey, Richard Hampshire, Keith Horner, Richard Ausden, Jonathan Preston, Katherine Henderson, David Sandham

Midnight return from the summit of Jiekkhevárri

Ullsfjord and the peaks of Troms county viewed on the descent from Jiekkhevárri

Panwali Dwar from Bauljuri – we climbed the right hand of the ridges

George Healey high on the South-East Ridge of Panwali Dwar

On the summit of Panwali Dwar with Nanda Devi behind

Martin with C.S.Pandey at Pindari base camp

The naked *rishi* of the Satopanth Glacier

Brede Arkless on our ascent of Shipton's Peak

John Shipton beneath
his father's fabled col

Ben Lovett climbing out of Eric Shipton's bamboo valley

The sacred peak of Adi Kailash in Kumaon Himalaya

The die-hards set out from Kuthi for the Nama Pass –
L to R: John Allott, Martin, Hari Singh and Mike Freeman

John Lyall at summit camp on Kamet with Mana peak and Kumaon ranges behind

Kamet emerges from the mists on the morning of our departure

Changuch (6322m) from the base of Longstaff's Col – we climbed the ridge between sun and shade

Rob Jarvis silhouetted on the final crest of Changuch

Martin leads his team along the final crest of Changuch with Nanda Devi's twin peaks behind (photo: Rob Jarv

The "famous five" at
Dhakuri Pass on the
homeward trek from
Traill's Pass;
left to right:
Paul Guest, Martin,
Ludar Singh, Rob Jarvi
Leon Winchester

Dave King and Allan Isherwood on the upper slopes of Eva's Peak with peaks on the Lahaul-Zanskar divide behind

Marching down the Zanskar-Kanthang Glacier on our "walk into nowhere"

Dave King climbing the ice nose on the ascent of Eva's Peak

Chapter 22

THE GATEWAY OF WINDS

Oh, if I had wings to lift me from this Earth,
to seek the Sun and follow him!
Then I should see within the constant evening ray
the silent evening world beneath my feet,
the peaks illumined, and in every valley peace,
the silver brook flow into golden streams.
No savage peaks nor all the roaring gorges
could then impede my godlike course.

Goethe (from *Faust*)

"Martin, you will love Pindari," Mr Pandey assured me. "It is absolute heaven."

Of all the peaks in India Nanda Devi is the most revered and singularly impressive. The 7816m summit is the twenty-fifth highest in the world. Her twin peaks are protected by a ring of 6000m peaks 90km in circumference. Within this circle is a glacial wilderness which drains through a profound chasm, the Rishi Gorge. The discovery of a route into this sanctuary by Shipton and Tilman in 1934 was one of the great exploits of Himalayan exploration[1]. The Indian Government closed the Nanda Devi Sanctuary in 1982 due to the environmental damage caused by trekking and climbing parties. However, the mountains on the Sanctuary's southern rim could still be approached through the Kumaon foothills and the Pindar valley. One peak above all here captured my imagination, the magnificent arrowhead of 6663m Panwali Dwar.

The name alone was enough to send shivers down my spine. Panwali Dwar translates as Gateway of Winds, a fitting role for a sentinel of the Goddess Nanda. Wilfred Noyce was the first mountaineer to admire her when he climbed the neighbouring peak of

Bauljuri (5922m) in 1944. A Japanese team made Panwali Dwar's first ascent by the South-East Ridge in 1980 and an Indian team led by Prajapati Bodane claimed the second in 1991. Both used siege tactics with fixed rope. Pictures in the *Himalayan Journal* revealed a slender pyramid of unrelenting symmetry that would challenge the best team I could assemble.

At the end of an enjoyable but ultimately unsuccessful trip to Gangotri in 1992 I booked both Panwali Dwar and Bauljuri with the Indian Mountaineering Foundation[2] for the following September. Bauljuri was to be our insurance policy, a lower and easier peak that all members could expect to climb.

Mr C.S. Pandey became my expedition agent with a campaign of charm and bludgeoning persistence. Prospective expeditions to India are inundated with letters of introduction from tour agents. Pandey's pitch was slightly more plausible than his competitors and I intimated mild interest. Whippet-thin, moustached and immaculately dressed, he appeared in my Delhi hotel room at 7.00 am on the morning of my arrival and spared me not an hour of peace until we left two days later. He seemed a troubling mix of Don Corleone and Mahatma Gandhi, but his rampant enthusiasm triumphed over my doubts.

"In India, Martin, we say *Atitha Devo Bhava*, Guest is God. And with my company safety is a major concern."

I placed the kinder interpretation upon this latter claim and signed him up to provide staff and ground services for our team of ten climbers and four guides on Panwali Dwar.

Kumaon district is famous for its hill stations, which provided summer sanctuary for the elite of the British Raj and have since become popular tourist destinations. Naini Tal, Ranikhet, Almora and Kausani are linked by a network of well-maintained roads and by mid-September the monsoon usually sinks away southwards. The following five weeks provide the best conditions for trekking and climbing before the cold winds of winter arrive.

Not so 1993! When our team arrived in Haldwani at the edge of foothills on 13 September, the local people were mopping up after the heaviest monsoon rains for seventy years! The deluge had continued unbroken for nine days. Dozens had died in the floods, landslides blocked every route and many sections of hill road were completely washed away. We had to journey 150km through Almora and Bageshwar to the road head at Song. The case seemed hopeless.

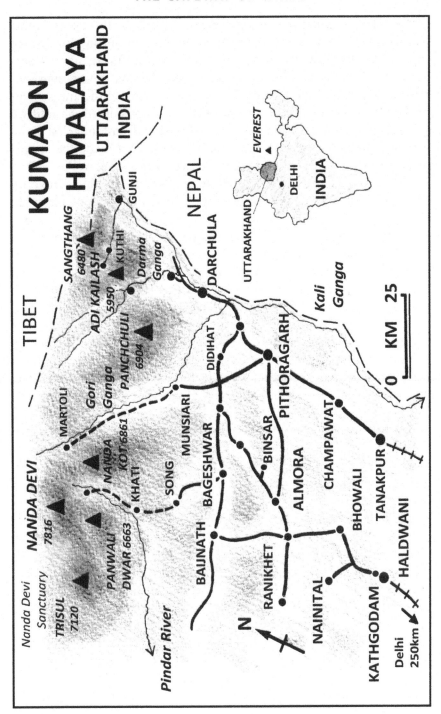

We holed up under the faux marble facades of the three-star Amar-pali Hotel for three nights, contemplating our diminishing supplies of rupees and the slow disintegration of our plans. Our team members entertained themselves by hiring bicycles and going for training jogs up and down the Civil Lines to Kathgodam, much to the amusement of the locals. Every conceivable scenario was considered. Should we go back to Delhi and head north-west to Manali in Himachal state, which might have escaped the rains? Eventually, I made the simple resolve to stick to the plan. If need be, we would walk to Pindari!

We despatched all non-essential kit back to Delhi, then drove up to the first blockage just past the apple-growing town of Bhowali. Here we hired a team of twenty-four Nepali porters to carry our gear over the broken roads. We passed our first night bivouacked on the veranda of Kainchi temple, which nestles in a green valley clothed in deodars. Kainchi is the spiritual home of Neem Karoli Baba, a revered maharishi who died in 1973. His rotund beatific face beams at travellers from countless posters and effigies in the district. Perhaps it was Baba's blessing that restored good fortune to our enterprise. Next day, we hiked twenty kilometres over a succession of landslips, passing hundreds of labourers hacking at fallen boulders with crowbars and shovels. Two decrepit bulldozers provided the only motorised assistance. We hit a clear road in the Kosi valley and commandeered an old bus that was waiting for custom. In evening gloom we swept up the curving hills over Almora top and down into the shadowed Sarju valley. Briefly, the grey clouds parted to reveal a jumble of snowy peaks on the northern horizon. Dozens of villages were lit by bonfires in celebration of a local religious festival. The road was empty. The tingle of optimism returned to our venture.

The village of Song lies in the upper Sarju valley at 1430m alti-tude and is the starting point for the Pindari trek. The route was established and popularised in the 1830s by George William Traill, the first British Commissioner of Kumaon. A stone-laid path forty five-kilometres long was built over the 2902m Dhakuri Pass and up the Pindar valley to the snout of the Pindar Glacier at 3800m. Traill's men then crossed the pass from Pindari to the Gori Ganga valley passing under the eastern ramparts of Nanda Devi. His hope of a lucrative trade route to Tibet was not fulfilled. Glacial recession has turned the upper Pindar Glacier into a chaotic icefall.

On 19 September we climbed 1400m over the pass to Dhakuri

bungalow accompanied by a caravan of twelve mules, each burdened with seventy-five kilograms of kit. The campground nestles under a canopy of Himalayan *banj* oak trees, and we awoke next morning to a panorama of the Sanctuary peaks, which towered above the forested valley. Amongst the throng the white tip of Panwali Dwar could be discerned, peeping from behind the broader bulk of Bauljuri.

The walk into Pindari was a time-shift into a medieval world. Contrasted to the architectural wastelands of India's burgeoning cities and the grasping lives that hundreds of millions endure down on the plains, one is inclined to conclude that it is a better world. Safe from the rapacious advance of the road-builders, the people of the valley pass peaceful existences growing buckwheat, tending vegetable plots and spinning wool. Their houses are roofed with thatch or slate, as yet untainted by the scourges of "quick-set" concrete and corrugated iron. The terraced fields are tilled by docile water buffalo.

However, Western eyes are easily deceived. Down at Khati the village headman, Ratan Singh, told us that the people were suffering from food shortages and would rely on Government aid to get through the winter. Our custom at the local tea stalls doubtless helped the locals to buy short-term security, but I envisaged that a flood of cash-laden trekkers would undermine the traditional way of life. That the Pindari trek could touch the springs of conscience is only a reflection of its loveliness.

From Khati the main valley path cuts northeast through a forested gorge for ten kilometres to a bungalow and grazing ground at Dwali. We arrived at Dwali in a drenching thunderstorm but at dawn next day the flaming turret of Nanda Devi East was framed at the valley head to our north. The path climbed steadily, its banks fringed with wild raspberries. Beyond a final resthouse at Phurkia the valley broadened and birchwood gave way to grass flats. The icefall of the Pindari Glacier swung into view and the mule path ended at the ashram of Kupidhaura. We crossed the river by a natural bridge of jammed rocks to make our base camp on the west bank, and by nightfall on 21 September our team was installed on a grassy site fed by freshwater rivulets. For all our tribulations, we were only three days behind our schedule, yet it seemed presumptuous to consider the ascent of a 6600m peak in the thirteen days left at our disposal.

Over the following days we stocked an advance camp on gravel terraces at 4430m under the Buria Glacier. The Buria is a shelf glacier, which flows from a 5331m col between Bauljuri and Panwali Dwar. We had a fine view over the upper Pindar valley to the lofty ridges of Nanda Kot and Changuch. We spent three nights of indifferent weather acclimatising here. A dismal day of non-stop snowfall drove us to paroxysms of boredom and hunger, especially our high-altitude porters, who were dropping into deepest gloom at our diet of dried hill-food. We did have radio contact with base camp, and called up cook Bhanu to order a batch of *paranthas*, topped with lime pickle.

Simultaneously, porter Rana set off for base and five hours later he reappeared with thirty of Bhanu's best, wrapped in tea towels and still warm from the pan.

Already creaking under their load of monsoon snow, the mountains were now capped with a further fifteen centimetres of fresh powder. We deferred any serious inspection of Panwali Dwar and opted for the gentler inclines of Bauljuri. A second camp was placed at 5250m just under the Buria col, and thirteen climbers made the climb to the summit on a morning so clear and still that it beckoned no comparison. As we reached the Buria col, Panwali Dwar was revealed in full glory. A pair of razor-sharp ridges, painted with virgin snow, made an elegant upward sweep to a needle-sharp summit. Here was the mountain of fantasy, but it seemed far beyond our grasp.

On return to base camp I dredged my knowledge of avalanche theory. Over a prolonged period a dry fresh snowpack will gradually consolidate and stabilise even though it remains constantly at sub-zero temperature. The process is termed equi-temperature metamorphism. As to how long this process actually takes I was unsure. With just five days of the trip remaining George Healey, Winky O'Neale and I were sufficiently tempted to go up on to Panwali Dwar and test the theory. The rest of the team declined to join a challenge, which, in my candid opinion, offered only a slim chance of success, and they opted to try shorter climbs on 5662m Lamchir.

George was a bluff Yorkshireman with an opinion on most things. He inspired optimism. Winky by contrast was deeply and quietly driven, immensely fit and stick thin. She was the wife of Kevin O'Neale, my deputy leader on the trip. We never saw Winky eat a hot meal, but she regularly nibbled at snack bars and her pace never lagged for want of energy.

Over two gentle days we climbed back up to the Buria Glacier and branched off right to make camp on a small snow plateau at

5200m at the foot of Panwali Dwar's South-East Ridge. The long hours pinned in camp under the burning afternoon sun tried our patience. My mood was tense rather than excited. I was pleased to be committed to the mountain. No other option could have brought me an ounce of peace or satisfaction. At 3.30 am on 2 October we left camp, carrying a one-person bivouac tent, one hundred metres of seven-millimetre-diameter hawser-laid rope, two snow stakes, three ice screws and half a dozen rock pegs. By contrast, the 1991 Indian team had taken 1100m of rope, twenty-five snow stakes, fifteen dead-men, thirty ice screws and ninety rock pegs!

The lower ridge was mixed and rocky, the flanks seamed with snow gullies. At half-height the snow took over and swept up to the summit point in a steep and corniced ridge. Initially the snow offered a supportive frozen crust. We climbed quickly across moonlit slopes then over steeper avalanche debris to gain the ridge. We pushed hard while the snow crust persisted, and at midday had reached 6000m, where the ridge became narrow and exposed. A steeper tower of rotten rock required pitched climbing and, as the outcrops diminished in size towards the commencement of the snow ridge, we found a tiny cove of snow banked under an overhang on the south side of the crest. In an hour of digging and chipping we fashioned a flat platform large enough to take our tent.

By sitting side by side and sticking our feet out of the front door we could get our bodies under cover and were able to attach ourselves to rock anchors through belay sleeves in the back wall of the tent. Once settled, we whiled away the steamy afternoon brewing hot drinks. Towards evening, as the sun's glare faded, the swirling clouds sank beneath our perch and resolved into solid cumulus galleons. With grey keels, billowing white sails and roseate bows they drifted gracefully across the lower peaks and foothills. An inky dusk engulfed the gorges and Bauljuri's ice capping glowed crimson through the sunset hour. We wriggled into our sleeping bags as the deadly cold of night clutched our camp.

At 3.45 am we emerged from the rime-crusted tent, fortified by a cup of hot orange squash and some glucose biscuits. The air temperature was –15°C and Venus was bright in the eastern sky. We climbed through the final rock outcrops to an incipient notch in the ridge where the snow formed a level corniced edge. Beyond this easement the South-East Ridge made no further concessions, sweeping up for several hundred metres to the apex of the peak. From the apex the south-west ridge dropped five hundred metres in a single rapier thrust. The snow face between the two arêtes dropped at a dizzy angle to a hanging glacier, and beyond that lay a void that spelt oblivion. There was no option but to traverse across the face under the cornice edge, with no protection other than an ice axe belay. If the slope fractured we had little chance of reprieve.

I dug out a large stance for George and Winky. No longer was the snow frozen as it had been lower on the mountain; rather it was dry and supportive, much in the mould of fragile windslab. I isolated a large test block and levered from behind to see how easily it would shear. The block simply disintegrated under load, so there was no obvious slab avalanche risk, but I could not be absolutely certain until I made my commitment to the traverse. Tentatively, I kicked steps leftwards, ready at any instant to leap upward or aside should a crack appear in the snow. The fate of the climb and our lives hung suspended.

Halfway across my heart muscles relaxed their grip and a fulsome pulse replaced the choking flutter of the first few steps. After running out the full 100m of rope I chopped a stance and belayed to my ice axe with the reinforcement of a vertically driven snow-stake. There remained the fear that if either George or Winky slipped I would be unable to hold their long swinging fall on such a skinny rope with just a waist belay.

The next five hours proved that the fearsome distant views of Panwali Dwar had not flattered to deceive. An initial riser of 55° angle took three full pitches. Above there was no significant ease-ment of angle, no resting places other than the stances we dug, and nowhere that we could get astride the crest of the ridge. I finished pitches as and when I became too exhausted to continue. Usually this came after running out between sixty and eighty metres of rope, and I then spent another fifteen minutes digging out a secure stance large enough for three pairs of feet before planting the axe and stake anchors.

The summit apex seemed to get further away the higher we climbed and the snow became softer and deeper. I began to dread the thought of descending this ridge late in the day when the snow would be rotten. How could I keep in control and look after my team? Close to midday my energies failed completely and I slumped over my axes in a wave of nausea. I gradually regained some rhythm in my breathing and forced down half a cereal bar mixed with snow, yet still felt dwarfed by the scale of the face. After fifteen minutes I forced myself to continue, making three steps at a time. My chest heaved with the strain but the flame of hope flickered once more.

There remained one big riser of snow before the apex. After two more pitches and two more hours the snow hardened a little and I sensed that the south-west ridge was getting tangibly close as it rose to meet our own arête. Suddenly and dramatically the pristine edges met. I ploughed up another few steps and plunged my axe over the joining point, then swung my leg over so that I sat astride the arms of the mountain in a pose of symmetric perfection such as only the gods should enjoy.

I sat in elevated silence for a minute or two, then shuffled *à cheval* along the crest to a point where the flanking angles relented, and rolled over to the north side. Here I felt secure to bring up George and Winky. At 2.30 pm we made the final steps to meet the gaze of Nanda Devi across the southern Sanctuary. Kindly shafts of filtered sunlight warmed the summit and the ridge was just sufficiently broad to allow us to sit. Indeed, it was the first and only oasis of the day. We gazed awestruck on Nanda Devi's southern wall and spied the rock tooth of Changabang with the floating castle of Kamet beyond, absorbing in precious minutes the scenes that would be our sustenance for years to come. Then we thought darkly of the descent: the tiptoe back to that fearful apex, the unrelenting slope of the plunging face, and the eleven long pitches that lay between us and the security of a rock anchor.

Our line of steps provided the lifeline. From each stance I belayed our rope round my waist and George and Winky back-climbed down the steps to establish the next belay. Then my turn came. I had to reverse each seventy-metre pitch without any protection. Some of the steps had softened in the afternoon sun and broke under my weight. My crampons incessantly balled up with damp snow, which could only be dislodged by a vigorous tap with my ice axe. By daggering both my axes up to their hilts at waist level I could compensate for any sudden loss of footing. Pitch followed pitch. The repetition coupled with a deep fatigue lulled me to a trance-like state. Hardly a word was spoken. In my reverie I became convinced for several hours that my companions were two completely different people,

Mike, my brother-in-law, and Heather, the wife of another guiding colleague.

Evening came. The snows of Panwali glowed amber then pink as the sun sank, and rainbow spectra glistened through the gossamers of ice crystals that floated above the slope. The scene was mesmerizing in its delicate beauty, and my mind drifted serenely, freed from any anchorage to the world beneath. At the same time the inner steel of the survivor kept my arms and feet to the unending task of climbing down. The stars were already well-advanced on their nocturnal wheel as we reversed the traverse under the notch to regain the rock outcrops at 6150m.

At 9.00 pm we reached the tent. Winky was plagued by headaches; George was strangely subdued and shivering with cold. We squeezed into the tent and I tried to brew some water, holding the stove in my crotch to keep the gas cylinder warm. Twice I drifted off only to be shaken back to life as the pan tipped and the stove flame flared. Finally, we got our warm drink and then we dozed through the midnight hours.

By 4.00 am my mind was buzzing with anxiety. I wanted to get moving before the snow was softened by the sun. My companions were sluggish and slothful. I spent nearly an hour stamping about outside of the tent waiting for them to dress and pack, and it was 6.00 am before left. We soon became impatient of the loose rock terrain on the ridge and took our chances in a snow couloir that ran down the east flank. After a couple of icy steps the gully broadened and eased. When the angle dropped under 50° we faced out and traversed back to the ridge, pinned under the glare of the risen sun. We clawed our way into the camp at 5200m at 11.35 am, made drinks with the last of our gas, and then lay in a sun-baked stupor shielding our faces with sunhats. With arrival of a cooling blanket of afternoon cloud we readied ourselves for the 1400m descent to base camp. The downhill torment was relieved by the arrival of Kevin, Phil, and porter Darwenda on the edge of the Buria Glacier. They took our loads, leaving us to stagger light-headed back to base. In just twelve hours the mules were due to arrive for the homeward march.

Panwali Dwar was, from that day, my mountain of perfection and the first climb on which I'd been close enough to the edge to see into eternity. Thus it has remained. The climber may return to high mountains many times in a quest to recapture that pitch of exaltation, but never quite succeeds.

Notes

1. Shipton described the exploration of the Sanctuary in his classic book *Nanda Devi*. Hodder and Stoughton (1936); reprinted by Bâton Wicks (2000).
2. All expeditions intending to climb mountains over 6000m in India must apply for permits to the Indian Mountaineering Foundation (IMF) and pay royalties according to the height of the peak and size of the party.

Chapter 23

SHIPTON'S LOST VALLEY

*". . . all of a sudden the fog rolled away from us and we found our-
selves looking down into the immense depths of a cloud-filled valley
at our feet. The glacier descended in a steep icefall for about a thousand feet, then flattened out into a fairly level stretch of ice before it
heeled over for its final colossal plunge into the gloom of the gorge six
thousand feet below us."*

Eric Shipton (from *Nanda Devi*)

On my first reading of *Nanda Devi* I was most enthralled by Eric
Shipton's account of his crossing of the Garhwal Himalaya watershed between Badrinath and Kedarnath temples with Bill Tilman and
three Sherpas in 1934[1]. They were spurred by the legend of a high
priest of ancient times who reputedly performed the *puja* ceremony
in both temples in the same day. As the direct distance between the
two is twenty-four miles and the 7138m peak of Chaukhamba stands
square in the way, the feat seemed improbable. Shipton and Tilman
allowed six days. They ascended the Satopanth Glacier and crossed
over a heavily glaciated pass into unmapped country in rank monsoon weather. The *denouement* was an epic. They became trapped
without food in dense bamboo forest in the gorge on the far side
of the pass. Their ensuing battle for survival, fording dangerously
swollen torrents and competing with black bears for the supply of
edible bamboo shoots, was a story of courage and endeavour against
the odds. They emerged fourteen days later twenty miles south of
Kedarnath. The direct link remained elusive.

Come the 1990s, no party had repeated the crossing. The secrets
of the route were preserved when the first part was designated to
the Inner Line security zone following India's conflict with China
in 1962. The only known attempt was that of two Bengalis who

had entered the bamboo valley from the Kedarnath side in 1984 and were never seen again. The promise of historic wanderings in a wilderness of exceptional ecological diversity inspired me to the point of distraction. Where in the Himalayas can you find a piece of country untouched since the days of Gandhi's resistance to the British Raj? I tasked my agent Mr Pandey with the tricky task of obtaining Inner Line permits to enter the area. Judging the challenge too serious for a commercial expedition, I searched out a team of volunteers.

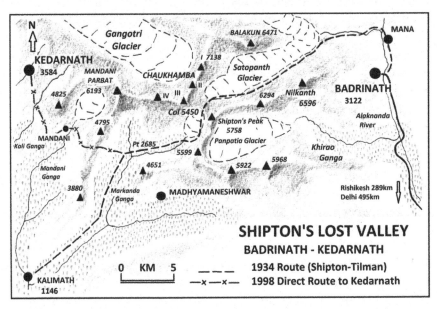

I first recruited John Harvey, a past client who loved Himalayan travel, and he co-opted Welsh caving enthusiasts Pete Francis and Ben Lovett, while I called in the expertise and passion of a guiding colleague Brede Arkless. Brede was a life force – the first female British and International Mountain Guide, mother of eight children, devout Catholic and vegetarian. Yet I wondered at her energies at the age of fifty-eight. Three months before departure I received a surprise call from John Shipton, Eric's son. He had heard of our plans and wanted to come along. John was a contented bulb grower in rural south-west Wales. The bug of mountain exploration had bitten late.

One of my father's stories always remained as an image of his special form of mountaineering, gleaned from memories of his conversations over dinner during childhood. The climbing of a difficult col, and seeing very far below what appeared to be a paradisical valley, which appeared to offer rest and a gentle route back to civilisation, but which turned out to be a hopelessly difficult and impenetrable jungle, had become a sort of personal legend . . .

Young Shipton first appeared in a state of dishevelment in the Heathrow departures lounge. With jutting temples and troubled brows he was the image of his father. His desert pants looked as though they had already spent a month in the field and he took slugs from his duty-free whisky while discussing recent football results. On arrival in India he transformed himself into ardent academic, learning Hindi and lending us the benefit of his fount of botanical knowledge. He was well aware of his father's reputation as a philanderer and joked that he expected ice-blue Shipton eyes to appear in the throng of every Garhwal village. Given the gift of eccentricity his want of mountaineering experience was hardly a drawback.

At 6.00 am on 24 May 1998 our team of ten sat cross-legged in an annex of Badrinath temple before its high priest.

"Work is worship," said the Rawal, "if you are determined you will reach your goal . . ."

The four Indian members, Pandey, Heera Singh, Naveen Chandra and Sobat Singh Rana, hung spellbound on his every word. The Rawal is revered by the tens of thousands of pilgrims who come annually from all over India to worship at Badrinath temple, following a tradition of over a thousand years. To have this private audience conferred symbolic significance upon our venture. Outside, in the chill air at 3000m altitude, we joined hundreds of pilgrims in a ritual bath from the hot water springs under the temple. Drum rolls, murmured chants and a cacophony of bells mingled with the roar of the Alaknanda River, and, some ten thousand feet above the temple, the snowcap of 6596m Nilkanth glowed in the first flush of dawn. Even British sceptics could sense the charge in the atmosphere.

Three kilometres north of Badrinath lies Mana village, last outpost before the great glaciers of the Kamet and Gangotri ranges and checkpoint to the forbidden land beyond the Inner Line. Our access permits, the fruits of six months of relentless paper-chasing by Pandey, were presented to the intelligence officers. After a friendly chat we were allowed the freedom to proceed. We estimated the distance from Badrinath to the Satopanth col at thirty kilometres with ascent of 2300m. We planned a slow approach in order to acclimatise, and took nineteen porters with us to ferry a supply of food to the base of the col.

Our path swung west into the Alaknanda Nala. After five kilometres we crossed to the south bank of the river by a snow bridge and some three kilometres further made camp on an old lake-bed directly opposite the free-standing falls of Vasudhaura. Here we encountered a bearded Rishi whom we had seen leaving Badrinath temple on horseback that morning. His arm was pinned above his head in a woven sock, in spiritual penitence, a position which he had maintained for thirty years in devotion to the god Krishna, who reputedly held his arms aloft for a hundred years in these mountains. His nut-brown body was unadorned save for a penis thong. The Rishi was once a guru of Indira Gandhi. He told us that he was sickened of the crowds and pollution down in Badrinath and was going to the mountains to be alone and die[2]. It was bad luck that the first Western expedition to the Satopanth Glacier for half a century should arrive on the day he began his retreat.

Our second day took us through meadows bedecked with primroses to the snout of the glacier where we gained our first glimpse of the col. Sheltered close under the massive hulk of Chaukhamba the pass looked hazily distant and insignificant, but we could decipher a considerable icefall guarding access. We battled through dwarf willow scrub along the lateral moraine for five kilometres passing directly under the north wall of Nilkanth and over the spring snowline to the summer grazing alp of Majna at 4200m. The pre-monsoon weather was clear and fine, in sharp contrast to the cloud and rains endured in August by the Shipton party.

Next morning our caravan made rapid progress over frozen névé past the frozen lake of Satopanth Tal and established a base camp under the col at a height of 4650m. The porters returned from here with Pandey, and we were left to contemplate an icefall some 600m in height which had caved in and ruptured from both flanks. The left flank was severely fractured and sported a slim leaning tower some sixty metres high that looked ripe for collapse, while the right side was menaced by any avalanches that might fall from Chaukhamba's huge south face. We opted to explore the centre and seven of us set out with fifteen kilogram loads. Towering cumulonimbus clouds that had gathered daily on the Kedarnath side of the range now spilled over the col and enveloped us in light snowfall.

Brede, John Shipton, Ben and Naveen dumped loads at 5150m and returned to camp. Heera, Sobat and I continued up into the jaws of the icefall. The 1934 party had made a camp hereabouts and in Shipton's words passed the night: *"to the accompaniment of an almost continuous roar of ice avalanches from the great cliffs of Chaukhamba above us. Several times I was brought to a sitting position, trembling, as some particularly large avalanche fell close at hand."*

I felt the creeping dread of objective danger as we entered an ice labyrinth via a tenuous snow bridge. Our way was barred by misted ice walls so we traversed left until stopped by a vertical jumble of broken ice blocks. A simple snow couloir lay just forty metres away, but I could see no safe way to reach its sanctuary. Suddenly, I wanted to be out of this place. We turned tail, repacked the kit, and with burdens of thirty kilograms ploughed back down the glacier. As we passed under the potential crash site of the leaning tower, an ominous crack echoed from its base and a shard of ice broke off. I reached camp with a clear conviction that we should not return.

As an alternative, I espied a line of snow ramps on the face of the peak of 5758m to the left of the icefall, from the top of which a traverse line led towards the col. The steepness of this was sufficient to persuade Shipton to go back, although he would have loved to tread in his father's bamboo valley. Pete Francis was troubled by a weak knee and decided to join John in returning to Badrinath together with Naveen and Heera. They planned to take buses a hundred miles round to the Kedarnath side of the range and then trek from Kalimath along the ridges bounding the far side of the bamboo valley. A team of five rather than nine would reduce exposure to risk on a route where a single sprained ankle could jeopardise everyone's life.

At midnight on Saturday 30 May our watch alarms sounded the assault on the col. Our twenty-five kilogram loads included one four-person tent, a week's worth of rations, static rope for abseils and river crossings, a "volcano" stove which could run on twigs and bark down in the forests, and a gigantic *kukri* knife for bushwhacking. There was one unbroken line of snow ramps on the 700m face. The torchlit climb was a torture of effort and a tense game of memory. A brilliant dawn caught us just two-thirds of the way up and we fought progressive enervation and fast-softening snow to gain a snow ridge, where we were delighted to find ourselves above the icefall.

Brede and Sobat led a short traverse to the crest of the col, which was a broad snowfield a kilometre in extent at an altitude of 5420m. Beyond its further edge we could see only a deep blue sky and a line of haze which hung above the foothills. Beyond was an infinite void, and I felt strangely empty of emotions. At once I yearned for the warm caress of the bamboo forest.

The col was menaced by séracs up on Chaukhamba's south face, so we moved down easy snow-slopes on the far side and made camp at 5100m where we could examine the delineation of the great valley below. The bounding ridges were some 4500m high and the valley itself cut a straight line westward from the glacier snout into deepening layers of forest. A thousand metres of unsighted icefall lay between us and the security of the woods.

Brede and I wanted to go back up and climb the shapely summit of Peak 5758. On the following morning while Ben, John, and Sobat moved camp down to the brink of the icefall we climbed on to gain the south ridge of the peak where we could view the ice plateau of the upper Panpatia Glacier and an assemblage of unclimbed peaks. Our ridge was composed of piled blocks, one of which moved under the weight of my arms and trapped my leg. Unable to shift the offending stone, I required Brede's assistance to escape the prospect of permanent entrapment. Near the top we traversed out to steep snow runnels and gained the summit ridge at a fortuitous break in an ice cornice. The summit bore no signs of previous visitors and the name Shipton's Peak was bequeathed to our conquest. We descended down the north face back to the col on 50° slopes of névé that were so firm and sure that we could face outwards. These were conditions one dreams of in the Alps never mind the high Himalaya!

The tables of fortune quickly turned. Thick clouds boiled down on the glacier and we groped our way down through the fog to join the others, their line of marker wands providing invaluable guidance. Once reunited an air of tension took hold of our party. How could we get down the icefall, of which Eric Shipton had written:

"We gazed down upon the head of a second and very formidable icefall. It was appallingly steep and for a long time we could not see

any way of tackling it which offered the slightest hope of success."

The glacial retreat of the previous sixty-four years was unlikely to have made the undertaking any easier. When visibility improved we went out to probe the options. A long gully dropped down the left side of the ice and was undoubtedly the route by which Shipton and Tilman descended. However, this chute was directly threatened by a hanging sérac. Examination of the right edge of the icefall brought an emphatic rebuff. The third option was to traverse directly under the hanging glacier then abseil down rock steps to gain snow-slopes beyond the risk zone. Despite its initial exposure to ice avalanches this route finally gained our favour.

At dawn we commenced the traverse while the splintered ice cliff above was still in shade. We skated nervously across the icy terrace and gained the reassurance of a rock spur. Here a large block offered the perfect anchor for a long abseil down to snowfields which effectively circumvented the icefall. The great forest beckoned. Straight as a die, the valley, which is called the Gandharpongi Gad, dropped below us into green woodland. We understood Shipton's optimism at so pleasant a sight after the tribulations of the col.

Dry ice and boulderfields led us quickly down to the glacier snout at 3650m where we floundered straight into dense birch wood, much of which had been bent or flattened by avalanches. Our camp that night was a clearing beside a running brook quilted with yellow corydalis and wild rhubarb. Great scrolls of white bark hung from aged birch trunks, fuelling John's volcano stove which brewed a constant supply of drinks. Lammergeiers swept imperiously up the valley between its soaring walls of vegetated granite. We spread out in the open and breathed that happiness with life that thinks not of the trials to come but only of the wonder of the moment.

A mile downstream from our camp the upper valley terminated in a pronounced downfall. In Shipton's words:

"The river disappeared underground for a short distance above the bank of the precipice and issued forth in a great waterspout to crash down into the depths below."

Standing on the jammed blocks spanning the river we peered down into a dense mantle of giant oak trees which fell away for 800m to the junction with the side river which the Garhwal West map[3] marks as spot height 2685m. Not only was this the lowest point of our planned route but the crossing of this side-stream was also the pivotal passage of the 1934 venture, the place where Sherpa Pasang was nearly killed by a falling boulder and two rain-drenched days were spent in finding a fording point.

At the lip of the downfall we hitched our ropes round juniper roots, and, trusting to their dubious strength, abseiled the steepest bluff. By cautious route-finding we descended steep oakwood and rock slabs without further recourse to the rope. Claw-marks on tree branches and large piles of droppings showed that black bears still roamed the forest. Our incessant noise, crashing through the undergrowth, ensured they stayed at a safe distance. Where a canopy of old trees shielded the sunlight the forest floor was open and the going was easy, but a dense scrub of dwarf pines and thorn bushes was fighting for space in every clearing, forcing us down on hands and knees. The twisting branches snagged our rucksacks, forcing us to push forward headfirst until we went crashing forward, propelled by the weight of the loads.

We kept sharp lookout for any traces of human activity and in the forest we found a rudimentary wire animal trap; then Sobat spotted an empty wood-framed shelter at a clearing. Outside was a makeshift shrine and inside we found goatskins filled with crushed roots and herbs. Sobat reckoned this to be the camp of illegal plant hunters. Some Himalayan roots have enormous value for medicinal purposes and there is a lucrative black-market trade to China. Such activity was unlikely to be detected in this gorge.

The side-torrent could now be heard pounding its path down a canyon to our right. For an hour we searched upstream for a crossing, but vertiginous walls of conglomerate prevented any access to the river. With mounting concern we hurried back down the spur to the confluence with the main Gandharpongi River at Pt 2685. A terrifying roar located the meeting point. We scrambled to the edge of a slimy crag overhanging the river and spied below a makeshift bridge of three wooden spars between raised boulders at precisely the point where Shipton and Tilman must have crossed in 1934. Thanks to the hunters our passage was assured, and a relaxed team made open camp and fire that night, happy to be couched by the crux of the route.

From Pt 2685 Shipton and Tilman had fought their way down-valley for five more days, emerging at Kalimath. Our aim to prove a direct link to Kedarnath temple involved breaking out of the gorge and crossing a series of three 4500m ridges. A thunderstorm broke early next morning as we abseiled down to the river. We crossed the bridge using a rope handrail for safety then ploughed into dense dripping undergrowth. Thick stands of bamboo now made their appearance. Our patience with the jungle was quickly exhausted and we struck directly uphill on a relentless climb of 50° angle. The exposure was such that we would have tumbled many hundreds of feet had we slipped on the muddy open ground. Occasional stands of gnarled rhododendron made pillars of security. Higher we re-entered bamboo forest and the pitiless climb continued, accompanied by constant birdsong from the tree-tops. We emerged from the forest at 3600m, and a drenching rainstorm began just as we were clearing a level patch for our tent.

The next storm arrived the following afternoon as we were traversing snow slopes towards a gap in the Dobra Khal ridge. We were working against the grain of the country. The physical effort, biting shoulder straps, and dwindling energy stores, gnawed at our confidence and patience. The Mandani valley lay over the ridge. With a trail and a temple marked on our map we imagined there would be a teashop there!

We crossed the ridge at 4400m in a blizzard but the sun reappeared as we descended a steep snow gully on the far side. We rushed down open snowfields and across carpets of yellow globeflowers, infused by the rich evening light. Then we hit steep slopes of rhododendron. Scanning the shadowed Mandani valley we could decipher stone buildings, but there were no signs either of smoke, light or animals. Our hearts sank and we made camp on a shelf three hundred metres above the valley floor. Morale was at a low that night. Kedarnath was still two ridges away. Sobat had long since despaired of our definition of a high mountain trek, and each day our diet shrunk while our consumption of body fats increased. No sooner were we fed than we slumped into an exhausted sleep.

Deserted and peaceful, Mandani might have been the most exquisite spot on earth that next morning. Grassy moraine shelves led up from a tiny stone temple to long glacier slopes and then the shapely twin summits of 6193m Mandani Parbat. Nobody is going to make a big name for themselves climbing in such remote places, yet this is how Himalayan mountaineering once was and can still be for those who shun the glory-seeking. We brightened considerably to discover a note from John Shipton at the temple door. The others had passed this way just the previous day. Then, as a gift to the temple, I offered the trusty kukri, carried so far by Sobat but never used in anger. I didn't realise that this temple was dedicated to the avenging goddess Kali. Who knows what curses she might bring down on our team for such an impudent offering.

Leaving Mandani all traces of path disappeared, leaving us enmeshed in a jungle of dwarf oaks, trailing brambles and giant juniper, the terrain complicated by a succession of side gorges – or *nalas*. We wished we had kept the kukri. Escape from the forest was imperative, and we bent our backs to a 900m climb up to the Simtoli ridge. On gaining a snowy crest at 4300m a sudden storm descended and a lightning bolt struck the ridge just metres above us. Kali must indeed have been angry.

We camped in a snow-filled corrie evocative of Scotland in early spring. The cheerful birdsong was prescient of renewed life. Our food was finally exhausted with a breakfast serving from a single packet of custard. A snow gully led up to the true crest of Simtoli Dhar at 4450m and we were greeted by a view of the dawn alpenglow striking across the Kedarnath ranges. Gentle slopes dropped into our last valley, the Kali Ganga, and on its far side we spied a grass gully which breached the Khalini Dhar, beyond which lay Kedarnath.

Brede used the last of our gas to brew up by the Kali Ganga, and with a conquering grin presented cups of ginseng tea to revive her flagging male companions. How could I have doubted her[4]? The ultimate climb was accompanied by the familiar symptoms of aching abdomen, strained back and leaden leg muscles. Sobat gained the ridge crest first and at last we looked down on the clustered buildings of Kedarnath 900m below. Hundreds of tiny figures could be seen plying the approach trail to the town. After eight days in solitary splendour we were due for a culture shock. The abode of Lord Shiva attracts as many pilgrims as Badrinath[5]. Unbroken snowfields dropped steeply towards the town. With a theatrical sense of occasion I broke into a succession of swooping standing glissades down to the lowest limit of the snow. After so much toil this was a fitting finale. Then we packed away our axes and quietly slipped into town. Among the throngs milling round the temple we spotted young Shipton. He, Heera, Naveen and Pete had got in just an hour before us, having followed a route from Mandani a little south of our own.

While our reunion was joyful our satisfaction was tinged with regret. In revisiting Shipton's lost valley and in proving the direct route from Badrinath to Kedarnath we had pierced two of the remaining myths of the high Himalaya. We can but pray that the valley will be as wild and beautiful when we too are dead and gone.

Notes

1. Eric Shipton and Bill Tilman were the pre-eminent British mountain explorers of the twentieth century – immensely tough, courageous and committed to the lightweight ethic. Although they were involved in several attempts on Everest, it is for their daring exploratory exploits, such as the first penetration of the Nanda Devi Sanctuary, that they have become icons to younger generations of alpinists.
2. The Rishi survived for eighteen months in a cave by the Satopanth Glacier at an altitude of 4500m, his food supplies replenished by his devotees, but perished during his second winter.
3. The Survey of India maps of the region were published by Swiss cartographer Ernst Huber as Garhwal East and Garhwal West at 1:150000 scale. Shipton himself contributed some of the original survey work in the 1930s. The Indian military authorities have refused to allow public access to more recent 1:50000 topographic maps of the Himalaya, such is their security paranoia.
4. Brede Arkless died of stomach cancer in 2006. She cycled the two hundred miles to her hospital in New Zealand to hear her terminal prognosis. I last saw her on Mont Blanc a year before she died. She had broken trail for eight hours in knee-deep snow to make the summit. Several French guides had stayed studiously behind.
5. In June 2013, at the height of the pilgrim season, Kedarnath was devastated by a flash flood and mudslides. Many hundreds of people lost their lives and only the temple was left untouched.

Chapter 24

JOURNEY TO THE EDGE OF TIBET

"Martin, Little Kailash is exceedingly beautiful trekking; the country here is most unspoilt." Agent Pandey was at it again, sowing the seeds of a new Himalayan adventure.

"Where on Earth is Little Kailash?" I thought. There is a thrill in being told of a hitherto unknown destination, perhaps a new Shangri-la. The peak was not named on the 1:200000 topographic maps of the Indian Himalaya. I delved into past journals and finally found its location wedged between the borders of Nepal and Tibet in Eastern Kumaon, the former kingdom of the Bhotia people. Harish Kapadia, a guru of Indian mountains, had trekked there in 1982 and his account included a picture of a pyramidal peak sliced by horizontal rock bands with distinct resemblance to Tibet's Mount Kailash, which in fact lies 110km to the north.

Little Kailash was thought to be 6321m high, and could alternatively be called Adi (*Old*) Kailash or Baba (*Holy*) Kailash. According to legend, Lord Shiva made it his home with his wife Sati. After a betrayal by other *devtas* (gods) Sati threw herself on the *puja* fire. Shiva married her reincarnation, Parvati, and together they left Adi Kailash and moved north to Holy Mount Kailash in Tibet. Kapadia's photo showed Adi Kailash to be attractive and challenging, and his account of snowbound passes, sacred lakes and plunging gorges set my pulse racing. The region had been closed to foreign visitors since the Chinese border incursions of 1962, and, so far as we knew, no peaks in the range had been climbed. We would need Inner Line permits, but by promoting ourselves as a joint Indo-British team, protocols and restrictions were less onerous. I liked the idea that our regular staff – Naveen, Hari, Mangal and Ajay – would be fully-fledged team members, whatever the economic truth of our relations.

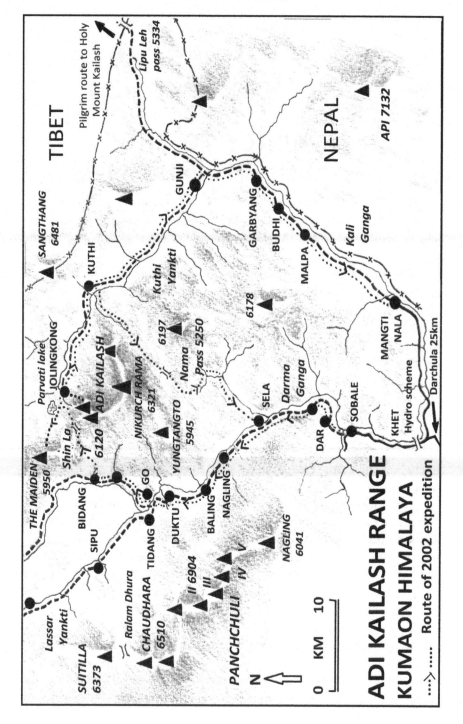

ADI KAILASH RANGE
KUMAON HIMALAYA
....>..... Route of 2002 expedition

On 20 September 2002 our expedition bus left the Indian plains at Kathgodam for the winding journey through the hills of Kumaon, our destination the town of Darchula on the Kali Ganga river, which forms the Indo-Nepalese border. We were tightly squeezed with eighteen members – twelve British and six Indian – plus all kit and food for our three-week trip right down to the last cabbage. After an intense monsoon deluge, the peaceful calm of early autumn reigned over the swathe of forested ridges. Passing over the 1800m top of Almora town, the snow giants of the high Himalaya appeared on the northern skyline, including Nanda Devi, the presiding Goddess of the Kumaon hills. The drive passed into a sylvan wonderland of spacious long-needled pines through which shafts of diffused sunlight lit the ground mosses to a brilliant emerald. Scattered villages and terraced cultivations blended timelessly into the dips and curves of the landscape. Through Binsar forest, Shere Ghat, where we crossed the clear-flowing Sarju river, Chaukori, Didihat and Ogla the journey unfolded like a dream. I felt the ultimate serenity that even should this day be my last all would be well with the world.

Arrival at Darchula was a free-fall from heaven. For five years past the town had been overwhelmed by the construction works for a major hydroelectric power scheme sited fifteen kilometres upstream at the foot of the Darma valley, just before it spills into the Kali Ganga. The fifty-two-metre dam, eight kilometre tunnel and massive turbine house would generate power for millions of homes down on the Gangetic plains. The site itself was a real-life vision of an animated computer game – hundreds of stone-breaking labourers, dozens of earth-movers, giant rock-crushers – all working in seeming chaos but doubtless controlled by a logistical mastermind somewhere among the ghastly ranks of tin huts.

The District Magistrate who authorised our Inner Line permits at Darchula was so pleased with our gift of Glenmorangie whisky that he was found fast asleep when the crucial documents were ready for his signature. We also reported to the local Army unit, who radioed our itinerary to all Border Police posts in the area.

The first twelve kilometres of our trek up the Darma valley followed a bulldozed jeep road, broken in several places by landslips. Modernity comes with a heavy levy on the environment. On turning a sharp bend to the north just past the Dar village, the slope dropped away into an incised trench four hundred metres deep and the road was replaced by a rock walkway carved into a sheer face. We ambled up ten kilometres of forested gorge to Sela village, gazing open-jawed at the dancing waterfalls that crossed the path.

Sela's folk provided memorable hospitality with tea, rice spirit and a visit to their Shiva temple. Nestled under huge chestnut trees this open enclosure was adorned with hundreds of bells. After we had paid due homage to Shiva's trident, the local boys grinned furtively and pointed to a large round boulder in the temple courtyard. Apparently all visitors are challenged to lift this 120kg monster. After a demonstration from the local experts, we each tried in vain, making excuses of slipped discs and weak knees. Humiliation loomed. Last to try was our team doctor, a sixty-year-old anaesthetist from Cornwall and oldest of our team, Mike Freeman. He got his fingers locked under the stone and hauled it off the deck.

From Sela at 2550m we walked nineteen kilometres up the valley to Duktu village at 3200m, sensing a subtle change in vegetation and scenery to the drier starker terrain more typical of Tibet than India. Below Duktu the Darma River carved a precipitous gorge through soft glacial sediments fringed by broad terraces sown with red-headed *kultu,* the local wheat crop. Thus far we had gained no more than the odd glimpse of snow peaks, but at Duktu a broad side-valley revealed "five cooking pots" of the Panchchuli range in full glory.

The Bhotia population only stays here between May and early November, moving down to villages near Darchula for the winter. Crops of root vegetables, medicinal herbs and hallucinatory plants supplement a healthy trade in goats and mules. Remarkably, the post is collected every day, but the absence of medical facilities condemns anyone suffering serious illness to a thirty-kilometre ride by mule to the roadhead.

The dawn of 26 September came with peerless clarity, the Panchchulis arrayed with such brilliance that it was hard to leave the scene and rejoin the main valley. The Darma forked north-eastwards and a mule trail contoured high above golden birch woods, then climbed steadily to the campground of Bidang at 3900m. Bidang was an important market for Tibetan traders before the border was closed. Enclosed by vast fields of scree the valley headed inexorably north into the wastes of Tibet.

Bidang became our base camp while we reconnoitred the western approaches to Little Kailash. No peak within our view remotely resembled the banded and isolated tooth of Kapadia's photograph. Other peaks, possibly higher, were blocking access and the shortcomings of a 1:200000 map were now apparent. Depressingly, we concluded that Little Kailash lay over the Shin La, a 5500m pass which was due east of Bidang. On its far side lay Jolingkong Lake in the upper Kuthi Yankti valley.

Kapadia had crossed Shin La in 1982 and locals told us that it was once a wedding route. Closer inspection revealed that this was no place for a bridal palanquin. We were confronted by a nine-hundred-metre wall of cliffs of alpine proportions, broken here and there by snow gullies and ramps. Doctor Mike was bullish at the prospect but warned me that there were some seriously worried people in our party. As leader I had seriously misjudged our approach. Our clients had been told to expect an adventure, but it wasn't easy to ask them to abandon the luxuries of our base camp so early in the trip. As we carried loads to an advance camp at 4500m, I spied a herd of *bharal* (wild sheep) trotting in file towards the Shin La access gully. Ten minutes later they were over halfway up the pass, ambling without concern on slopes that we had estimated as 50° in angle. Instantly the spell of apprehension was broken.

We planned to shift ten days' worth of food, tents and climbing kit over the pass. Starting at 1.30 am our first group of twelve divided into four roped teams and ventured into the gully, a place that would become a death-trap from stonefall after mid-morning. Shaded from moonlight the onward way was unclear and rock walls appeared to block any exit until a narrow snow shelf led to a ramp. The sunrise gave due deference to Nanda Devi as the highest of the ranges to our west, flooding her twin sentinels with pink glow for a precious minute before casting the myriad of other peaks in a slightly paler rendition. We threaded a weaving line off the ramp and gained a 40° band of snow leading rightwards to the pass, which was guarded by a hundred-metre fortress of red gneiss on its north side.

To our bafflement, the expansive view did not include the elusive Little Kailash. While seven members continued down to Jolingkong with bulging packs, five of us returned down the gullies to the advance camp and made a second load ferry the following morning. The mystery of Little Kailash was solved with blinding impact a hundred metres down the far side of the pass. The full flush of the mountain's banded north face came into view, skirted by a graceful fringe of parallel glacier tongues, all powdered in fresh snow. I could hardly catch my breath so sudden was the revelation and I knelt a few minutes, camera in hand, in prayerful gratitude. Topographically, Little Kailash was exposed as a subsidiary peak of a larger mountain which had blocked our view from Bidang[1], but was no less alluring for its deception.

Our camp at Jolingkong lay on a huge expanse of cropped grass sprinkled here and there with boulders. At one end a few tin huts, built by the Kumaon tourist authority as a resthouse for pilgrims, made the sole blemish on a landscape of lonely intensity. On the eastern horizon a coxcomb of orange pinnacles, known as Parvati's Crown in honour of Shiva's wife, guarded the Tibetan frontier.

A sociable visit from the Border Police procured an invite to visit their post and we accepted a challenge to take them on in a game of volleyball. The Police spend six months at a stretch up here patrolling the border wastes and catching any Tibetans who try to get into India illegally. With little else to do they were likely to be well-versed in volleyball skills. Despite fielding our tallest and most athletic members we received a thorough thrashing. Playing on a sun-baked pitch with an encirclement of resplendent mountains, we hardly cared.

Jolingkong temple, and the neighbouring lake of Parvati Kund, lie at 4625m altitude. The lake is a kilometre across yet its water was surprisingly warm for a brief swim. While our Indian colleagues made offerings of fruit at the Shiva temple we marvelled at the montage of lake and mountain and wondered why so lovely a place should be utterly deserted when Indian trekkers have open access. Meanwhile, the indefatigable Mike had discovered that the limestone rock strata hereabouts were crawling with fossils. These had lived in the seabed before the uplift of the Himalaya. Ignoring our protestations of vandalism he collected several fine ammonites.

With cultural preliminaries complete we turned our attentions to mountaineering. At 3.00 am on 3 October six of us left camp bound for a snow peak lying at the head of the side valley which feeds Jolingkong lake. The tension of night navigation was heightened in our knowledge that armed police were out on patrol in the vicinity. We had informed the commander of our planned climb but wondered if our message had been passed down to the troops. A trek of five kilometres up snow-covered moraines led to an active glacier and steep snow face. By now we were committed, and despite the direct heat of the morning sun we pushed on up a couloir of 50° angle. With a final wade through powdery drifts we emerged on the main watershed between the Darma and Kuthi Yankti valleys a couple of kilometres north of the Shin La. A succession of three false summits tested resolve and patience to the limit, but brought an ever-widening panorama, including the unmistakeable outline of Holy Mount Kailash which floated on the Tibetan plateau seventy miles away. The authorities had forbidden us to bring a GPS device and, without any accurate altitude calibration, we guessed our height as 5950m. I've seen a few mountain views in my time but never one to rival this in its expansiveness and intrigue. From 7756m Kamet round to the Tibet's sleeping giant, 7728m Gurla Mandhata, an array of unknowns spanned the horizon.

Back at base camp Tom Rankin, who had led much of the final climb, asked if we could call this mountain The Maiden after one of Scotland's loveliest and most remote hills A'Mhaighdean. We asked our Liaison Officer, Sharma, for a Hindi translation and he came up with "Kuanri Ladkhi". Literally, this means "unfertilised woman", which was not quite so romantic! So we settled for Rajula, The Princess, in reverence to a legendary *rani* of the Bhotia people.

While others climbed a snow-peak just north of Jolingkong, I readied a team of three for an attempt on Little Kailash: Mike, Pat Harborough and James Gibb. We aimed direct for its north face, which commenced just a few hundred metres from camp. In the twilight, just two hours into the ascent, our confidence was crumbling.

"Well, this is a load of bollocks! It's hardly going to improve, is it?" stated Mike.

A crust was breaking under every step, depositing us knee-deep in bottomless powder snow. We staggered drunkenly towards a steeper glacier tongue. Here, we encountered impenetrable and glassy ice. For sixty metres we had to hack and swing our way using belays from our two ice screws until the angle eased. Then we reverted to trenching in deep powder. We crawled up the steeper sections on knees and elbows, our suffering exacerbated in the knowledge that we were too late to correct our error of judgement. These northern slopes were getting only four hours of oblique sunlight a day. With air temperatures pegged at −5 to −10°C the snowpack had not consolidated since the monsoon blizzards of three weeks earlier.

By midday we had ploughed ourselves to exhaustion. We set our camp at 5600m, 150m below the crucial rock band. We had spied a way through the barrier at its thinnest point. The weather remained impeccable as we climbed through a second dawn. With the team safely belayed under an overhang I tackled the band. Orange gneiss gave way to disposable black shale, requiring a double-clearing operation. Before each move could be made I had first to shovel heaps of powder snow clear and then dismantle the underlying rock in sizeable chunks. The protection in such material was sparse and dubious.

After two hours of painstaking effort I stepped on to the upper snowfields, only to be thrown off balance by an angle far steeper than anticipated. The snow was hip-deep and utterly devoid of substance. My crampons grated alarmingly on the underlying shale. Scattered outcrops of rotten rock offered no belay anchors. Although the summit was less than two hundred metres above, I obeyed my instant intuition. The ground was lethal. With sadness I called the retreat and, protected by a single piton, climbed carefully down to rejoin the group.

We had undertaken not to tread the final metres of Little Kailash in respect to its status as a sacred peak, but, even on the most generous interpretation of this promise, we were about 150m short of success![2] Lord Shiva had made clear pronouncement upon our endeavours and we returned to Jolingkong that evening tired and frustrated.

Waking to the first breath of sunlight on our frosted tent next morning I cleared crusted eyelids and thought of a first cup of coffee. Poking my head outside, I saw Mike, up and dressed, stalking round camp and chanting a new mantra – "Nama, Nama, Nama, Anyone for the Nama Pass?" Just twelve hours after crashing in from the Little Kailash debacle, he was trying to persuade his wilting colleagues to undertake one last adventure before heading home. No amount of red wine and Viagra could account for such energy.

The Nama Pass lies ten kilometres south of Little Kailash and provides another link between the Kuthi Yankti and Darma valleys. There was no record of a crossing by any mountaineering party. The Nama was an optional conclusion to the expedition, but some folk had already decided they preferred to trek out by the valley route to Gunji, where the main pilgrim route to Tibet and Holy Mount Kailash is joined, and thence down the Kali Ganga back to Darchula.

Though seventy-five kilometres in distance the trail is paved and could be done with surety in four days.

By contrast the Nama Pass route involved an ascent from 3700 to 5200m, and a ten-kilometre stretch of unknown high mountain terrain. If trapped up there by storms we would be unable to retreat in sufficient time to catch our flights home. That morning the whole team walked thirteen kilometres down the valley to Kuthi village, arriving in a wet mournful snowfall. We had some pretty hardy mountaineers in the team, but the list of defections from the Nama plan grew steadily until only Mike was left. My fellow-guide John Allott, Hari Singh and I were the only diehards, who, like him, wanted to squeeze the last drop of excitement from the trip.

Happily, the following day dawned clear and fresh. Kuthi was revealed as the most charming village of our trek. The doors, balustrades and window frames of its clustered houses were adorned by exquisite woodcarvings which are two centuries old. Before leaving we questioned the locals about the Nama. An army captain said that the Border Police had only crossed the pass once in the last eleven years and a wizened local warned of mazes of crevasses.

Bidding farewell to the rest of the team we crossed the Kuthi Yankti river and headed south-west up the Nama valley into the unknown. Barely recovered from the efforts on Little Kailash I lagged behind; even so it was inspiring to see yet more new glaciers and peaks. We camped at 4650m as clouds massed into an imminent storm. A thunderous deluge fell that evening in surrounding valleys, but by chance of fate we were spared. At dawn the sky was once more clear and we marched onwards on a solid crust of snow towards two horns of rock which marked the watershed. All crevasses were filled or hidden. On the last mile the snow began to give way and we trudged wearily under a hanging glacier towards the col. The view ahead was clouded and obstructed by intervening ridges and we turned briefly to bid farewell to the Nama valley. Suddenly a great crack issued from the hanging glacier and a large shard of ice plunged down the face sending its cloud of dust and splinters straight across the tracks we had made just ten minutes previously.

We exchanged knowing looks but nobody said a word. We were simply relieved to set our sights downhill. Six hours later, after a relentless 2500m descent, we plunged through thickening forest and back into Sela. Nothing had changed during our fortnight's absence.

The same old men sat contentedly on the terrace as the village matriarch prepared our tea. Mike's enquiries for alcoholic succour elicited a large carton of *chang*, and with the additions of two kilos of freshly dug potatoes, a carton of salt and a rest-house bed, our homecoming was complete.

Notes

1. In 2006 we returned to make the first ascent of this higher peak, which we named Ishan Parbat (6120m).
2. In 2004 a follow-up expedition led by Andy Perkins and Martin Welch found an easier route to the summit of Little Kailash on its south-west flank (AD alpine standard), but left the final ten metres of the peak untouched. The summit altitude was estimated at 5950m.

Chapter 25

KAMET – ONE STEP TOO FAR

What adventure can be greater than a struggle against the Himalayas?
Amidst the prosaic things of life, the memories of those days spent in
Garhwal, the beautiful heart of Himachal, will last us for all time.
Corporal Ralph Ridley (1937, *The Ice Soldiers*)

Since the 1990s high-altitude mountaineering in the Himalaya has
been dominated by commercial expeditions. These are not guided
in the conventional sense of the word. The organisers provide the
full range of ground services; Sherpas are provided to make trail, fix
ropes and set camps; and the paying members move independently
without direct link to a qualified Western guide. I have viewed this
style of climbing with some disfavour. The mountain is subjected to
prolonged assault with the encumbrance of fixed ropes and damage
to the environment. The members assign all logistical tasks to the
staff, which runs agin the spirit of adventure and personal responsibility that is the underpinning of genuine mountaineering.

However, a mountain guide is hardly best-placed to criticise
assisted mountaineering, and no system evolves without good reason.
My early Himalayan trips had achieved many ascents up to 7000m
with traditional guiding methods, but at extreme altitudes the ability of a guide to look after both self and clients on the rope breaks
down. Instead, the provision of security is entrusted to the fixed line.
I've never liked the idea of devolving my duty of care, but was willing
to put my ethical misgivings to the test for the chance to attempt one
iconic high peak.

The granitic obelisk of 7756m Kamet stands in proud isolation on
the northernmost frontier of the Indian Garhwal ranges. Being one
of the highest peaks of the British Empire, Kamet was subject to early

investigation. In 1913 C.F. Meade and guide Pierre Blanc reached the 7138m col to the north-east of the summit. In 1931 a strong British team, led by Frank Smythe, followed Meade's approach and completed the climb to achieve the world's highest summit success to that date. Smythe was a prolific author with commercial sensibilities, and triumphantly entitled his account of the climb *Kamet Conquered*.

In 1937 five British regular soldiers of the East Surrey Regiment secretly attempted to repeat Smythe's climb during their summer leave. They told their officers that they were going trekking, and left with the most rudimentary kit, including "21 pounder" tents and felt-lined boots made by the regimental handyman. They reached nearly 7000m without Sherpa assistance before retreating. The effort of these "Ice Soldiers" was forgotten until the discovery of their pho-tographic film-rolls in the 1970s[1]. More recently Kamet became a regular target for Indian military expeditions, and during one such enterprise in 2003 a helicopter rescue was undertaken at a record-breaking height of 7000m, just under Meade's Col.

We were the first commercial Western organiser to book the peak, and in spring 2005 I recruited a large party with varied credentials. The German couple, Hartmut Bielefeldt and Claudia Bäumler, had summited Everest the previous year in a remarkable lightweight climb from the Tibetan side in which they used only one Sherpa. Mike Freeman, Tom Rankin, Steve Ward and James Gibb were regular Himalayan clients, but none had been above 7000m. Neil Lindsey wanted to rediscover his altitude legs after a long lay-off from the Himalaya. Others were unproven at altitude: John "Rock" Hudson a sixty-year-old geologist, and David Hasdell and Hazel Hunkin, who were the babes of the team in experience and age.

My deputy leader, John Lyall, was a strong and steadfast Scottish guide from the Spey valley whose mountain passion encompassed an intimate knowledge of Himalayan flora and fauna. We recruited Sherpas Thukpa, Urgen and Phurba from Darjeeling, plus two Indian high-altitude porters. With the addition of two cooks, a kitchen boy and a Liaison Officer, this was never going to be a lightweight affair.

The road journey to Kamet is of mind-boggling length. We cut out the first six hours by taking a train from Delhi to the holy city of Haridwar and bathed in the Ganges to allay the searing heat of early May. Entering the foothills at Rishikesh, we passed a road sign indicating 426km in distance to the Niti Pass, which lies thirty kilometres east of Kamet. We followed the main Ganges valley, then the Alaknanda tributary to Joshimath and finally the Dhauli Ganga side-valley to the roadhead at Gamsali, just thirty kilometres from the Tibetan border. We should not have complained of the bumpy ride, for in 1931 Smythe's team walked three-quarters of this distance!

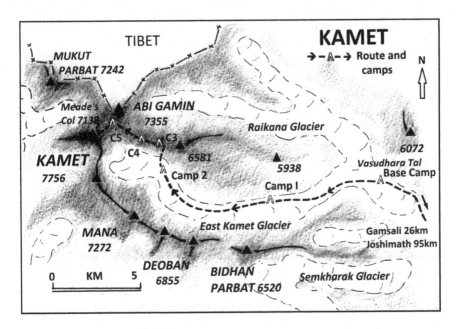

On a day of biting wind and spitting snowflakes the scenery of the Dhauli Ganga was oppressively wild. Snowdrifts blocked the road four kilometres before Gamsali and we made our first camp at Bampa. A fine morning revealed our true location in the midst of stunning physical geography. Down the valley, pine forests swept elegantly up concave slopes to jagged peaks. The distant ice crown of Dunagiri poked over the top of this lower horizon. Looking upstream, the valley gorges of the Amrit and Dhauli rivers met in a confluence choked with a vast layer of glacial debris, washed and layered into a level surface through which the milky blue rivers had eroded deep trenches. Great slabs and prows of virgin rock towered six hundred metres above.

After presenting our Inner Line permits at the Gamsali post of the Border Police, we trekked through the Dhauli gorge to Niti village at 3400m. The village was deserted apart from a few Intelligence Bureau personnel. The native Bhotia people did not arrive from their winter settlements until the second half of May. A shortage of porters posed our first organisational crisis. Only forty-eight of the eighty requested had turned up. Many men from the Joshimath area preferred to enjoy the marriage season in their home villages, and Nepalese porters, normally so reliable, were not allowed into Inner Line areas. Without double-carries or double-loads we could never get all our kit the twenty-five kilometres to base camp.

The Dhauli forms another beautiful gorge above Niti. The winter snows had been the heaviest for thirty years and the valley bottom was choked with huge drifts of avalanche debris. We had to ford the Dhauli river eight kilometres higher up and trusted that similar snow-bridges would allow us easy passage. Above the gorge at Khal Khurans the last straggling birch trees gave up the survival fight and the narrow *nala* broadened into a majestic arid valley.

The designated crossing point of the Dhauli Ganga lies just above its confluence with the Raikana river, where the Dhauli valley cuts north-eastwards in its final rise to the Niti Pass. We were confronted by a raging torrent, swollen by the snowmelt, and lacking any accessible bridge of snow. A fall into these waters promised certain drowning. A few rusty box girders lay scattered on the bank, presumably left by the Public Works Department in anticipation of this predicament.

Scouting skills were required. Those who had passed their back-woods badge set to work to lash three sections of girder together with some of our fixed rope. The resultant six-metre span was lowered across the stream with ropes and at the instant it touched the far bank Sherpa Thukpa risked his life and skipped across. Seconds later the bridge was swept off its lodgement. Three times we pushed the bridge out over the flood and each time it was carried off downstream, until on the fourth try Thukpa was able to make an anchorage. We built up stone abutments around the girder-ends before retiring to a nervous camp.

By morning the river level had dropped half a metre, but left the girders coated in verglas. We scattered sand over the ice, fixed a rope handrail and watched anxiously as the porters crossed. We left the bridge in place, with a prayer that it would survive four weeks until our return.

Our next camp at Nand Kharak was a delightful alluvial plateau at

4400m, covered in spring grass and fringed by juniper. The boulder-covered snout of the Raikana Glacier lay just above. I put up my tent and stretched out. The stress of the river-crossing was beginning to recede when a biting blizzard blew in. One by one our porters arrived, their woollen clothes caked with snow and each with a load of forty to fifty kilograms. Normally the porters erect makeshift tarps under boulders and set up stoves for a long session of chapatti-making, but now they were stranded and some looked hypothermic. We tore into the loads and extracted, then erected, every one of our expedition tents for their shelter. Come the morning a dozen defected. We could hardly blame them. The remaining gang of thirty-six nobly agreed to do two carries three kilometres up to base camp.

It would be hard to imagine a less hospitable place than Vasudhara Tal base camp. A string of frozen lakes is besieged by a wilderness of boulder moraines, devoid of vegetation, still half-covered by snowfields and raked by chilling winds every afternoon. Long icicles hung from flanking cliffs and a lofty range of 6000m snow peaks rimmed the skyline of the Raikana Glacier. Recent military teams had abandoned piles of tinned fruit and had painted ugly graffiti on nearby rocks. Our Sherpas built a stupa and at dawn after our first night they held a *puja* ceremony, blessing our team and making offerings of juniper and food to assure our safe passage to Kamet. With their prayer flags fluttering above our tents we began to feel more at home, though our evening comforts hardly compared to those described by Smythe in 1931.

Shipton manipulated the gramophone, and the well-remembered tunes floated out into the still night, whilst we sat around puffing at our pipes, at peace with the world.

Our first foray towards Kamet took us across firm snowfields and round a little rock peak forming the cornerstone between the Raikana and East Kamet Glaciers. Here the north-eastern walls of Bidhan Parbat, Deoban and Mana were suddenly revealed, plunging 1500m in tiers of glacial aprons broken by ice cliffs. The East Kamet Glacier squeezed through a vertical canyon beneath these precipices, a sombre but immensely beautiful "valley of death". Kamet herself lay out of sight where the glacier twisted down from the north. Our planned site for Camp 2 at 5600m lay twelve kilometres up this trench.

Our team set to work ferrying loads up the glacier. After 10.00 am the glacier became a furnace, trapping all the radiation refracted from the surrounding peaks. The daily journeys up the glacier combined fear and leaden exhaustion, but gradually we adapted to the scale of our surroundings and within a week had occupied Camp 2 directly under Kamet's pyramidal south-eastern wall. Throughout this phase westerly winds blew hard over the top of Kamet, sending snow plumes streaming off the summit. This instability extended to lower levels, producing regular afternoon snow flurries and a variable breeze. Until the jet stream weakened we could not hope to live on the higher slopes.

Above Camp 2 fierce walls of red granitic gneiss line the east side of the glacier. There is only one gap in these defences where a narrow side-canyon spills into the main valley. Halfway up the canyon is a vertical glacier snout which can be by-passed by steep mixed terrain on its right side. We fixed eighty metres of rope here and continued up the glacier slopes above to a broad plateau at 6150m. Having surmounted the defensive wall of the main glacier we were now surrounded by a further cirque of smooth cliffs and ice walls. A blizzard chased us back to base and continued for the next eighteen hours, laying thirty centimetres of fresh snow above 5000m. We rested pensively for two days at base. Already our team had splintered. Hazel was suffering severe skin rash and she and David opted to return to Joshimath to go trekking. Neil was laid out with a back strain, unable to get out of his tent. I was about to summon a helicopter rescue when one of our Indian high-altitude porters, Govind, offered to give his spine a massage. We dragged Neil out of his tent flat on his campmat. After a few minutes of pinching and pummelling, Govind elicited a squeal of relief as a trapped nerve was released. Neil was free to join the summit bid.

On 25 May we were all back up at Camp 2. Thukpa, Phurba and I occupied Camp 3 the following day just as another blizzard set in. A three-hundred-metre mixed face rises above the camp to a prominent shoulder at 6550m and forms the technical crux of Kamet, a climb of *assez difficile* standard where ropes are usually fixed. When the storm abated I went out on my own and broke trail to the foot of the face. Judging the face to be dangerously loaded with fresh windslab I turned tail, but my gesture galvanised Thukpa and Phurba, who had lazed through the morning incanting prayers and clipping their toe-nails. My initiative had pricked their conscience. They immediately loaded up sacks of fixed ropes and headed up my tracks. I warned them not to go on to the face, but they pushed on regardless. The next time I looked out of my tent they were perched motionless sixty metres up, alongside the crown-wall of a fresh slab avalanche. Thankfully they took the hint and returned to camp.

The following morning was brilliantly clear. We should perhaps have obeyed the twenty-four-hour rule[2] and left the snow to settle another day, but progress was needed. I led out our first rope, moving gingerly past the slab fracture-line and up to the security of a rock wall. Traversing up and right I gained a narrow balcony of snow, where old ropes were visible. In the lead I could be sure that strong anchors were placed but the Sherpas felt that this should be their task. Thukpa led through and fixed our lines eighty metres across the balcony and up a ramp. The route was tenuous and gave an exposed but simple passage to a headwall of steep snow. We decided to leave this open final slope alone for another day for fear of avalanche. After six hours of upward push we descended our three-hundred-metre line of ropes in just forty-five minutes. Meanwhile the rest of the team had arrived at Camp 3 and the next day John Lyall and Thukpa successfully anchored the final rope on the levelling which would become Camp 4.

We now had more bodies than tents at Camp 3. Rock had given up the game and descended back to Camp 2. The onset of another storm was particularly ill-timed. We were pinned in our tents for the next thirty-six hours. Steve and Tom became respectively petulant and despondent, squashed with John and I in a tent designed for three. With the aid of his pee bottle John completed a full twenty-four hours without leaving the tent. Fearing further defections I got up and stalked about camp every few hours trying to rally the troops. Having sold this trip as an achievable objective my conscience was stretched at this juncture and I exerted all my persuasive powers to convince Tom to go on. When the skies cleared on 31 May we had just a week left to make the summit. To our surprise Hartmut dropped out. Perhaps his trials on Everest were too-well remembered.

For the first time the high-level winds fell light. On 1 June we made the move to Camp 4 at 6550m. Kamet's final dome lay just a kilometre away across the gulf of her 2000m South-East Face, but the nearby corpse of an Indian soldier leant the campsite a macabre ambience. Dawn on the 2nd revealed a stunning vista of the peaks of Kumaon and western Nepal and we set off up the glacier ramp towards Meade's Col. Within an hour James complained of tightness in his chest and turned back, leaving us with five climbers, two guides and our three Sherpas who ploughed up the ramp in deep fresh snow. The only technical difficulty was a 40° ice slope where we prusiked up old sections of fixed rope. At 4.00 pm we sited Camp 5 at 7080m under Kamet's upper east face just short of Meade's Col. Scanning the vast blanket of fresh snow clothing the face I realised that tough trail-breaking would be required, yet the route looked technically simple. Surely a summit climb of just 670m was not beyond us? Our Sherpas, however, thought otherwise. They had been here before with Indian Air Force and Navy teams. On those occasions they had climbed diagonally rightwards to gain the arête bounding the snow face on the right, known to them as Chinese Ridge as it demarcates the Tibetan border.

Neil, Mike, John and I squeezed into the largest tent. Claudia, Tom and Steve were next door and the Sherpas a couple of metres beyond. For three hours I coaxed our MSR kerosene stove, trying to rehydrate the team and fill bottles for the next day. As the temperature dropped condensation formed on the flysheet and the drips of water extinguished the stove every couple of minutes, filling the tent porch with noxious fumes. Finally my temper snapped and, swearing loudly, I switched power to the feeble flame of our gas stove.

All through the night the tent flysheets flapped violently in a gusting breeze. We had hoped to get started before dawn but could do little until the sun rose and the wind dropped. The Sherpas were adamant that we should take the Chinese Ridge. John and I feared it would be dangerously icy for an exhausted party. They felt it their right and duty to lead the route, but we held the direct responsibility for the safety of the team and I exerted my authority. Urgen and Phurba took the decision badly and offered no help with trail-breaking. Only Thukpa would share the lead.

In six hours we reached 7500m where the slope steepened. We had overtopped Kamet's closest competitor, 7355m Abi Gamin, and could look down on an uninterrupted view of the snaking glaciers and sandy foothills on the Tibetan flanks. In afternoon shadow the air temperature was close to −25°C. A major push was needed to get to the ridge bounding the left side of the face. I took over and gave my all to make a thigh-deep trench up the drifted slope. I reached the ridge at 3.20 pm, but there was no thinning of the snow.

As John took over the lead Neil turned back with Phurba. For twenty minutes John waded at a steepening, unable to progress. The remainder of the team became progressively colder. Tom slipped under the bulge and crashed down into me. Steve dropped a mitten and reported a loss of all feeling in his toes. Mike and Claudia looked drawn and wasted. The final cornice winked defiance. With just two hours of daylight left we needed to get off the mountain with all speed. Whatever the coming torments of regret, only survival mattered here. We turned tail at 7650m, just one hundred metres short of the top.

In the steely chill of evening we ploughed down our tracks, staggering from side to side. Some of the team could barely stay upright. We bundled into the tents on Meade's Col and began the process of melting water for drinks. Neil was gasping for breath and feared he had contracted pulmonary oedema. I administered a cocktail of Diamox and Nifedipine and prayed he would recover. Bereft of other treatments team doctor Mike felt his best recourse was to recite Psalm 23, and then Psalm 121 . . .

I will lift mine eyes up to the hills, from whence cometh my help. My help cometh from the Lord, which made heaven and earth . . .

We were hardly reassured! From their tent Tom and Steve reported frostbite damage to both toes and fingers. After four hours everyone had been supplied with two warm drinks. I turned off the stove and crashed into glorious oblivion for eight hours.

Morning brought bright sunshine and a revival in Neil's condition. Our sole imperative was to get down to Camp 2 in a single day. As we set off I took a last poignant look at the simple slopes of Kamet's crown.

The descent to Camp 4 was torrid. Baked by sunlight and befuddled by altitude it took massive concentration to make downhill steps. At the icy step the team was so shaky that John and I lowered everyone down on an eighty-metre top-rope. Yet once we reached the top of the fixed ropes our energies recovered. The ropes gave a sure passage to the lower slopes. Without them we could not have coped. Coming down last I asked Thukpa and Urgen if they could strip some of the lines. I helped as best I could, but these Darjeeling boys took my request to heart. They removed every fixed rope plus several pegs and nuts and ambled down to the plateau of Camp 3 with loads of over twenty-five kilograms! If only they had pulled together in a similar fashion on the summit day.

Descending the gorge back to Camp 2 I watched enthralled as the evening mists played across the great north-east face of Mana Peak. The beauty of the scene would have been so sweet had we shouldered success, but instead it was tinged with the ache of sadness and the weight of a heavy pack. At Camp 2 our Nepali cook Saroj welcomed us with sweet tea and noodle soup, and we breathed thick healthy air once more.

In the morning an examination of Tom and Steve's toes revealed significant frost damage[3]. If they allowed their feet to thaw they would be unable to walk out. Bravely, they headed straight down to base camp while others shared their loads. A painful journey and long spell of treatment lay ahead. My heart ached with a sense of responsibility, but after so many trials and traumas one simple fact remained. We had gone two weeks too early. Whatever we felt we deserved, I'm afraid that big mountains don't play by emotional logic.

Five of us stayed a day at Camp 2, clearing and packing for the final pull-out. On 6 June, a morning of ethereal mist and pleasant chill, I viewed Kamet for the last time as we trekked round the bend of the glacier. She reared her unblemished pyramid above the tendrils of fog, proving that by any measure of God's earthly wonders, she had been worthy of our efforts.

Notes

1. The film rolls were discovered in tobacco tins in a house in Blackpool and were published by Blackpool and Fylde College *The Ice Soldiers* (2002).
2. A basic rule of avalanche avoidance is to stay off slopes for twenty-four hours after a major snowfall.
3. Significant tissue damage and deeper frostbite to the first and second toes was incurred, resulting in two amputations of terminal toe phalanxes.

Chapter 26

EAST OF NANDA

There are few treasures of more lasting worth than the experiences of a way of life that is wholly satisfying. Such are the only possessions of which no fate or cosmic catastrophe can deprive us; nothing can alter that fact if for one moment in eternity we have really lived.

Eric Shipton (*Upon that Mountain*)

At 1.00 am we zipped the tents of Camp I, shouldered our loads and traversed to the base of the couloir. A thousand vertical metres above us lay the narrow notch known as Longstaff's Col. For four hours we inched our way up ribbed and fluted snow slopes in a succession of zigzags, bowed under eighteen kilogram loads. Dawn caught us just over halfway up. The first flush of sunlight was welcome but in the coming hours the couloir would become first a cauldron and then an avalanche chute. Our porters had to get down before the avalanches commenced. Rob and I swapped leads with increasing regularity as we encountered soft drifts. The angle crept up to 50°. When it seemed inevitable that the porters would have to dump their loads and return, a fog fortuitously rolled in, cooled the air and saved the crisis. At 10.00 am we staggered up the final metres to the 5910m col. Burning radiation filtered through the soup of cloud. Mangal and Heera dropped their loads and turned tail while there was time to safely descend, and we slumped in enervation.

To our dismay the col was a knife-edge. The thought of camping here initially induced terror. Preliminary probing revealed hard ice half a metre down. How could we hope to get two tents securely lodged? The orange turret of the first pinnacle soared a hundred metres above and mocked our dithering. The mountain's twin peaks basked in the sun a couple of miles away. Welcome to the domain of the Goddess Nanda[1].

Although Rob Jarvis and I felt ourselves to be at a cutting edge of our profession by taking four clients to such a wild place, mountain guiding in the Himalayas is nothing new. Indeed, in 1905 Tom Longstaff took his Swiss guides Alexis and Henri Brocherel out to India and climbed to this same spot in search of a route into the Sanctuary of Nanda Devi. They too faced the challenge of lodging a tent. Their hopes of finding an easy passage down into the Sanctuary on the west side of the col were dashed at the sight of long ice slopes, but they climbed on to the pinnacled ridge that rose towards the 7434m eastern summit of Nanda Devi. Longstaff was confident this could be climbed if supplied with a few days' worth of food and fuel, but lacking resources they retreated, so ending the first remarkable foray on one of the world's great mountains.

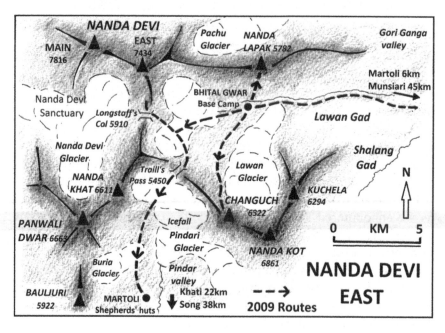

Two years later Longstaff tried to get into the Sanctuary from the west up the formidable Rishi Gorge, but was beaten back. Instead, he ascended Trisul on the Sanctuary's outer rim, the first proven ascent of a 7000m peak. After Shipton and Tilman found a way up the Rishi in 1934, Tilman returned with a joint British-American team in 1936 and ascended Nanda Devi's 7816m main peak with Noel Odell. Tilman recorded their summit moments with typical self-restraint:

I believe we so much forgot ourselves as to shake hands on it.

Nanda Devi East was a tougher proposition despite its lesser height. Four young Polish climbers came in 1939 and eclipsed Tilman's achievement by completing the route from Longstaff's Col. This was much the hardest ascent achieved in the Himalaya before the Second World War. Their success had a tragic aftermath. Two of the team were later killed in an avalanche while attempting Tirsuli peak, and the others found their return to Poland barred by the outbreak of war. Jakub Bujak never saw his family again. He joined the RAF and died in unexplained circumstances while climbing on Cornish sea-cliffs in 1945.

Nanda Devi East received a second ascent in 1951 by a French team which included Sherpa Tenzing Norgay. Although his world-renown came with Everest, Tenzing later recalled that Nanda Devi was much the hardest climb of his career. Subsequent ascents were few. All required extensive fixed-roping along the initial pinnacled crest to 6500m^2. Our plan was to do the same, but without a secure camp on the col we could not hope to progress.

We roused ourselves and began chipping at the ice to fashion platforms. By early afternoon the tents were pitched, with guy-lines anchored to snow stakes on either side of the ridge, lodgings of a sort so long as the wind didn't blow. Leon Winchester and I took the smaller bivouac tent while Rob, Jim Finnie and Paul Guest occupied the larger site four metres away. Cocooned in my sleeping bag with a brew of tea to hand, the place began to feel vaguely domestic.

In the evening the clouds thinned and the air sharpened so that we could look down into the Sanctuary. A vast meltwater lake has developed at 5000m altitude at the foot of Nanda Devi main peak, a totemic sign of global warming. From there the South Ridge of Nanda rose in an unbroken sweep of nearly three thousand metres. The setting sun burned through a sea of boiling cloud lower in the basin and the silent snow queens of Devtoli and Trisul lined the further horizon. The scene was more alluring in the knowledge that this has been forbidden country since closure of the Sanctuary in 1982. This was my dream domain and thus I fear it will remain as the years slip by.

Rob, Paul, Leon and I pushed our route over the first three pinnacles over the next two days. The splintered flagstones of rock were still thickly piled with winter snow, but a recent Polish expedition, led by Bujak's grandson, had fixed new lines[3]. The terrain was of alpine *difficile* in standard, the exposure sensational and the onward terrain lacked any obvious camping ledges. At midday on the second sortie Rob and I left Leon at a sheltered gap and climbed a rock step on to a hogsback of steep snow. Huge cornices forbade us to venture on the crest and we were forced on to the western flank where convex slopes slipped away into an abyss above the Nanda Devi Glacier. The fixed ropes ended and we kicked into ice under the rotten surface snow. A stream of unhappy conjectures filled my mind. We could never trust our porters to carry loads over this terrain. There was no prospect of an early camp. Only two out of our four clients were ready for this sort of challenge.

Rob Jarvis is a vibrant young guide and not given to wavers of conviction. I didn't want to show weakness but felt compelled to express my doubts.

"You know, I don't think this is going to go."

Immediately, he replied, "Funny you should say that; I was just thinking the same thing myself!"

We turned a little short of 6100m. Back at the col we packed and stowed thirty-five kilograms of surplus kit for later collection. As soon as the couloir was chilling in shade we set off down. Our first steps sheared a big slab of surface ice-crystals which funnelled down the gully with an alarming hiss. We followed the avalanche trail, but the underlying snow was icy and Jim was nursing an injured knee. Facing into the slope, each step took him several kicks and progress was achingly slow. An hour after dark I suggested that he simply sat on the slope and slid while I reined him from above on a short rope. My knees strained to the point of buckling as I manipulated this sledge ride to the foot of the slope. A half-moon glimmered through the cloud as we limped back to camp. There are times when one must accept that a mountain is beyond one's powers.

I might not have renounced Nanda Devi East so emphatically had I not divined alternative objectives. Spared the stress of the siege we could now be freebooters in the Goddess's back garden. South of our base camp in the Lawan valley lay one of the last major unclimbed peaks in Kumaon Himalaya, 6322m Changuch. The mountain had rebuffed three attempts from the southern Pindari flanks. Changuch displayed a series of sharp gable-edges along her north-west ridge which rose to a pristine summit point. Not only did we deem Changuch highly desirable but when we spied a route up the north face to reach a shoulder on the ridge we felt a delicious sense of broaching the possible.

The feasibility of switching objective depended on the disposition of our Liaison Officer. Happily, the Indian Mountaineering Foundation was no longer assigning officious military men to this role and instead was giving keen civilian mountaineers a chance to shine. Our LO was an enthusiastic youth from Kullu called Ludar Singh. On first introduction he stated:

"Martin, from now on you are my guru; wherever you go I will follow."

With the promise that he could follow me up Changuch, Ludar was quickly persuaded to the change of plan. John Venier and Jim Finnie were struggling with acclimatisation and injury and decided to go home early, leaving a team of five, Liverpudlian Leon, pig-famer Paul Guest, Rob, Ludar and me. We quickly gelled and styled ourselves fancifully as "the famous five".

Before we could tackle Changuch a thorny problem reared its head – our pile of kit up on Longstaff's Col. As leader I could have delegated the task of retrieval, but the fair solution was to draw lots. I got the short straw, and while Rob surveyed the defences of Changuch I commenced a gruelling nightshift with high-altitude porter Heera Singh. Five hours into our climb, balanced on the ice slope a hundred metres under the col, Heera reported that he had lost a crampon. I had only brought a fifteen-metre length of rope, so could not lower him. We were stranded. Praying for a stroke of fortune I climbed down past him and scanned the slope. There, twenty metres lower, lay the missing crampon.

At midnight we reached the col and spent an hour loading our sacks to weights close to twenty kilograms. I struggled to stand up. Heera is a hardy chap, unflinching in every situation we'd encountered in eleven years of expeditions together; but when he got to his feet and I motioned him towards the 50° headwall of the couloir, he gave me a wide-eyed look of horror.

"Sir, load is too heavy."

His confidence was shot and neither he nor I trusted his ill-fitting crampons. Holding the rope tight, I coaxed him to face in and try the crucial first steps. The alternative was to jettison his sack and search for the pieces a thousand metres lower. For three hours we crept down the slope until the silhouette of the Tibetan border ranges had taken shape against the lightening sky. Desperate to avoid the heat of the rising sun I pleaded with Heera to try facing outwards. Gradually, his confidence returned and his crampons stayed on. Fifteen hours after departing we returned to base camp in time for breakfast. Longstaff's Col was abandoned without regret.

In the night of 6 June Rob, Leon and Paul attacked the face and ramp which gave access to the Changuch ridge. They climbed a steep gully then hopped over a succession of avalanche runnels in a leftward diagonal ascent of five hundred metres to gain the ridge. Meanwhile, Ludar waited eagerly for me to recover from my escapade on the col. Stuck all day in a sun-baked camp at 5000m, a stultifying torpor plagued my spirits. We set off at nightfall and immediately my fatigue and demoralisation evaporated. I felt motivated and happy again, and was buoyed by the infectious charm of Ludar, who responded with a competent display of crampon-work. Life is simple and fulfilling once commitment is made. We reached the ridge at 2.15 am to find the team's two bivouac tents perched on tiny platforms. Ludar squeezed in with Rob while I built a bed of flat slates and bivouacked outside.

We decided to rest a day and tackle the six-hundred-metre summit climb the following night. I stretched out in the morning sun, alternately browsing Huxley's *Brave New World* and savouring the panorama of the Pindari peaks. Our virgin ridge rose above in three angular steps. This was the Himalaya at their sublime best.

Just after midday, cumulus clouds rose in sudden fury to envelop us in a blizzard. I dived into my bivouac sack and commenced a claustrophobic afternoon. Several inches of snow built up around my couch and an insidious chill seeped through my layers. At nightfall a bitter cold replaced the storm. Rob sounded reveille at 11.00 pm and we left at half past midnight. At once I realised that I was stubbornly cold. The initial ridge of mixed rocks failed to boost my circulation. I couldn't move fast enough to regenerate body heat and burning pain engulfed both hands. This was not the brief sting of hot-aches, but the start of a grim unending torment. I calculated five hours to sunrise.

Leaving the security of rocks we made an unprotected traverse of steep snow and ice slopes. Rob and Leon went ahead, while I followed, tied close to Ludar and Paul. With relief I reached Rob's ice screw belay at the end of the traverse. Rob then led up five long pitches to gain the next levelling of the arête. The purple tinge of dawn smudged the eastern skyline, and, six miles to our north, Nanda Devi's twin peaks emerged from slumber, first in ghostly white raiment, then in a crescendo of rosy splendour. Even in the throes of suffering I was struck to reverential awe. On the west side of the ridge we faced a longer wait for the sun's caress. Alternately, I stuffed my bare hands in my armpits then beat them together to stimulate some blood flow and save my fingers from frostbite.

Rob balanced across an elegant corniced edge towards the third and final rise, his silhouette etched between brilliant white snows and dark shadow. At 8.00 am we reached the summit crest and at last could enjoy the sun's blessing. My torture was over. The summit lay thirty metres along a slender arête perched on a rocky turret. We took turns to traverse out and claim our prize.

Four hours later as we regained our tents on the shoulder, the daily blizzard commenced. I squeezed in with Rob and Ludar. The single-skin tent was the size of a dog kennel. We sat with knees stuffed under our chins until I was seized by violent thigh cramps. Only by unzipping the tent door and standing upright could I gain any relief. The snow poured in and the tent became a squalid mess of split food bags, soggy sleeping bags and slush. Unless we moved that evening we would be trapped for another day. New snow was blowing over the ridge, creating the risk of windslab avalanche on our descent route.

Come 6.00 pm the snowfall abated and we made our move. We dug out the frozen tents, and, from used "poo-bags" to tent pegs, we stripped the site. I tied our two sixty-metre ropes together and belayed the team as they climbed down to the slopes. Once Rob had established ice-axe anchors in the snow I dropped the rope and soloed down. There was no point tying on. Had I fallen from above while roped I would have pulled the whole party off the face. Rob dug a test snow-pit and pronounced the slope safe for the descent back to the entry couloir. At 11.00 pm we quit the face and walked into a phantasmagorical moonlit world. Billions of fresh snow crystals glistened on the surface while fathomless shadows plunged into every hollow. We traversed dreamlike across curvaceous mounds of pristine powder, our silhouettes marching a hundred metres ahead of us towards the lonely black dot of our tent, and arrived, victorious, a little after midnight.

Four days later at 2.45 am I was jarred out of slumber as my alarm rang. We were on the move again. Why waste the last week of the trip in languor? A legendary glacial col links the Lawan and Pindari valleys. Traill's Pass was first explored in 1830 under the direction of Kumaon's British Commissioner, George William Traill. Due to glacial retreat the route fell in disuse in the twentieth century and the last-known crossing was made in 1994. The prospect of a Shipton-ian mission to force the route and walk out of the mountains by a different valley was enticing. The "famous five" duly assembled in the mess tent for porridge and pancakes and embarked in pre-dawn fog at 4.00 am. Forty square miles of empty wilderness lay between us and the Pindari trailhead. I considered the thousands who, at that moment, were clogging the arteries of Nepal's Khumbu valley, and toiling in file on Island Peak or Everest, and thought ourselves the luckier. After three hours of meandering in moraines we found a steep snow gully, which led us to the northern end of the pass at 5312m.

A level glacier stretched three kilometres to the brink of the great icefall above the Pindari valley. We set camp and readied ourselves for the commitment of the crossing. Paul and Leon were wonderful companions, solid in every situation, but after four weeks in the field personal idiosyncrasies can grate. Whenever I passed Leon a brew he would slurp contentedly and pronounce:

"That really hits the spot".

Tiring of this Scouse banality, I implored him to think of some-thing else to say. When the next brew was handed over he paused a moment and declared:

"That's really spot on, mate."

There was no point in further argument.

We stirred in shock at 3.30 am, two hours behind our scheduled alarm call. Initially, fog shrouded the plateau. We set compasses at 220° and immediately hit crusted snow. At every step our feet detached pancakes of sun crust which slowly sank into underlying mush. An oppressive lethargy dogged our progress. Even Ludar lost his habitual bounce. Long mountain experience has taught me that all things must pass, but this stretch probed the limits of our resolve while taking us into a no-man's-land, from which retreat would be problematic. After three hours we reached a rock spur at 5450m under which the Pindari Glacier commenced its 1600m downward plunge.

The morning sun burned with cruel intensity. Clouds were boiling on the Pindar flank. In mid-June valley temperatures regularly exceed 30°C by day. Vicious thunderstorms are inevitable. Knowing the Pindari icefall to be impassable we sought a route down its western flanks. Time was of the essence, but of necessity we brewed a drink of hot lemon squash before we moved on. A 55° ice gully dropped off the spur and we descended in four pitches of down-climbing to gain a glacier shelf, where we met the rising storm-clouds. Growls of thunder reverberated in the valley and light snowfall commenced. We ploughed down the shelf in hope of a quick solution while visibility lasted, but became stranded at the brink of a band of vegetated cliffs. A diagonal snow gully cut down the face into the mist and offered the only possibility of progress. Though we couldn't see the bottom we had to take our chance. I scouted ahead while Rob short-roped Leon, Paul and Ludar behind. The gully debouched in a near-vertical wall of muddy shelves devoid of any solid rock for a belay.

Wearing crampons I threaded a zigzag route down overlapping turfs and landed on gravel moraine in a blizzard of wet snowflakes. Our altitude was 4800m. We still had a thousand metres to go. The snout of a substantial side glacier now blocked our passage. Shrinkage of the glacier had left a desolation of boulder-fields and ice craters. We straggled across, probing several blind alleys before a passage was granted.

On the far side a grassy ramp dropped teasingly towards the valley but the fog cut any downward view. Though we yearned to be down on the Pindari pastures, we knew that a blind descent could trap us on the vertical walls of moraine bounding the main glacier.

Instead, I suggested we climb over the adjoining ridge in search of shepherds' tracks. With a silence that spoke of heavy hearts the team obeyed and we trudged uphill for 120m to meet an abrupt arête. Vertiginous grass slopes covered in wet snow dropped down the far side.

With Rob scanning the ground and shouting directions I traversed off the arête into the next couloir and scrambled eighty metres down a water-worn gully which ended at an overhang within a slide and a jump of grass slopes. Again I demurred. Not so much as a sprained ankle could be risked here. With patience close to snapping I scrambled back and Rob called me over to an easier alternative route. As the others followed, the clouds cleared revealing rich green pastures and shepherds' huts in the valley some six hundred metres below. Simultaneously we chanced on a genuine path, which lent us new vigour. We bundled downhill for 200m, but the cloud curtain closed once more and, in our haste, we lost the trail at the rim of another cliff band. By now we were beyond any thought of re-ascent.

We traversed until a ramp of tangled shrubs and wet slabs led diagonally towards a canyon. There could be no turning back, and at last God showed mercy. At 6.00 pm, after thirteen hours on our feet, we stood in the stony bed of the gully at 3800m altitude, with nought but a shrubbery between us and the Pindari meadows. We plodded down gratefully to flats of close-cropped grass, criss-crossed by a myriad of freshwater streams. A dozen horses with their foals grazed nearby and our nostrils filled with the pungent scents of sheep dung and wood-smoke.

While we brewed tea Ludar disappeared to the shepherds' huts and procured an invitation to dinner. Night fell and a dense canopy of stars delineated the bounding walls of the valley as we squeezed into the cosy hearth of shepherd Amar Singh's summer home. After a month on high hills we could at last savour the joy of the journey's ending[4].

Notes

1. Nanda Devi, the bliss-giving Goddess, is the presiding deity of the peoples of Kumaon and Garhwal, which collectively form Uttarakhand state.
2. In 1994 British guides Julie-Ann Clyma and Roger Payne made an alpine-style ascent. They benefited from the ropes put in place by other expeditions operating concurrently on the peak, but this was still a remarkable achievement.
3. The 2009 Polish expedition celebrated the seventieth anniversary of the first ascent of Nanda Devi East. Despite taking a very strong team they encountered heavy snow conditions and failed at 6900m.
4. Paul Guest died in a fall from Zero Gully on Ben Nevis in February 2012.

Chapter 27

A WALK INTO NOWHERE

*Is this the summit, crowning the day? How cool and quiet! Have we
vanquished an enemy? None but ourselves. Have we gained success?
That word means nothing here. Have we won a kingdom? No and yes.
We have achieved an ultimate satisfaction ... fulfilled a destiny ... To
struggle and to understand – never this last without the other ... such
is the law.*

George Leigh Mallory

Afternoon shadows lengthened across the dusty main street of
Udaipur town. A tractor rumbled through the bazaar, its exhaust
belching black clouds of diesel residues. Groups of girls, with their
hair neatly plaited and gaily dressed in sky-blue pinafores and cardi-
gans, walked home from school. Groups of old woman, wrapped in
shawls, squatted on verandahs and gossiped. The wizened *chowkidar*
sat outside the hotel, thumbing through his duplicate book of Form
Cs, the much-cursed registration document that every foreign tourist
must complete on check-in. In the ancient Marikula Mata temple[1]
our *puja* blessing was in progress. Mr Pandey joined in via mobile
phone link from Delhi, and the priest's devotions were relayed with
an accompaniment of ear-splitting static on the outside speaker
system. On either side of the enclosing walls of the Chandra Bhaga
valley snowy peaks of 6000m glowed pink in the declining rays of
the sun. We were at the threshold of another Himalayan venture in a
happy state of prescient anticipation.

We had come to Himachal Pradesh state, and to the region of Lahaul,
a vast tract of high mountains split by a striking valley trench ninety
kilometres in length, the Miyar Nala. Our aim was to follow the
Miyar from Udaipur up into the borderland peaks of Zanskar and

Kishtwar, and make a circuit of three difficult five-thousand-metre passes, exiting back to Lahaul down the Sural valley, a distance we estimated at 150km. I had thrown in the lure of making an unofficial attempt on one of the dozens of unclimbed six-thousand-metre peaks that were reputed to lie along these divides. To simplify logistics and add a twist to the challenge, we planned to dispense with porters on the Miyar Glacier and spend fourteen days behind the ranges with only a cook, Sherpa and two high-altitude porters for support.

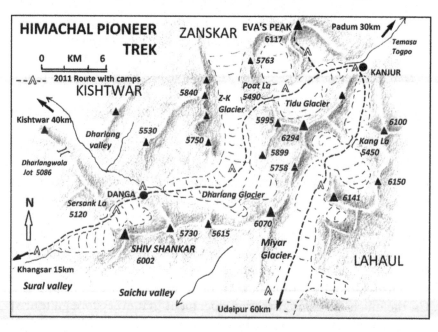

Counting back, this was the thirtieth Himalayan trip I had organised and I had led eighteen of them. As usual I fretted over the devil's bargain that must be struck between adventure, service and profit on a commercial expedition. Our clients, asked to shell out the better part of £4000 to join our trip, might expect better facilities than those offered by the filthy Amandeep Hotel, and the onward schedule offered a high probability of slow starvation in the outback. Yet without the wilful severance of the umbilical cord what would they gain? I shouldered the burden of their trust.

For four days we ambled happily through bucolic villages and fields in the lower valley and then strode along open alluvial shelves of cropped grass. At the Miyar Glacier snout the terrain abruptly changed. The glacier squeezes through a valley so narrow that there are no lateral moraine crests to offer easier walking. The lower glacier is steadily sinking and the monsoon floods of 2010 had triggered countless rockslides and avalanches on the sidewalls. We spent much of the day picking our way through fresh rock debris.

Our sixteen porters, variously clad in flip-flops or plimsolls, were strung out over a wilderness of scree-coated ice moraines. They were all from Nepal. Their daily wage for carrying a twenty-five-kilogram burden was 350 rupees, a touch short of £5, and that was before the *sirdar* Sham Singh took his cut. Every Himalayan expedition is morally compromised by the portering contract, which is a good example of Ruskin's principle of unequal exchange whereby *one man is able to give what cost him little labour in return for what has cost the other much*. Our seven team members each managed around fifteen kilograms, enough to salve the conscience while nurturing gradual acclimatisation. One porter, flamboyantly dressed in a turquoise jacket and matching hat of brushed wool, clutched an empty bottle of Red Knight whisky. He was an exception. Gambling, not alcohol, is the main vice of these porter bands. For some a large slice of their season's earnings would be dissipated before they got home to their families.

At 4400m we reached a highway of smooth dry glacier and made a chilly camp, ready to start the final push to the 5450m pass of Kang La. Only fifteen porters turned out next morning to make a last carry for us, the whisky *wallah* having been floored by a headache. We initially made steady progress past a succession of hanging glaciers and chiselled granite walls, but the pace flagged against a chilling breeze. The porters were cold and had to return that evening. Although we had hoped they would dump loads just under the pass, we were forced to stop four kilometres short at 5060m on a bleak and clouded afternoon.

From here we would be on our own. My co-leader Robin Thomas and I had already demanded major economies of food and equipment, but now a selection of kit and food was spread out far in excess of our carrying capacities. In half an hour the surplus had to sorted, packed and sent down. If we misjudged we could face severe malnutrition over the next two weeks or else be doomed to fail under crippling loads. Our mess tent was replaced by a large nylon "tarp" to string from boulders. Cook Saran would not be parted from either of his two kerosene stoves, but some pans and serving dishes were prised from his grasp. Sherpa Thukpa looked crestfallen when we removed dozens of tin cans from the onward stockpile. Our Indian high-altitude porters, Govind and Mangal, fought bravely to hold on to their bags of potatoes and vegetables. Had these Westerners gone mad? This behaviour was far removed from the indulgent norms of the expedition business!

Our team members were not spared. Zoom lenses were traded against down clothing. Some, fearful of spending two weeks in plastic boots, hid sturdy trekking shoes under their flysheets. The merits of a Kindle over paperbacks were hotly debated. The team whisky was ceremoniously decanted into Sigg bottles. When night settled we were leaner in weight and, at last, committed. I sensed the joy of freedom and slept in peace.

On most expeditions there is one member who works in a different time zone to everyone else. Gustavo, an Ecuadorian living in Texas, was our laggard. He pitched up late for every meal, walked at a slower pace and simply loved being in mountains rather than working towards deadlines. He was allowed to carry a lighter load and garnered more assistance from our staff than the more agile members, who, inevitably, began to harbour a slight resentment. Gustavo had been the last to book the trip and, effectively, his fee was my profit for the journey. I was inclined to be tolerant.

The sun had not long risen over the Kang La before he was hanging down a crevasse. In a dry year the Kang La is clear of snow in summer and trekking parties cross without a rope, but a heavy monsoon had laid a foot of fresh snow on the upper glacier. Our loads weighed close to twenty-five kilograms. The crevasses were narrow, but Gustavo missed a jump and slithered three metres down a slot. I placed an ice screw anchor in the underlying ice, and rigged up a Z-pulley system. After a couple of metres hoisting, I needed a rest so we relaxed our grip, expecting my Ropeman[2] back-up clamp to take the load. Alarmingly, the rope kept slipping. Gustavo screamed "I'm going down!" and disappeared from view. Only then did I realise that I had put the Ropeman on the wrong way round! We grabbed the rope and, after frantic rearrangement of the clamp, established upward movement once more.

Kang La was a wild spot, unadorned except for the upturned carcass of a bharal sheep. The pass lies on the watershed of the Greater Himalayan Range and we looked north into a domain both arid and savage. This was the fabled land of Zanskar. Among a cluster of skeletal rock peaks a stately snow queen sailed on the horizon. Under her summit diadem, an ice nose and curving glacier shelf made an elegant robe and train. She stood fifteen kilometres away across the Tidu valley and possessed the imperious looks of a 6000er. There was no way that we could walk past her.

Two nights later seven of us were bivouacked at 5000m on open gravel flats under her glacier snout. We had expended significant reserves of energy and willpower to ascend a 500m boulder-chute up from the Tidu Glacier the previous afternoon. The night temperature was around –10°C and we were condemned to rise at midnight. Robin emerged with a fever, shivering and coughing gobs of phlegm. He could barely stand, still less climb a mountain, and, while we dressed, he wrapped himself in extra sleeping bags to better survive the remaining six hours of night.

Without a moon to guide us we navigated by intuition and vague awareness of a silhouette of rock spires against the star-filled sky. A lilac dawn found us up amongst the waves of the glacier shelf exactly where we had planned. In distant views the hanging ice nose halfway up the face promised an unpredictable crux to our route. Only now, as it emerged from the shadows three hundred metres above, could we discover our fate, and there was a route, straight up a runnel in its crest.

As we approached the nose Gary markedly slowed. He had suffered severe nausea on a training climb in the Alps and knew that he was susceptible to acute mountain sickness. We could take no risks of a recurrence. The rules of safe glacier travel prescribed that someone else descend on a rope with him, but the other four had invested much in this climb. I judged that the snow on the glacier was firm enough to allow a safe solo retreat, so long as Gary kept strictly to our tracks of ascent.

With Gary wandering *sans corde* down the glacier and Robin stricken with fever at its base, I pondered the scenario of a rescue. We were a thousand metres above and six kilometres from the camp where Gustavo and our support crew waited. The Tidu valley was otherwise deserted. The nearest road-head was close to Padum, thirty kilometres to our north, and from there any victim could look forward to a twenty-four hour jeep ride to hospital in Kargil or Leh, followed by a flight back to Delhi. It would definitely be preferable if nobody got seriously ill or injured.

On my rope I had the pleasure of re-acquaintance with Allan Isherwood, with whom I had shared a traverse of the Grépon four years previously, and David King, a fast-learning novice. Steve Birch and Mike Timar formed their own rope, following our line and using our ice screws. We pitched up the 60° ice nose and gained an easement. As the sun built some power the frozen crust started to give way and our rhythm was destroyed, but as the slope steepened again we found that by flexing our feet sideways we could spread our weight and stay afloat. The angle increased to 50° and I led a long pitch on fragile fibrillations of snow to gain the summit ridge.

The panoply of peaks on the southern horizon included dozens of impressive 6000ers along the Himalayan watershed that have barely been identified still less explored. Now we could see to the north and west over rocky castellations and high white glaciers towards Kishtwar. With a huge cornice to the north and with a pitch of brick-hard ice on the south flank the final ridge proved delicate. Steve and Mike followed. They probably knew as well as I that there was little hope of holding a slip on the ice. We gained a crowning protuberance of snow at 11.20 am and measured our height at 6119m. I suggested that we call the mountain Eva's Peak, after Mike's baby daughter.

The crux of our descent came at the ice nose. We arranged a fifty-metre abseil and while I fixed an ice thread, all of us hung suspended from a single back-up screw. The other four dozed off while I fumbled hopelessly to thread misaligned holes. Eventually a stack of five abseil plates was rigged and we made our escape. Robin and Gary had waited back at the bivouac. The others opted for a second night on a gravel bed while I pushed back down the boulder gully and into the dark in search of *rajma* stew and tented lodgings.

Twelve hours later the team was reunited and huddled on a draughty medial moraine on the Tidu Glacier. Yesterday's fatigue still lay heavy in our muscles when Allan dropped his bombshell.

"I don't know where I left them, but they must be up there somewhere."

He had lost his crampons up on Eva's Peak, and hung his head in abject shame.

"I simply don't believe it, Allan!" I fulminated with frustration. There are occasions when feigned patience is misplaced, and it is best to clear the air.

We still had two ice passes, Poat La and Sersank La, and twenty kilometres of glacier to cross, a little far for chopping steps. Within a couple of minutes my mood calmed from outrage to grim acceptance of the predicament.

"I'll have to go back up and look; I'm the only one who can remember the route."

While the others headed up to set a high camp under Poat La I turned back towards Eva's Peak and bowed my body to repeat the slog up the stone couloir. Finding nothing at the bivouac site I continued up to the glacier snout at 5200m. The search was fruitless. Rueing the waste of four hours of precious energy, I returned to the Tidu Glacier. Our next camp was four kilometres uphill. Afternoon clouds boiled over the glacier and I set off at a vapid plod. I had nothing left to give. After thirty minutes the lanky silhouette of Mangal appeared out of the mists.

"Sir, please give me load. I have given Allan spare crampons." I stopped in astonishment. Despite my orders to dispense with surplus kit before Kang La, Mangal had smuggled over an extra pair of ancient crampons with leather straps, as if in divine premonition of this very fix. My efforts may have been wasted but our enterprise was saved.

At dawn the prayer flags adorning the 5490m crest of Poat La streamed horizontally in a bitter east wind. With this crossing we moved from Zanskar to Kishtwar district. A ramp cut down through vertical cliffs on the western flank. The onward march unfolded in grandiose fashion. We descended eight hundred metres to the Zanskar-Kanthang Glacier, an ice-stream of singular magnificence. A series of burnished rock peaks split by tumbling glaciers and icy couloirs filled its western walls. On the east side a fabulous prow of rock opened up, apparently holdless save for a single gigantic flake at half-height. A replica of the Matterhorn occupied the onward view. To our knowledge none of these had ever been named or attempted. Forgetting the strain of our twenty-kilogram loads we strode like lionhearts down the long incline of dry ice.

At 4500m the Z-K Glacier joined the Dharlang Glacier and swung westward. Our smooth promenade ended with entry into a labyrinth of stone moraines, just as the efforts of a ten-hour day sapped our reserves. The team became split and mutinous mutterings were voiced when I expressed a determination to push on to nightfall.

Even Thukpa was struggling under a load that was close to thirty kilograms. I forged on through the desert of rocks and dead ice hoping to find a grassy oasis for a camp. After two hours I gave up the search and stopped on a barren rocky glacis close by a glacier river. The team staggered in. Some made beds on top of flat boulders. Others dug out couches in the gravels. Immediately, our Indian team got to work, building a wall shelter and erecting our tarp. Within an hour Saran had cooked up soup and the dhalbhat was steaming in our pressure cooker. As the stress of the day receded, a slim new moon rose and we settled to a peaceful sleep under the stars.

We had five days in which to find and cross our third pass, Sersank La. The Dharlang valley was a trap, twisting northward for forty kilometres to the ethnically troubled towns of Kishtwar. The last party known to have attempted the Sersank icefall had turned back in face of "a near-vertical maze of 800–900 metres of extremely treacherous ground". The stakes were high.

Robin and I left at dawn and forged a route through the remaining miles of moraine. By midday we reached deserted grazings at 4000m at Danga. Round the corner lay the Sersank valley and the denouement of our adventure. We climbed on to a sharp lateral moraine and entered the jaws of the valley. The lower icefall had crumpled into a hopeless sea of overlapping ice towers. However, we spotted a ramp of screes and grass running up its right side above a rock band, which gave the sole chance of passage. Next morning we returned with Govind, Mangal and Thukpa, weaved an exposed line through the rock band and romped across the ramp. At its end we were forced on to the glacier above the lower fall. The crevasses were huge but we linked a series of snow bridges to gain a second icefall. We tackled this direct, fixed a rope, and then snaked through a crevasse field to a flattening at 4800m. The Sersank La came into view two kilometres away with no intervening obstacle other than a final shale wall. With a combination of luck and intuition we had found a way. Exhilarated, we dropped loads and hastened back to Danga to report the success.

Team spirits brightened at the news. Food supplies were running low, and Saran's cuisine had acquired a minimalist theme. Allan had barely eaten or spoken for a week since Eva's Peak and was absorbed in silent dreams of lamb chops and Lancashire hotpot. Gary was mid-way through a nine-kilogram weight loss, while Gustavo needed reassurance that he was capable of the Sersank climb. Even the Indians were glad to leave some kitchenware and surplus kerosene in a shepherds' cave, ready for the final push. By 4.00 pm on the following day we were all settled in a high camp under the pass. Though evening clouds threatened a change in the weather the night was bitterly cold. We packed in twilight and moved towards the pass in the shadow of the north wall of 6002m Shiv Shankar. Robin led a diagonal line up two pitches of 60° rubble and at 10.15 am on 6 October we reached the col. Our altitude was 5120m and to our south we looked down on the gentle folds of the Sural valley.

I watched Mike and Gary as they scanned the valley of our escape. Were they richly contented from the adventure, or merely thankful that its trials were soon to be over? Would they have preferred a porter caravan and a known objective? Through half a lifetime of guiding I had been convinced that my clients would always share my pleasure in discovery. Only now, as we stood at the threshold of fulfilment, did I feel doubt.

With another journey nearly done, I wondered if I would ever abandon my personal quest to cross new peaks and passes. Could I renounce my will and still find happiness? In truth, climbers pursue a path far removed from the spiritual ideal of abandonment of the self. They will happily read the *Bhagavad Gita*[3] at base camp and think themselves wiser, yet climb on regardless, seething with ambition, ever-driven towards fresh goals. The difficulty is that mountain travel is simply too enjoyable to relinquish without a fight. It would take real courage to jump off the carousel, but with age there will come a time when one has no choice.

The birch woods down the Sural valley glowed to autumnal rust; a day's march and we'd be down in green pastures, breathing the muggy air of lower climes and dreaming of home . . .

Notes

1. The temple is dedicated to the Pandavas and is thought to be 1400 years old, one of the earliest Hindu shrines in the Himalaya.
2. The Ropeman is a lightweight hinged clamp that provides an alternative to using a prusik cord. The Ropeman grips when loaded in one direction and slips when loaded in the other.
3. The sacred Hindu scripture, revered as the true source of spiritual knowledge.

Part Six

REFLECTIONS

Chapter 28

A JOB FOR LIFE

A few hours' mountain climbing make of a rogue and a saint two fairly equal creatures

Friedrich Nietzsche

Mountain climbing, in its finest guise, is a triumph of human spirit over the shackles of convention. It is spontaneous, thrilling, occasionally reckless, and it bucks the norms of society. The profession of mountain guiding introduces a strand of commercialism that can easily corrupt that ethos. As long ago as 1890 Mummery took a jaundiced view of guides:

> The constant repetition of the same ascent has tended to make the guide into a sort of contractor. For so many tens or hundreds of francs he will take you anywhere you would like to name. The skill of the traveller counts for absolutely naught; the practised guide looks on him merely as luggage.[1]

By Mummery's cynical yardstick, a client pays a guide solely to get to the top, and this base level of contract has been the tradition of guiding in the Alps. The daily summer bedlam on the Matterhorn exemplifies a guiding scene shorn of aesthetic sensibility. Heaven forbid that this bleak view should predominate in the public's perception of our profession. The true mountain guide offers companionship, the sharing of adventure, discovery of the natural world, the coaching of skills and the mastery of self-confidence, while generating an enormous amount of fun in the process.

When a client's ambition to succeed predominates to the exclusion of all else, the relationship with both guide and mountain is easily soured. Guiding relationships work best when conducted with mutual trust, patience and realism. I'll do everything in my power to help my regular clients reach their goals, because I know that they will forgive a failure.

Guiding needs the spark of ingenuity and the expression of individualism that makes real mountaineering so intoxicating. I'll gladly accept the accusation that I have used my job to pursue my personal satisfaction in the mountains, and indeed I have reaped rich rewards, but never have I treated my clients as baggage, neither on my thirtieth ascent of the Matterhorn nor my hundredth of the Inaccessible Pinnacle. I can vouch that most of my colleagues in the British guides' association profess a similar philosophy.

When I qualified in 1985 our IFMGA carnet was a passport to work in nearly every country of the world. Since then our profession has been squeezed by the insidious creep of protectionism and regulation. Every instinct of lawmakers and bureaucrats pushes us closer to the guiding style so abhorred by Mummery, and our individual powers of judgement and responsibility are progressively eroded. We are subjected to local laws telling us how many clients we can take on a route; we are required to acquire meaningless *cartes professionelles* if we want to take our clients on a trip into France; we are bullied and bamboozled by Indian *desk-wallahs*. The fear of legal action has stoked an industry in professional liability insurance and stalks our every step. All this makes it harder for us to pursue our passion with untrammelled joy and independence. We are lucky that, compared with many countries, the United Kingdom has retained a *laissez-faire* approach to mountain activities, and our civil court judges take the sane view that participation in mountaineering involves a wilful exposure to risk, irrespective of whether a guide is in charge of the party. Nevertheless, our profession faces a battle to preserve its freedom.

Few mountain guides are rich. Subjected to seasonal trade, the vagaries of the weather and the whims of their clientèle they face a yearly struggle to make ends meet. A guide must strike a compromise between scraping a conventional living while transmitting the spirit of an alternative lifestyle. Post-war climbing culture evolved as a rebellion against middle-class values, a challenge to a society that was increasingly risk-averse. The recent boom in outdoor activities has turned this process on its head, and it is now the middle-class who are spending their income in an addictive pursuit of mountain adventure. This trend is entirely healthy for the human condition and the mountain guide has a vital role to play in its expression. Ultimately, we are all bound by some sort of convention, but on the mountains our clients can taste of another plane of consciousness. We can lead them to a state of exalted exhaustion at the summit, and help them sense what Bill Murray described as *the evidence of things unseen.*

Of my many clients, I have most admired those who reveal their humanity through their climbing; the Munro-baggers who steal precious weekends to pursue their task; the friends who support each other's goals to the exclusion of their own; the alpinists who revel in climbing a snowy *facile* in the aftermath of a storm as much as a top-notch *grande course*; those who are enthralled to see new horizons; and all who sustain their sense of wonder in life through the hills.

William Blake had intuition of a later truth when he wrote:

> *Great things are done when men and mountains meet; this is not done by jostling in the street.*[2]

Mountains do bring out the best in people, and we can all descend to petty squabble and temptation if we are not inspired by the beauty of wild places or united in face of danger. Nonetheless, I have been endlessly inspired by the ingenuity, endurance and passion that drive the daily lives of my clients, and mountains are only one part of that. After thirty years of guiding people from most walks of life I am persuaded of the inherent decency and goodness of humanity.

Those who turn to the mountains find enlightenment through their experiences on higher ground. That truth is not in doubt, and what greater reward is there in a career than to have helped people make some sense of their lives?

Notes

1. *My Climbs in the Alps and Caucasus* p 111.
2. A gnomic verse written around 1793, seven years after modern mountaineering began with the first ascent of Mont Blanc.

Appendix I

GLOSSARY OF TECHNICAL TERMS AND CLIMBING GRADES

Technical Terms

Abseil Sliding descent of a rope, usually using a friction plate for control *(Ger)*

Aid-climbing Using placed or fixed metal anchors to make progress rather than the natural rock

Anchor Piece of hardware placed in rock, snow or ice and then used for security

Belay System of security protecting a moving climber; the belayer controls the feed of rope, usually by means of a friction plate, and is tied to one or more anchors

Bivouac Overnight lodging without overhead shelter

Bolt Metal anchor drilled into rock

Bosse Bulge of snow or ice *(Fr)*

Brèche Narrow gap *(Fr)*

Cam Rock protection device operated by two opposing sets of retractable metal cams; developed in early 1980s and bearing a variety of trade names (eg *Friends, Camalots*)

Dièdre Vertical rock corner or open-book groove *(Fr)*

Fixed rope Static rope left in place on a climb

Graupel White hail, a product of winter squall precipitation *(Ger)*

Harness Integrated webbing of waistbelt and leg loops, universally worn by modern climbers, providing equalised energy absorption in event of a fall

Hoar-frost Surface ice crystals formed by deposition of vapour in very cold temperatures

Ice screw　Tubular ice protection anchor with thread and bits, screwed into the ice

Jumar　Moveable and lockable metal clamp for ascent of fixed ropes

Karabiner　Steel or alloy snaplink with opening used to connect anchors and ropes

Mantleshelf　Technical move in climbing to gain lodgement on a narrow ledge; the climber must lock elbows into a downward-pushing support then raise the foot level with the palms.

Moving together　Moving roped without fixed belays, but often using intermediate anchors between the climbers as running protection.

Névé　Generally used by climbers to describe consolidated snow with frozen surface crust, the term more properly refers to a compacted snow band in the first stage of glacier formation *(Fr)*

Nut　Tapered metal wedge placed in rock cracks for climbing protection; also called a "wire"

Peg　Metal pin, blade or angle hammered into rock cracks for climbing protection; also known as a piton

Piton　French term for a peg

Prusik cord　Thin rope cord (usually 5mm diameter) tied into loops of up to a metre in circumference, used for ascent of fixed ropes, crevasse rescue and protection of abseils

Prusik knot　Sliding knot by which a Prusik cord is tied to the main climbing rope

Quick-draw　Two karabiners linked by a short sewn tape, used to connect the rope to protection anchors for running protection on a climb

Rime　Surface deposition of atmospheric vapour, creating feathery formations of ice crystals on windward mountain faces, formed when cool moist air rises over a sub-zero mountain massif

Rognon　Ice-smoothed rock ridge protruding from a glacier *(Fr)*

Runner　Intermediate anchor point clipped into the rope, which provides running protection as the climber moves above

Sérac　Ice cliff, typically formed under a hanging glacier *(Fr)*

Short-roping　Moving together on the rope, typically less than five metres apart, without intermediate protection, the simplest and fastest system of movement on Alpine climbs and a fundamental guiding technique

Sling　Knotted or stitched loop of rope or tape, used for anchorage on a rock spikes on round a rock chockstone

Snow stake   V-profiled alloy stake, typically 70cm in length, driven into hard snow for anchorage, essential for belays and fixed-rope anchorage in Himalayan mountaineering

Spindrift   Blowing cloud or wave of snow crystals, obscuring visibility at surface levels

Sport climbing   Climbing style whereby pre-placed bolts protect the ascent. Developed in the late 1970s, its facility and security enabled a massive leap in the gymnastic standards of climbing performance

Thread   Belay attachment using a sling threaded around a natural rock chockstone wedged in a crack

Traditional climbing   Climbing style in which the climber places most or all of protection and belay anchors during the ascent; also known as "adventure climbing", and ethically the only acceptable style up to 1980

Tyrolean traverse   Suspended horizontal traverse of a fixed rope, used to access a sea stack across a sea channel or to bridge a gap between rock pinnacles

Verglas   Black ice, often invisible to the eye, formed by freezing of a thin film of surface moisture *(Ger)*

Waist belay   Traditional belay method whereby the climber feeds the rope around the waist to provide friction and control in event of a fall, superceded by metal belay-plates in the modern era

Windslab   A layer of homogenised pulverised snow grains deposited by the wind, forming a cohesive and unstable band in the snow-pack and the cause of many avalanches

Wrist-loop   Hand-loop or leash tied to the ice axe, and adjusted to give the climber wrist support when climbing, and providing security against dropping the axe

Climbing Grading Systems

British rock grades

Scrambles: Scrambling is defined as requiring use of hands as well as feet in progression, and scrambles are graded from 1 to 3. A grade 3 scramble equates to a Moderate or Difficult rock climb, and most scramblers are glad of a rope for protection on grade 3 scrambles.

Traditional rock climbs: Traditional climbing grades run: Easy (a simple scramble), Moderate, Difficult, Very Difficult, severe, Very

Severe, Hard Very Severe, Extremely Severe (the E-grade is divided numerically from E1 up to E10 or 11). These grades reflect all factors influencing the challenge of a climb, encompassing technical difficulty, lack of protection, continuity of difficulty and length.

A supplementary numerical grade for pure technicality of the hardest moves is appended to the overall grade of harder climbs: 4a, 4b, 4c, 5a, 5b, 5c, 6a, 6b, 6c, 7a, 7b.

As an example of a combined grade The Old Man of Hoy Original East Face route is E1, 5b.

Sport climbing grades: Confusingly, a separate numerical grading system, adopted from France in the 1980s, is used for climbing wall and outdoor bolt-protected sport rock climbs. This runs from 4a up to 9b, with supplementary sub-division of each grade by a + suffix. Sport grades refer to pure technical difficulty, without clear distinction as to how long or sustained is the route. A sport 6a or 6a+ equates approximately to a trad 5b climb

Winter and Ice Grades
Scottish winter climbs: The overall grade of winter climbs follows the Roman numeral system from grade I through to grade X. Simple 45 to 50° snow gullies are grade I. A classic ridge climb such as Tower Ridge of Ben Nevis would rate grade III or IV on the scale. Benchmark steep ice routes such as Poachers Fall on Liathach or Point Five Gully on Ben Nevis are grade V.

In addition there is a simple numeric technical grade as a supplement to the harder climbs, running from 1 to 10. So Tower Ridge has a combined grade of IV, 4; Poachers Fall V, 5; and The Godfather on Beinn Bhan VIII, 8.

Continental ice routes: Pure ice routes frozen waterfalls are denoted by a Continental/Canadian system of technical grades – Water Ice (WI) 1 up to 7, with a supplementary + suffix. WI4 is approximately equivalent to Scottish technical 5.

In addition Norwegian waterfalls have traditionally used an overall Roman numeral grade – a seal of overall challenge. These grades are rather stiffer than Scottish grades – a Norwegian VI would equate to a long and sustained Scottish VII.

Mixed winter climbs where difficulties are climbed on rock

placements are given an international M-grade from M1 up to M12 and beyond.

Alpine Mountaineering Grades

The French-language Alpine system is widely recognised and used worldwide by European climbers. The grades refer to overall difficulty, encompassing length, variability of condition, seriousness of retreat and descent, technical difficulty and continuity of difficulties:

Facile (F), *Peu Difficile (PD)*, *Assez Difficile (AD)*, *Difficile (D)*, *Très Difficile (TD)*, *Extrêmement Difficile (ED)* with the additional sub-division denoted by the + suffix.

Classic routes on the ridges of the major peaks climbed in the nineteenth century were typically PD, AD or D in difficulty, eg: the Hörnli Ridge of the Matterhorn is AD and the Italian Ridge of the Matterhorn is AD+. The successful completion of *Assez Difficile* climbs still represents a benchmark of all-round mountaineering competence. Major North Face climbs are typically TD or ED in standard. The ED grade is now subdivided numerically, eg: the Eiger 1938 Route is graded ED2.

Appendix II

QUALIFICATIONS IN MOUNTAIN GUIDING AND INSTRUCTION

British Mountain Guide (BMG) and International Mountain Guide (IFMGA)

The Guide qualification is technically the premier level of mountain qualification in the world. The International Federation of Mountain Guides Associations (IFMGA) is the umbrella administrative organisation supervising the Guides' training schemes and mutual interests of over twenty-five constituent member countries. The British Mountain Guides (BMG) association has been affiliated to the IFMGA since 1979 and has over 160 full-members. Each member country of the IFMGA administers its own training and assessment scheme, with variations according to its geography, climate and climbing traditions. Upon qualification the British Mountain Guide automatically becomes an IFMGA Guide and carries an equivalent carnet and badge.

Entry requirements: To commence training for the BMG qualification the candidate must present a climbing c.v. which includes extensive experience in all disciplines of climbing, mountaineering and ski-touring:

UK Rock Climbs: lead ascents of over fifty rock climbs at E1 or harder grade, spread over a variety of climbing areas

UK Winter Climbs: lead ascents of over fifty winter climbs of grade III and harder, including twenty routes of grade V standard or harder

Alpine Climbing: at least four seasons of alpine climbing, encompassing at least twenty routes and summits in different regions of the Alps, and ten routes of TD or ED standard.

Ski-Touring and Off-Piste Skiing: at least thirty days of off-piste and ski-touring, including several multi-day tours in a variety of areas of the Alps.

The training scheme: Upon acceptance as a registrant to the training scheme the candidate completes Induction courses to check on essential competencies in each discipline of the qualification, then proceeds to formal training and assessments:

Summer Rock Climbing: two training courses and a six-day assessment, usually undertaken in North Wales.

Winter Climbing: training course and six-day assessment undertaken in Scotland; upon successful completion the candidate becomes an Aspirant Guide.

Ski-touring: ski-technique course, touring training course, avalanche theory course, an Aspirant working apprenticeship of fifteen days minimum with a full Guide and a six-day assessment in the Alps.

Summer Alpine Climbing: training course, two summer seasons completing a minimum of thirty days' work as an Aspirant apprenticed to full Guides, and a six-day assessment in the Alps.

The Guide must also maintain a current certificate in wilderness first aid, and complete courses in coaching skills and in the legal aspects of mountain guiding.

The training scheme takes a minimum of three years and involves undertaking over a hundred days of courses and assessments.

The British Mountain Guides web-site www.bmg.org.uk gives full details on how to become a Guide.

UK Mountain Leader and Instructor Qualifications

A series of awards for application in the British hills is run by Mountain Training UK www.mountain-training.org. MTUK is run by volunteer boards comprising leading bodies in each constituent part of the UK (eg. British Mountaineering Council and Mountaineering Council of Scotland). MTUK is part-funded by grants from Government-funded organisations such as Sport England. The emphasis is on instructional skills rather than pure mountain guiding.

Summer Mountain Leader Award (summer ML): This award validates competency to lead hillwalking groups in summer conditions. There is no roped climbing involved, other than use of a safety rope in an emergency situation. The award was established in 1964 and is now regarded as an essential requirement for teachers and youth group leaders intending to lead parties in the UK hills.

Winter Mountain Leader Award (winter ML): The winter ML extends the summer ML to the leadership of hillwalking parties in winter conditions. Assessment covers a multi-day snow-holing expedition and exacting requirements for navigational competency. Basic use of ropes is included on terrain up to 45° angle.

Single Pitch Award (SPA): This award tests technical competence in management and supervision of groups on single-pitch rock climbing cliffs and climbing walls. Candidates for assessment must have twelve months minimum rock climbing experience and personal lead competency to a minimum of Severe standard.

Mountaineering Instructor Award (MIA): The MIA covers the skills for instructing summer mountaineering including all aspects of summer rock climbing, the coaching of lead climbing, and scrambling. All candidates must first hold the summer ML award and submit a c.v. containing a minimum of twenty lead routes at VS, 4c standard or higher. The award is held by well over a thousand instructors and is a basic requirement for employment with most outdoor centres and guiding companies in the UK.

Mountaineering Instructor Certificate (MIC): MIC holders are validated in the skills for instructing in winter climbing in the UK and before undergoing assessment all candidates must first hold the winter ML and MIA awards, as well as presenting a c.v. containing lead ascents of at least ten routes of grade III and above plus twenty logged days of party leadership in winter conditions.

Holders of the MIA and MIC awards may join the Association of Mountaineering Instructors (AMI), which promotes their professional development and safeguards their status.

International Mountain Leader Award (IML): This award has growing status as a requirement for worldwide trek leading and low-angle winter treks on snowshoes. All candidates must first possess the summer ML award and a c.v. of international mountain walking and UK winter hillwalking. No climbing or skiing is involved in the qualification. The British Association of International Mountain Leaders (BAIML) www.baiml.org represents the interests of IML holders and is a member of the union of international mountain leader associations (UIMLA). The training and assessment is administered by MTUK.

INDEX

Locators in italics show diagrams within the text, those followed by n show information contained in footnotes.